EDUCATIONAL PSYCHOLOGY FOR LEARNERS

ANGELA L. VAUGHAN
BRETT D. WILKINSON

SECOND EDITION

CONNECTING THEORY, RESEARCH & APPLICATION

Kendall Hunt
publishing company

PREFACE

PURPOSE OF THE BOOK

A quote generally attributed to the Greek philosopher Socrates and quite popular in educational circles, asserts that "Education is the kindling of a flame, not the filling of a vessel." That is to say, education is the active pursuit of impassioned inquiry rather than the passive acquisition of knowledge. The flame is kindled by curiosity and engagement because meaningful learning is not a passive activity, it is an active one.

This book serves as a guide for becoming a more active, intentional, and engaged learner. It also lays the groundwork for students to become more effective across a variety of important educational activities. From enhancing regular study practices with improved memory retention and test-taking abilities, to balancing a busy schedule and maintaining motivation in the face of personal challenges, the basic purpose of this book is to equip students with a versatile yet reliable toolkit of skills and strategies for lifelong achievement. It is designed to kindle the flame of learning.

Becoming an effective learner requires self-reflection and experimentation. It doesn't happen automatically or by chance. When students take the time to evaluate what works and choose to try out new skills and methods, the outcomes of learning can be radically transformed for the better. Furthermore, when students equip themselves with knowledge about learning and research-based learning strategies, they are finally able to take control of their academic experiences. Our desire is to help students make the most out of their college education by outlining many of the vital points of knowledge and skill that lead to greater academic and professional success.

Research-based theories, concepts, and strategies are presented as the foundation for advanced learning. Rather than provide students with a laundry list of skills and techniques, we emphasize the broader relationship between successful learning strategies and the theories that underlie them. In doing so, students can grasp not only how enhanced learning occurs, but why certain learning approaches are more effective than others. This generates an opportunity for students to build intentionality or purposeful decision-making, into their own learning process. It also lends additional credibility to the strategies, skills, and techniques throughout this book. The approaches detailed herein are research-based means to increase your effectiveness as a learner.

There are three key terms that you will discover repeatedly throughout this text: deep learning, transferrable learning skills, and self-regulated learning. Although different in scope, each is similar in purpose. All are tied to the idea that critical thinking, self-control, and focused effort are essential features of learning. If there is any larger purpose of this book, it is to offer students the chance to recognize the inherent value of learning methods that go far beyond rote memorization and mere preparation for exams. Regardless of your educational background and experience, it is possible to transform your potential into a concrete reality. As a student, you are preparing for a lifetime of learning. Learning how to learn *well* is the first crucial step towards success.

INTENDED AUDIENCE

Although the framework of this book is specifically tailored to the needs of new college students, the intended audience includes all learners who would like to gain the skill and insight needed to conquer the challenges of both academic and professional life. Making the most of learning experiences has as much to do with self-awareness and self-control as it does to how well specific tasks and activities are accomplished. The benefits derived from advanced learning skills can extend well beyond the realm of a college education, leading to greater adaptiveness and self-sufficiency in the professional world. Whether seeking to be hired by an employer or to become a self-made entrepreneur, the proficient learner is always one critical step ahead in the game of life.

This book is also intended for university program directors, faculty and staff who seek to deliver an academically rigorous course, substantiated by research, to support entering students' transition. As described earlier, students' educational and professional success goes beyond surface-level learning. Providing access to students also means providing the educational experiences and foundation that will promote their ongoing development such that they can meet the demands of higher education and the expectations of a global society.

CLUSTER PREVIEWS

CLUSTER 1: THE BIG PICTURE—EDUCATIONAL PSYCHOLOGY AND RESEARCH IN HIGHER EDUCATION

The first module describes educational psychology and how its theories and principles provide the foundation for effective learning. It then goes further to describe how institutions of higher education have evolved over the years to provide the environment and the context to be successful both academically and professionally. This includes adopting general education requirements that embody the liberal arts as a means to building life-long transferrable skills. For those of you who are entering freshmen (or those of you who have already taken these courses), it is helpful to understand the purpose and value of these requirements.

Some of the transferrable skills that you will develop include effective written communication and critical thinking; therefore, one of the tasks that you will face regularly within your education is the research paper. The second module provides guidance on selecting a topic, recognizing scholarly sources, and avoiding plagiarism. This module was included early in the textbook to support written tasks that you will most likely have for the entire semester.

CLUSTER 2: A PLAN OF ACTION—EFFECTIVE GOALS AND GOAL SETTING

Goals direct behavior and promote higher levels of motivation. As such, this cluster was included early in the text to help provide the road map for your semester and your education. The first module describes the research and provides specifics on useful goals and intentional goal-setting techniques that will drive action and give you purpose.

The second module provides detailed examples of useful goals that incorporate helpful goal-setting techniques in three domains: academic, personal, and social. After each example, a blank template is included, with some prompts to guide your thinking, so that you can complete your own goal in each of these domains. Although it is likely that you will set many more than three goals, this module guides you through the process so that you can then set effective goals on your own.

CLUSTER 3: MAXIMIZING ORGANIZATION—AN INTERACTION OF GOALS, MOTIVATION AND TIME MANAGEMENT STRATEGIES

Most college students would agree (as well as many working professionals) that time management is one of the more difficult challenges they face. The first module explains how time management is all about attention management, and explores how gaining control of your time will help you prioritize and minimize procrastination. The second module describes how to build routines and develop a schedule that supports your goals. Detailed examples are included to show you how to utilize a Master Calendar and an Ideal Schedule. The last module provides over 30 strategies that are directly related to you gaining control of your time, creating balance between work and leisure, and establishing an environment where you can maximize your learning.

It is likely that some of the techniques included throughout this cluster are unfamiliar to you and the availability of so many strategies may feel overwhelming; however, it is recommended that you select a few strategies, adopt them, change them to fit your needs, and then select a few more to experiment with over time.

CLUSTER 4: UNDERSTANDING MEMORY—INFORMATION PROCESSING FOR THE LONG TERM

Learning is much more than simply studying so that you can do well on your exams. Although performing well on exams may be the goal of most students, learning and processing information should allow you to encode, store, and retrieve new information over the long term. For many entering college students, the strategies of the past take too much time and are often inadequate for meeting their professors' expectations or learning vast amounts of information in a realistic amount of time. Therefore, the first module describes memory processes and how different types of learning strategies contribute to efficient and effective long-term storage and retrieval. This module also includes a laundry list of learning strategies that go beyond reading, reviewing, and creating flashcards.

The second module explains why strategies that incorporate visual imagery are a powerful learning tool. Two specific strategies are described: the Memory Palace and graphic organizers. Several examples are shared to illustrate the use of these tools. The last module describes how to use many of these strategies to promote active reading and optimal note-taking.

CLUSTER 5: MONITORING COMPREHENSION—MEANINGFUL LEARNING AND SUCCESSFUL TEST-TAKING

Comprehension monitoring is a self-regulatory process that allows you to actively engage in your course material, as well as to identify gaps in your knowledge. This is an important skill considering the number of times you will be assessed (e.g., taking exams) over the course of your college education and professional careers. Put simply, these strategies help you to answer the questions, "What do I know?" and "Am I ready?" Some of these strategies include incorporating self-testing and learning taxonomies (e.g., Bloom's Taxonomy) to help you monitor your comprehension.

The second module provides specific strategies to help you maximize your performance in the assessment process (i.e., taking an exam). These include minimizing anxiety, predicting future exam items, and improving your testwiseness.

CLUSTER 6: THE FUNDAMENTAL CAUSES OF BEHAVIOR— YOUR MOTIVATION

Cluster 6 describes motivation and was intentionally included later in the textbook. Many students feel highly motivated at the beginning of the semester; however, motivation tends to lag towards the middle of the semester, once examinations have begun and the workload has started to become more overwhelming. Like many other ideas in this book, this cluster describes not only how you can become more aware of your motivation, but how you can take control.

There are numerous theories and principles supported by decades of research that provide explanations for motivation and how it relates to academic and professional success. Therefore, the first two modules help you build awareness by describing in detail the more significant theories (e.g., self-efficacy, growth mindset, attribution theory, etc.) related to learning. The last module provides prompts and strategies in several different areas (e.g., coursework, time management, information processing, etc.) that can help you take control of your motivation.

CLUSTER 7: METACOGNITION AND SELF-REGULATED LEARNING: PROMOTING DECISIONS THAT IMPROVE LEARNING AND OUTCOMES

This cluster takes many of the concepts previously described in the textbook and identifies how metacognition and self-regulation allow you to incorporate the appropriate strategies for your tasks, evaluate their effectiveness, and make changes when needed. As you continue in your education, more will be expected of you. Metacognition and self-regulation will help you to continue to improve and develop your skills.

The first module focuses on metacognition and describes the relevant features of metacognition. An activity is included to help guide you through this often unfamiliar process. The second module focuses on self-regulation and describes two learning models that can help you optimize your learning and achieve better outcomes. It also includes an activity that guides you through applying one of these models to your goals.

CLUSTER 8: UNDERSTANDING AND EXPERIENCING DIVERSITY—AN INTRODUCTION

The purpose of this module is to provide an overview of important topics related to diversity while stressing the importance of understanding how personal experiences are socio-culturally informed. The first module explores the meaning of diversity as well as key terms in the diversity literature and the second module examines important concepts that represent barriers to an open and just society including prejudice, discrimination, oppression, and privilege. Finally, the cluster concludes by identifying the benefits of expanding social identity. This cluster serves as an introduction to these topics to build a foundation of knowledge, which serves to help you think critically and learn more deeply.

CLUSTER 9: WELLNESS—ADVANCING PERFORMANCE, LIFE SATISFACTION, AND CRITICAL THINKING

The purpose of this cluster is to enhance your understanding of wellness, including how to monitor and to take charge of your personal well-being. Whereas self-care involves taking care of yourself by engaging in healthy and revitalizing behaviors, wellness is a more encompassing concept that includes six broad dimensions: physical, emotional, social, spiritual, occupational, and intellectual. The information in this cluster will assist you in establishing and maintaining all six dimensions by refining your sense of how wellness impacts both performance and life satisfaction, both of which are key to maximizing your educational experiences in the short and long term.

The first module will define wellness and its six dimensions and the second module applies a holistic wellness perspective to nutrition, exercise, sleep hygiene, stress management, and social media use, while also examining the role that critical thinking and mindfulness play in maintaining personal wellness.

ACKNOWLEDGMENTS

Angela Vaughan—I would first like to thank all of the students and teachers who I have had the pleasure to work with over the years. In addition to gaining a rewarding career, I have learned so much from you about what it means to learn and to teach. I am also grateful for Brett, my coauthor, who easily instills passion and wisdom into everything he does. He is an incredible teacher, author, and scholar. Our program at UNC has missed him. I would also like to thank Kendall Hunt Publishing for their timely support and providing the means to makes this textbook a reality in such a short time.

Additionally, the original textbook and this new edition has been made possible by the contributions of several essential people. I appreciate Jesseca Manson (University of Northern Colorado) who provided critical feedback as we completed the original text. For this edition, Michael Graham and Alexis Hauck were instrumental in developing our two newest clusters. Michael Graham helped write our newest cluster on diversity and Alexis Hauck helped write the cluster on wellness. Currently, both are leaders and instructors in our first-year seminar program at the University of Northern Colorado. In addition to successfully serving the students in our program, Michael and Allie's work here will allow others to benefit from their expertise, passion and creativity. Lastly, I would like to thank my family. My children have been incredibly supportive and patient. Their love makes it all worthwhile.

Brett Wilkinson—My deepest gratitude goes out to Angela, my coauthor, who is driven with profound determination to improve the lives of college students. Your vision and work ethic is inspirational, and it has been such a pleasure working with you every step of the way. I would also like to thank the support team at Kendall Hunt for their hard work and accessibility. Finally I would like to thank my wife and children for their love and patience. You are the wellspring of my hope and inspiration.

ABOUT THE AUTHORS

Angela Vaughan earned her PhD in Educational Psychology from the University of Texas, Austin. Currently, she is the Faculty Director of the University 101 program at the University of Northern Colorado (UNC) in Greeley. Dr. Vaughan first developed the program at UNC to support first-semester freshmen; however, it has now expanded to serve all students and support their intellectual and professional development. She began her 20-year career as an educator while serving as a United States Air Force Officer. From there, she has taught and developed curriculum at the high school, community college, and university levels. In her present position, she focuses on undergraduate student success, as well as helping current and future teachers develop their practice and become more effective. Dr. Vaughan has delivered numerous campus workshops and conference presentations and has authored multiple articles on student learning, success and retention, and effective teaching. Currently, Dr. Vaughan consults with other first-year programs across the country who want to transform their current programs into an academically rigorous research-based first-year seminar. This includes designing and delivering comprehensive instructor and faculty professional development and training. She also serves as member of the editorial review board for the Journal of College Students Retention: Research, Theory & Practice.

Dr. Brett Wilkinson is an Assistant Professor of Counselor Education at Purdue University Fort Wayne. He earned his Ph.D. in Counselor Education and Supervision from the University of Northern Colorado with an emphasis in couples and family counseling. During his doctoral studies, Dr. Wilkinson served as a course instructor and researcher for the University 101 program led by Dr. Angela Vaughan. He has authored numerous journal articles on educational theories and practices related to cognitive complexity, phenomenological training methods, and humanistic values. Dr. Wilkinson actively presents at state, regional, and national conferences, serves on the editorial board for a national counseling journal, and facilitates professional workshops on advanced learning strategies, interpersonal skill-building, and professional development. He is also a licensed professional counselor in the state of Indiana with nearly 10 years of experience working as a mental health therapist with couples, families, and at-risk youth.

THE BIG PICTURE: EDUCATIONAL PSYCHOLOGY AND RESEARCH IN HIGHER EDUCATION

CLUSTER OVERVIEW

One of the greatest abilities an undergraduate student can acquire through higher education is learning how to be an effective learner. Everyone learns, certainly, but not everyone is effective in the learning process. Effective learners are adaptive and critical thinkers, who know how to seek, retain, and synthesize information. They are engaged, self-regulated, creative, and organized in the learning process. They define priorities, establish practical goals, and structure their time in ways that align with their personal vision of education. They cultivate learning skills that can be transferred from one situation to the next, and this adaptiveness gives them a professional edge over less effective learners.

In short, an effective learner is the person every professor wants to teach and every employer wants to hire. This is the sort of person each and every student should aim to become. Where is the magic elixir? What does it take to become an effective learner? Hard work, self-control, open-mindedness, curiosity, and a desire to learn how to improve oneself are a good place to start. That is to say, there is no magic elixir. There is no well-defined path. However, there is an incredible amount of knowledge and research to achieve effective learning skills for those who choose to pursue it.

This may sound overwhelming to some learners. A more practical person will consider this: effective learners tend to earn higher grades, graduate more quickly, and possess skills that today's employers actively seek in recruits. The adaptiveness and efficiency of effective learners symbolizes an acquired skill that can lead to greater productivity, work satisfaction, and

1

lifelong career earnings. In short, effective learning skills serve as the foundation for personal and professional prosperity.

Educational institutions have understood this principle for some time. The liberal arts and general education requirements maintained by most institutions of higher education today reflect this understanding. Educational psychologists who bridge the gap between psychology and education practices, recognize the value of lifelong learning skills. Grounded largely on the principles and research of educational psychology, this book illuminates the path for undergraduate students towards these effective learning skills. Each cluster provides an overview of theories, concepts, and practices that can be leveraged to enhance learning. The first cluster has two modules delivering an overview of higher education concepts and research practices that are relevant for undergraduate studies.

The first module provides a basic description of educational psychology, the history, and purpose of modern research universities and liberal arts traditions, the merits of transferrable learning skills, and a review of general educational requirements in higher education. The second module explores components of information literacy and scholarship for undergraduate students, including methods to identify and assess the credibility of scholarly works, how to develop a research question and thesis statement, methods for finding and evaluating information sources for research papers, as well as how to appropriately cite source materials and avoid plagiarism. In summary, the first cluster provides a foundation for understanding the role of higher education in effective learning, the scholarly climate in which learning occurs, and other technical skills students need to develop along the way.

CLUSTER OBJECTIVES:

- Describe the function of educational psychology in examining processes of learning for individual learners.
- Describe the history and guiding purposes of modern research universities, liberal arts traditions, and general education requirements.
- Outline the various benefits of acquiring transferrable learning skills, engaging in high-impact educational practices, and becoming a self-regulated learner.
- Explain the relationship between information literacy and scholarship.
- Outline the purpose and characteristics of scholarship in terms of scholarly works, original source materials, general scholarship types, and specific criteria for evaluating scholarly works.
- Describe how to prepare a research paper in terms of choosing topics, developing thesis statements, finding and evaluating sources, and using citations to avoid plagiarism.

EDUCATIONAL PSYCHOLOGY AND THE MODERN RESEARCH UNIVERSITY

CLUSTER 1 OBJECTIVES COVERED IN THIS MODULE

☐ **OBJECTIVE:** Describe the function of educational psychology in examining processes of learning for individual learners.

☐ **OBJECTIVE:** Describe the history and guiding purposes of modern research universities, liberal arts traditions, and general education requirements.

☐ **OBJECTIVE:** Outline the various benefits of acquiring transferrable learning skills, engaging in high-impact educational practices, and becoming a self-regulated learner.

WHAT IS EDUCATIONAL PSYCHOLOGY?

EDUCATIONAL PSYCHOLOGY: The scientific study of teaching and learning.

The field of educational psychology focuses on the scientific study of teaching and learning. Drawing ideas from the broader field of psychology and applying them in educational settings, educational psychologists seek new and innovative ways to improve teaching methods and student learning outcomes. This includes the exploration of individual differences in a wide range of areas like motivation, self-efficacy, information processing, self-regulation, memory, and cognitive development. It also involves the development of new instructional design approaches, assessment methods, and pedagogical principles that can be used to enhance learning in classroom environments.

Going beyond applied methods in school settings, educational psychology also explores learning across the lifespan. As people spend their entire lives learning new things and adapting to new situations, understanding how the learning process works at different stages and situations is extremely important. The basic process of learning is thus a central feature of educational psychology research and practices from early childhood to adolescence, and onward, throughout the entire lifespan. Illuminating the cognitive, emotional, and social processes of learning at various life stages also serves to inform the way in which a society designs its educational systems, public services, and policy initiatives (Myers, 2010).

Through scientific research and the development of theories and applied methods, educational psychologists seek to improve both teaching practices and learning methods in a systematic and empirically-supported way. There is tremendous scope in this endeavor, as the study of educational psychology consists of the individual learner, the process of learning, the learning environment, the ideal objectives to be learned, and the methods used to teach those learnings. However, these various considerations are constrained for the purposes of this book. Moving forward, the focus will be on the process of learning for individual learners.

OUR FOCUS IS ON LEARNERS, NOT TEACHERS

Most educational psychology textbooks are written for teachers-in-training. They are generally designed to guide college students towards becoming effective teachers themselves. This makes sense when considering the importance of learning theories and the powerful influence of educational psychology research on instructional practices today. If a society wishes to build optimal learning environments that serve the best interests of students, then it must equip its teachers with the knowledge and skills necessary to generate positive learning outcomes. Achieving this task obviously requires training new teachers in how to teach well in accordance with the most recent evidence-based methods.

However, evidence suggests that the very best teachers are those who not only understand theories, skills and techniques, but who embody characteristics of the so-called "self-regulated learner" (Paris & Winograd, 2003). In other words, self-regulated teachers have learned how to be effective learners themselves, often evidenced in terms of their own academic performances (Greenwald, Hedges, & Laine, 1996) as well as their general tendencies towards reflectiveness and adaptiveness (Zeichner & Liston, 2013). The importance of such abilities stretch beyond the realm of teaching, as research consistently shows that professional competence and career success are closely connected to traits such as self-awareness, adaptiveness, impulse control, concentration, and a readiness to learn (Goleman, 2006). The entirety of this book explains how effective, self-regulated learning improves the outcomes of students and professionals in a broad spectrum of majors and careers.

Learning does not end with graduation. Whatever the future career, the ability to learn and the adaptability to new challenges serve as the foundation for a successful career. Hence, the focus of this book is on learners rather than teachers. By gaining insight into significant theories, skills, and techniques, research has shown to improve academic outcomes; it becomes possible to improve one's lifelong learning practices. Becoming an effective learner is much more than the use of study plans and memorization techniques. It requires the investment of time and effort to discover new learning processes, to examine one's own standard approaches to learning, and to experiment with alternative learning methods.

FOUNDATIONS OF THE MODERN RESEARCH UNIVERSITY

The 21st century has ushered considerable changes to our collective understanding of scientific, economic, socio-political, and technological endeavors. We live in a globalized world. The transformation has occurred swiftly with immense impact and the complex web of factors involved is extremely difficult to untangle and decipher. Once rigid geopolitical borders and ideological boundaries have become more accessible, and as a result, ideas flow freely creating an interconnected global community that has transformed not only commerce, politics, and science, but the various arts and humanities as well.

Pioneering this global movement are the modern research universities. These institutions have long been founded on the principles of borderless knowledge, freedom of thought, and unbiased scientific inquiry. They also represent the provision of intellectual and scientific services for the public welfare. The pursuit of knowledge, insight, growth, and positive social change serve as the foundation for the vast majority of academic activities. Research universities contribute to scientific and technological development, socio-political and business analysis, and various educational, ethical, humanistic, and artistic endeavors. Globalization heavily relies upon the ideas and breakthroughs made within the walls of research universities on a daily basis.

Yet, a majority still have a limited understanding as to how university-based research and practice is contributing to the betterment of society. With so many technological advancements made by—and publicly promoted from within—the private business sector, the role of university-based research is often underreported and misunderstood. Furthermore, the purposeful evolution of modern colleges and universities is a mystery to most people and students, who attend these institutions.

To clarify the role of higher education in the world today, the following section will provide the major differences between basic and applied research conducted at modern universities, the historical purposes of higher education in relation to the changing needs of the workforce, and the invaluable role higher education currently plays in helping students develop transferrable learning skills.

CONDUCTING BASIC AND APPLIED RESEARCH

Modern universities stand at the epicenter of medical, technological, and socio-cultural knowledge advancements in the world today. Although private companies and industries once contributed to a large portion of research efforts, the broad shift of major industries away from core manufacturing efforts to refined technology and financial management systems in the late 20th century fundamentally altered this role (Davis, 2009). Rather than maintain costly private laboratories, companies solicited support from established university research facilities (National Research Council, 2012). Today, a vast majority of contemporary research efforts are conducted in universities and include two major types: basic and applied.

BASIC RESEARCH:
Research used to expand knowledge, satisfy curiosity, and develop theoretical or conceptual frameworks about the world.

Basic Research: This is knowledge-driven and often has limited short-term commercial value. Scientific questions on the age of the universe, the neurological basis of dream states, the phonetics of 16th century French literature, and the genetic variations in rhesus monkeys are unlikely to make scholars or researchers either rich or famous in the near future. Instead of contributing to immediate real-world problems or commercial advancements, basic research efforts add knowledge that enriches future research efforts and expands our general understanding of the world and the human condition.

However, the importance of such research should not be underestimated. Basic research is foundational, rooted in curiosity and improves the base of scientific knowledge. It requires the collective work of many researchers doing innumerable studies to grow a scientific field and make important conceptual advancements. In this respect, most basic research studies are like small pieces in a large complex puzzle. Each piece of the puzzle contributes to the larger picture, even as the big picture cannot be reduced to its individual pieces. Furthermore, these small pieces form the building blocks, without these there would be no core knowledge upon which to grow applied research efforts.

APPLIED RESEARCH:
Research used to develop practical solutions for real-world problems.

Applied Research: This is practical and focuses more on immediate solutions to real-world problems. Scientific questions about the effect of pharmaceuticals on depression, the influence of advertising on body image, the current rate of ice sheet melt in Greenland or the impact of new agricultural modernization efforts in Zimbabwe are directly related to contemporary issues and real-world concerns. Additionally, such studies have both commercial and reform-oriented potential. Because they are related to practical problem solving, their conclusions yield groundbreaking products, develop useful interventions or build transformative social and cultural initiatives.

In combination, the basic and applied research conducted at modern research universities serves to promote human knowledge and expedite positive real-world change. This is precisely the larger mission of the modern research university. Whether by conducting invaluable research or training the next generation of professionals, scientists, politicians, artists, and academics, the platform of higher education is meant to impart democratic values and enhance the welfare of the general public. The flow of ideas and information from modern research universities serves a larger public wellbeing and benefits our global citizenry.

THE ROLE OF HIGHER EDUCATION IN PREPARING THE WORKFORCE

As the globalized economy has evolved over time, so too has the system of higher education adapted its roles and purposes in parallel. Universities were not originally designed to prepare students for such a wide variety of specialized professional vocations. Prior to the 19th century, European universities almost exclusively trained doctors, lawyers, and theologians while American universities focused on classical and theological studies rather than educational support for advanced professional pursuits (Wellmon, 2015). Furthermore, a college education was widely perceived as a class-based luxury that conferred prestige among the elite. Although relatively inexpensive compared to today, the combined loss of time and money to attend college was prohibitive for most American colonists.

The Humboldtian university model—named after the Prussian reformist and philosopher, Wilhelm von Humboldt, who founded the University of Berlin in 1810—was the first large-scale attempt to merge research and specialized areas of collegiate study. In America, the transition from small, traditional liberal arts colleges to modern research universities was guided by the Humboldtian model. Support for innovative research and an expanded set of professional studies was given primary importance. Yet the first U.S. land-grant universities of the mid-to-late 19th century went still further by building specialized departments, expanding administrative support, and advocating for democratic values and academic freedom (Wellmon, 2015).

Even so, there remained little incentive for workers to seek a degree in higher education. It simply was not necessary for most occupations. Before the mid-19th century, most trade-based vocations required some form of one-on-one apprenticeship rather than a college degree. With the rapid growth of the industrial revolution following the Civil War, the workforce shifted away from trade-based apprenticeships to wage-based labor positions that demanded on-site training. By the 20th century, although many institutions conferred professional degrees in areas such as teaching, medicine, engineering, and business, college degrees were not yet legally required to enter these emerging fields.

Degree opportunities expanded rapidly following World War II as Americans returned to civilian life, the job market diversified, and more professional job opportunities were created. The higher education boom had arrived, providing an official gateway to the middle class. Student enrollment doubled between 1950–1960, 1960–1970, and 1970–1990 (Snyder, 1993). However, the earnings gap between college and high school educated workers remained small through the 1970's, when only 28% of jobs required a college education (Carnevale, Smith, & Strohl, 2013). As degree options and accessibility proliferated so did their market value. By 2020, it is estimated that nearly 65% of American jobs will require some form of college education (Carnevale et al., 2013).

THE ROLE OF HIGHER EDUCATION IN BUILDING TRANSFERRABLE LEARNING SKILLS

The proliferation of post-secondary degree requirements in the modern economy has led to an increasingly competitive job market and an evolving set of expectations held by employers. As universities seek to prepare students to meet these challenges, new priorities and principles have begun to change the landscape of higher education. According to a report by the Association of American Colleges and Universities (2007), adapting to the conditions of the 21st century global workforce requires that students become "intentional learners" who are proficient in the following broad areas:

- Inquiry and analysis
- Critical and creative thinking
- Written and oral communication
- Quantitative literacy
- Information literacy
- Teamwork and problem solving

These are called *transferrable learning skills*. The list reflects employer's expectations from prospective employees, and consequently, how colleges and universities now view the role of higher education. Factual knowledge in a specialized field is often not sufficient to get a job in a competitive market when most applicants have about the same level of technical expertise and specialized education. Employers want to hire people with strong transferrable learning skills because these core abilities signify adaptability, self-sufficiency, and growth potential. The real-world challenges and daily tasks of a profession are rarely based on factual or technical skills alone.

The good news is that colleges and universities recognize this fact and their core curriculum is designed to build transferable learning skills. While majors tend to focus on developing *hard skills*, liberal arts and general education courses tend to emphasize *soft skills*. Hard skills include the factual and technical learnings of a specialized area of study such as developing a balance sheet in accounting or performing a lab technique in chemistry. Soft skills have less to do with what you know and more to do with how you think and behave. Self-management, critical thinking, and interpersonal communication abilities are soft, transferrable skills that include decision-making, problem-solving, and relationships.

Moving from a hard skill to a soft skill mentality can be difficult for students. A college degree indicates that the basic hard skills of a profession have been acquired. However, the modern workforce is complex and diversified, meaning that it takes more than factual knowledge to be a competent and well-respected professional. While some people are naturally exceptional in soft skill areas such as communication, critical thinking or leadership, some would benefit from further development in these areas. Taking advantage of college or university liberal arts and general education requirements can be a big step towards becoming the type of rigorously intentional learner that is sought by modern employers.

What soft skills do you have that are well developed? Which skills do you think need more development?

LIBERAL ARTS AND GENERAL EDUCATION

Standing alongside and operating within the modern research university is the concept of the liberal arts and the value of general education practices. Liberal arts colleges exist as a counterpart to modern research universities. At the same time, the notion of a liberal arts education has played a significant ideological role in the shaping of modern universities, as well as the mission set forth by modern institutions to ensure students receive a general education that imparts transferrable skills. The following section provides an overview of the historical and contemporary views of liberal arts, its categories used in higher education, and the role of general education requirements in higher education today.

HISTORICAL VIEW OF LIBERAL ARTS EDUCATION

While the concept of *liberal arts* was first expressed in the Middle Ages, it was derived from the ancient Latin phrase *artes liberales*. In Greco-Roman times, *artes* meant "skills" or "body of knowledge", while *liber* meant "free". As such, *liberales* referred to those free people who received formal education, namely those who could afford a life of contemplation because they were unconstrained by the necessity of physical labor. In this respect, *artes liberales* can also be understood as "mental skills" in contrast to the *artes vulgares*, or "commonplace skills" that require physical exertion such as weaving, masonry, cooking, or blacksmithing.

The liberal arts of antiquity primarily consisted of the so-called *trivium*: logic, grammar, and rhetoric. The purpose of the trivium in Greco-Roman societies was to produce an educated citizen who could participate in democratic life and perform civic duties. The Greek polis or city-state, was democratic from about 500 to 300 BCE. Prior to this period, democratic principles held sway in Rome from 300 to 50 BCE. It was during these times that the liberal arts educational model came into widespread acceptance. Despite the patriarchal and aristocratic biases in choosing who could participate (only free adult male citizens in Greece and free adult male citizens of privilege in Rome), the ideal has shaped our modern view of the relationship between education and free societies.

Beyond the trivium, there was also the mathematical arts known as the *quadrivium*: astronomy, arithmetic, geometry, and music. Although these bodies of knowledge had been developed and studied during Greco-Roman times, their formal use in the liberal arts educational structure was not introduced until the early Middle Ages. At that time, the literary aspects of the trivium was considered a necessary prerequisite for mathematical studies in the quadrivium, together they formed the seven areas of liberal arts in medieval Europe.

Although the purpose of a liberal arts education in medieval times was to adequately prepare students for theological studies, the liberal arts structure was effectively preserved and the foundation set for a resurgence of its original purposes in contemporary times. The traditional liberal arts framework was further augmented by classical studies in Greek and Latin languages at early American colleges. The traditional liberal arts approach was replaced by the Humboldtian university model in the mid-19th century in universities as stated earlier. However, many smaller liberal arts colleges practiced traditional liberal arts approach well into the 20th century and some still use it today.

With a rapidly modernizing American society, colleges and universities had to adapt to the needs and expectations of the public, without discarding the traditional liberal arts format altogether. In order to preserve the guiding tenets of a liberal arts education, its foundational elements were built into the broader university curriculum. This led to the modern notion of general educational requirements that reflect the principles of a liberal arts education while also supporting academic mastery in specialized areas of study.

CONTEMPORARY VIEW OF LIBERAL ARTS EDUCATION

According to the Liberal Education and America's Promise (LEAP) strategic initiative developed by the Association of American Colleges and Universities (AAC&U),

> In a world marked by global interdependence, turbulence, and problems that are both urgent and complex, there is an opportunity to build widespread recognition that the learning outcomes fostered by liberal education have become more valuable to individuals and society than ever before, and therefore that liberal education should be reclaimed and repositioned as providing Americans with a comparative global advantage in preparing for work, citizenship, and lifelong learning (2012, p. 6).

The idea of a liberal education upheld by the AAC&U is broader than the liberal arts tradition, but includes it as such. It aims to bridge the basic principles guiding the liberal arts to a set of general educational priorities. The LEAP initiative draws attention to the benefits and values of the liberal arts in higher education and promotes essential learning outcomes for students. Apart from transferrable skills already discussed, they also go beyond them to emphasize other important areas of personal development such as civic responsibility, ethical reasoning, cultural awareness, and lifelong learning skills.

CATEGORIES OF LIBERAL ARTS EDUCATION

In higher education today, the divisions of liberal arts are quite different from the *trivium* and *quadrivium* of ancient and medieval times. However, the driving purpose remains much the same as that seen in Greco-Roman times, albeit with an aim towards enabling all the opportunity to participate in education. While liberal arts divisions are often structured by each college or university in a unique way, four major categories are generally in use: humanities, social sciences, natural sciences, and formal sciences.

Category	Discription	Examples
TABLE 1.1.1 LIBERAL ARTS DIVISIONS		
Humanities	The humanities involve the critical and speculative study of human experience in terms of history, culture, meaning, and expression.	Philosophy, Literature, Music, Foreign Languages, Religion, Ethics, Speech, and Visual and Performing Arts
Social Sciences	The social sciences involve the scientific and empirical study of human behavior, culture, society, and relationships.	History, Politics, Psychology, Sociology, Anthropology, Gender Studies, and Geography
Natural Sciences	The natural sciences involve the scientific and empirical study of the physical world in terms of principles, laws, and phenomena.	Archaeology, Astronomy, Biology, Botany, Chemistry, Geology, and Physics
Formal Sciences	The formal sciences involve the theoretical study of formal systems in terms of rules and definitions without the need for empirical observations.	Mathematics, Logic, Statistics, and Theoretical Computer Science

MODERN GENERAL EDUCATION REQUIREMENTS

As noted earlier, general education refers to those common learning outcomes that are upheld as educational priorities for all students including both transferrable skills and liberal education principles. Many colleges and universities employ the general education requirement through a broad core curriculum. It is important to recognize that this is an opportunity to gain crucial learning skills rather than an impediment to gaining specialized knowledge in a particular area of study. By taking full advantage of general education courses, it is possible to gain transferrable and lifelong learning skills that not only expand employment opportunities, but also grow appreciation for the complexities of life.

Despite this, general education goes beyond the notion of a liberal arts core curriculum. Other areas, collectively termed *high-impact educational practices*, have also been shown to greatly improve college student outcomes (Kuh, 2008), prompting colleges and universities to seek ways to expand student involvement in these areas. Such practices create more opportunities for students to engage in a collaborative work with peers and faculty, to gain experience with real-world applications of knowledge, to develop refined skills in solving purposeful tasks, and to reflect on personal development.

Research clearly shows that high-impact educational practices are linked to higher grade point averages, higher graduation rates in less time, and higher levels of student satisfaction with their college experiences (NSSE, 2007).

What current courses are you taking as part of your university's general education requirements? How do you think they will support your personal and professional development?

HIGH-IMPACT EDUCATIONAL PRACTICES:
Alternative teaching and learning methods that have been shown to increase student engagement, knowledge, and self-awareness.

From the 10 high-impact practices outlined by Kuh (2008) and endorsed by the AAC&U (2007), four are briefly outlined below:

First-Year Seminars and Experiences

Different forms of first-year seminars and experiences are one of the most widespread high-impact educational practices used by colleges and universities today. The most effective seminars emphasize the importance of transferrable learning skills, collaborative learning, intensive writing practices, and the basics of research and scholarship (Kuh, 2008). High school to college transition can be a challenging experience for any student, first-year seminars and experiences have been established to support students in this transition and further prepare them for the academic and personal rigors of a college education.

Undergraduate Research, Capstones, and Internships

Research opportunities for undergraduates are meant to build engagement and enthusiasm by giving students an opportunity to actively contribute to a discipline. Involvement in research with direct guidance and feedback from faculty and others also fosters a better understanding of the relationship between conceptual knowledge and applied practices. Similarly, capstone projects require students to complete an individual project that integrates the knowledge gained from their college experience, such as a research paper or an art exhibit. Finally, internships involve supervised placement in a work environment to provide insight into the real-world experience of potential careers.

> Are you familiar with the research opportunities that are available on your campus?

Learning Communities

This involves a group of students taking two or more integrated classes in different disciplines where the course topics are both intentionally overlapped and often related to real-world issues. Through intensive collaboration with peers and professors, students analyze the course topics from the viewpoint of different disciplines and seek to integrate their understanding of the real-world topics and common readings through the lens of unique disciplinary approaches. By participating in learning communities, students engage in collaborative learning skills, integrative learning skills, and critical thinking skills.

Service or Community-Based Learning

Connecting course work to community involvement is the goal of service or community-based learning. Applying what is learned in the classroom, students get an opportunity to directly experience how those ideas are applied in real-world settings and assess their real-world experience back in the classroom. This process is also meant to close the gap between theoretical and applied knowledge. The larger purpose is thus twofold:

a) to recognize the value of giving back to the community
b) to understand the relationship between abstract problems and real-world applications of those problems.

TODAY, TOMORROW, AND THE YEARS TO COME

A Brief Recap: Educational psychology studies how people learn and how to improve learning outcomes. Research universities actively encourage ongoing acquisition of knowledge and innovation by means of scientific, speculative, and empirical methods. The liberal arts are designed to promote foundational learning methods and foster critical inquiry. Employers in the modern workforce are interested in hiring people who possess the adaptiveness that comes from transferrable learning skills. Colleges and universities today are seeking ways to provide students with a general education and experiential opportunities to cultivate skills such as self-awareness, critical thinking, and interpersonal engagement.

In light of what has been discussed so far, the purpose of this book is clear. While the process of learning is more than the sum of its parts, understanding the parts can lead to a more complete knowledge. In less esoteric terms, one can say that learning how to become a more effective learner can be the most valuable component of a college education. Facts, theories, and application techniques are certainly vital aspects of higher education as well; just remember that whatever the area of study, there will always be more knowledge to gain and more ideas to consider. In contrast, the ability to flexibly, creatively, and thoughtfully handle new information and challenges is the hallmark features of a lifelong, well-adjusted learner.

The task at hand for undergraduate students is conceptually simple, but challenging in practice. How to acquire such refined learning skills? First and foremost, it requires that the student view learning as a significant and valuable pursuit. If learning itself is not regarded as important, then there is little reason to believe that a person will dedicate the time and energy necessary to grow their learning skills. Commitment to the idea that more effective learning practices will be beneficial in the long run is a personal decision. It requires a willingness to remain an active participant in the learning process. This involves asking questions, taking time to consider what and why one is learning, and making the process of learning a priority. Finally, it requires developing a reasonable degree of self-control.

Evidence to support the first point—learning how to learn is a valuable endeavor—has been laid out in this module and has been supported continuously throughout this book. However, it should be reiterated that this is ultimately a personal decision to invest in one's own learning. There are no techniques or strategies to imbue an individual with this understanding. As for the second and third points regarding active participation in the learning process and the value of developing self-control, these can be summarized in terms of a key concept: self-regulated learning. If a broad idea encompasses what it takes to get the most out of college and what is gained by doing so, self-regulated learning may well be it.

Supporting evidence on the power of self-regulated learning is provided throughout this book as it signifies the natural consequence of becoming an active participant in the learning process and the end result of developing self-control. It is both a skill and a habit that is forged through the use of optimal learning strategies over time. It involves the ability to set useful goals, analyze tasks, select strategies, assess performance, sustain motivation, etc. Even more broadly speaking, it is an indicator of one's ability to clearly understand and effectively adapt to changing features in the learning environment.

The path to becoming a self-regulated learner is also the path to acquire transferrable skills and achieve the goals set forth by the liberal arts or general education programs. In other words, the major topics addressed thus far all point in the same direction: towards becoming an adaptive, civic-minded, critical thinker who proactively forges his or her own path in life. With this goal in mind, the concepts and strategies in this book will attempt to provide some basic foundations for transforming this extraordinary ideal into an attainable reality.

MODULE 1.1 SUMMARY

- The field of educational psychology studies the processes of teaching and learning.
- Modern research universities are the cornerstone for basic and applied research practices driving technological innovations, scientific inquiry, and social progress.
- Liberal arts education originated in Greco-Roman times, it provides a foundation for the ideals and practices in much of higher education today.
- Transferrable learning skills related to communication, interpersonal abilities, and critical thinking are becoming important sought criteria among employers.
- General education requirements are primarily designed for undergraduate students to acquire transferable learning skills.
- Major liberal arts education categories include humanities, social sciences, natural sciences, and formal sciences.
- Involvement in high-impact educational practices like capstones, first-year seminars, learning communities, and service-based learning is linked to better grades and higher graduation rates.

KEY TERMS

- **Applied Research** – Research used to develop practical solutions for real-world problems.
- **Basic Research** – Research used to expand knowledge, satisfy curiosity, and develop theoretical or conceptual frameworks about the world.
- **Educational Psychology** – The scientific study of teaching and learning.
- **Hard Skills** – Skills derived from objective knowledge or technical abilities that are used to perform specific learning tasks.
- **High-Impact Educational Practices** – Alternative teaching and learning methods that have been shown to increase student engagement, knowledge, and self-awareness.
- **Soft Skills** – Skills derived from self-knowledge or interpersonal abilities that are used to perform general learning tasks.
- **Transferrable Learning Skills** – Fundamental skills that can be transferred from one job, career, or area of expertise to another.

REFERENCES

Association of American Colleges and Universities. (2007). *College learning for the new global century: A report from the National Leadership Council for Liberal Education & America's Promise*. Washington, D.C.: Association of American Colleges.

Association of American Colleges and Universities. (2012). *Big questions, urgent challenges: Liberal education and Americans' global future*. Washington, D.C.: Association of American Colleges.

Carnevale, A. P., Smith, N., & Strohl, J. (2013). *Recovery: Job growth and education requirements through 2020*. Washington, D.C.: Georgetown University Press.

Davis, G. F. (2009). *Managed by the markets: How finance re-shaped America*. Oxford: Oxford University Press.

Goleman, D. (2006). *Emotional intelligence*. New York: Bantam.

Greenwald, R., Hedges, L. V., & Laine, R. D. (1996). The effect of school resources on student achievement. *Review of Educational Research, 66*(3), 361–396.

Kuh, G. (2008). *High-impact educational practices: What they are, who has access to them, and why they matter*. Washington, D.C.: Association of American Colleges and Universities.

Myers, D. G. (2010). *Exploring psychology* (8th ed). New York: Macmillan.

National Research Council (U.S.). (2012). *Research universities and the future of America: Ten breakthrough actions vital to our nation's prosperity and security.* Washington, D.C: National Academies Press.

National Survey of Student Engagement. (2007). *Experiences that matter: Enhancing student learning and success.* Bloomington, IN: Indiana University Center for Postsecondary Research.

Paris, S. G., & Winograd, P. (2003). *The role of self-regulated learning in contextual teaching: Principles and practices for teacher preparation. Contextual teaching and learning: Preparing teachers to enhance student success in the workplace and beyond* (Information Series No. 376). Columbus, OH: ERIC Clearinghouse on Adult, Career, and Vocational Education; Washington, DC: ERIC Clearinghouse on Teaching and Teacher Education.

Snyder, T. D. (1993). *120 years of American education: A statistical portrait.* Washington, D.C.: U.S. Department of Education, Office of Educational Research and Improvement, and National Center for Education Statistics.

Wellmon, C. (2015). *Organizing enlightenment: Information overload and the invention of the modern research university.* Baltimore, MD: Johns Hopkins University Press.

Zeichner, K. M., & Liston, D. P. (2013). *Reflective teaching: An introduction.* New York: Routledge.

INFORMATION LITERACY— SCHOLARSHIP, RESEARCH, AND SOURCES

CLUSTER 1 OBJECTIVES COVERED IN THIS MODULE

☐ **OBJECTIVE:** Explain the relationship between information literacy and scholarship.

☐ **OBJECTIVE:** Outline the purpose and characteristics of scholarship in terms of scholarly works, original source materials, general scholarship types, and specific criteria for evaluating scholarly works.

☐ **OBJECTIVE:** Describe how to prepare a research paper in terms of choosing topics, developing thesis statements, finding and evaluating sources, and using citations to avoid plagiarism.

INFORMATION LITERACY

While an interest or desire to learn is a valuable characteristic of lifelong learners, the ability to find, evaluate, and utilize information to accomplish goals is even more fundamental. It is inconsequential if one enjoys learning or not if one does not know how to search for answers and determine the legitimacy of those answers discovered. According to a strategic report from the American Library Association Presidential Committee (1989):

> Ultimately, information literate people are those who have learned how to learn. They know how to learn because they know how knowledge is organized, how to find information and how to use information in such a way that others can learn from them. They are people prepared for lifelong learning because they can always find the information needed for any task or decision at hand.

In many ways, finding information has become easier with the advent of computers. The internet is overflowing with information, and organized digital databases provide access to countless resources. Imagine the time and

INFORMATION LITERACY:
An ability to both determine the need for additional information and to find, evaluate, and use that information appropriately.

legwork involved in searching for every document in print form on a library shelf! Very few people would wish for a return to the old analog methods of using card catalogs and microforms at the local library.

At the same time, with access to such a vast trove of information today, the legitimacy of these sources is questionable. The internet is flooded with personal opinions, poorly researched ideas, inaccurate explanations, skewed data, and incorrectly-cited source materials. While many blog posts, social media snippets, and even journalistic sources can be readily identified as opinion-based pieces, many other sources are quite artfully disguised. Even as information technology has ensured widespread access to knowledge, it has made the art of discernment an even more valuable skill.

For example, encyclopedia entries once written by qualified professionals on contract have been replaced with wiki articles written by anyone interested in making a contribution. This shift has expanded our access to knowledge, but it has also blurred the credibility of source materials. Such ease of accessibility can make discerning quality information from misinformation very difficult. Unfortunately, convenience often belies a lack of credibility or as the old adage goes, "just because you read it does not make it true."

Becoming a good consumer of information requires perceptiveness and due diligence. It means taking time to understand not only what constitutes high quality source materials, but also knowing where to find those sources and utilizing them. Forming good information literacy habits in college can help ensure that future research inquiries made for work or personal reasons are of the highest quality. Additionally, learning how to effectively find, evaluate, and cite legitimate source materials can make writing research papers a simpler and less stressful process.

This module will provide some tools for enhancing information literacy. It is divided into three sections. The first examines ways to discern between scholarly and non-scholarly source materials along with evaluating the legitimacy or credibility of a source. The second explores how to develop a research topic into a thesis statement and the appropriate steps for conducting research. The third section provides insight into how academic journal articles are organized, how to accurately cite source materials using professional citation styles, and tips for avoiding plagiarism.

UNDERSTANDING SCHOLARSHIP

Scholarship is a term many students equate with college financial support. For academics, scholarship denotes the important research contributions made by professors, scientists, and other professionals to a field of study. Students at colleges and universities are thus expected to learn how to access, evaluate, and utilize this knowledge base when writing research papers. In other words, undergraduate research is a means of developing information literacy skills. Because this is a new and challenging task for students, it is important to understand exactly what scholarly works look like and precisely how to distinguish genuine scholarly works from others.

SCHOLARLY VERSUS NON-SCHOLARLY WORKS

Scholarly sources of information are research-based and published in peer-reviewed or refereed publications. To grasp the difference between scholarly and non-scholarly sources, one has to understand what constitutes "research-based" as well as "peer-reviewed or refereed":

- *Research-based publications* both use and cite other research-based publications in an ongoing, scholarly process of refining scientific and academic knowledge. Such scholarly publications are written for other scholars and researchers rather than popular audiences. A scholarly article aims to contribute to the refinement of a particular field of study. Therefore, research-based articles make consistent references to other scholarly articles as proof of legitimate research practices. This ensures that ideas are not misrepresented and other scholars are given due credit for their contributions to the field.

- *Peer-reviewed or refereed publications* are scholarly source materials that have been reviewed and edited by other scholars, experts, and editors. Every article written by a scholar is not accepted for publishing. After writing an article, the author or authors will usually submit it for peer-review to an established journal publisher. Every field of study has its own diverse set of journals and each is staffed with editors and reviewers who are experts in the field. These reviewers and editors review the submitted articles and decide whether or not each is worthy of publishing. Once an article is published, it is considered a scholarly work.

Non-scholarly sources of information do not go through any such peer-review process. This may include books published by commercial publishers, magazine or journal articles (that do not go through a review process), and most online publications. Non-scholarly publications are generally written by people who are not considered experts in a field of study, professionals who have experience in a field but do not feel the need to reference their source materials, and organizations with a particular viewpoint or agenda.

SCHOLARLY SOURCES:
Research-based articles written by credentialed experts that have been published in peer-reviewed or refereed journals.

ORIGINAL VERSUS SECONDARY SOURCES

Remember playing the "telephone game" as a child? If not, it is like this: one person whispers a phrase into a second person's ear, who then whispers that phrase to a third person, who in turn does the same to a fourth person, and so forth. After a certain number of people have been involved in this process of repeated whispers, the last person repeats the phrase aloud to the rest of the group. Without fail that final phrasing only vaguely resembles the original message. The more people involved in the process, the more distorted the original message tends to become.

As in the telephone game, most original ideas and phrasings tend to deteriorate or devolve over time, if the original source materials are not referenced. If every child in the telephone game had gone to the first person to verify what he or she heard, then surely no information would have been lost. The same thing happens with academic concepts. When a scholar develops an idea, he or she publishes a peer-reviewed article to communicate this idea to other scholars. When a second scholar directly reads that original idea, he or she may decide to expand upon it and thus cites the original article in a new peer-reviewed article.

But what happens when a third scholar reads about the original idea in the second article and then cites it without ever reading the original? This is where the deterioration begins. Just like the telephone game, the original information can be lost through misinterpretation. By the time a fourth, fifth, or sixth reference to the original idea comes along without anyone having actually read the original article, nuanced aspects of the original idea might be lost. The only way to clear this is to find the original source and read it directly. So the reason instructors prefer that students use original source materials rather than secondary sources is to help students avoid misunderstandings that arise when original ideas are even subtly misrepresented.

> How do you find the original article when it has been cited in another article?

REDEFINING SCHOLARSHIP: BOYER'S MODEL

Through most of the 20th century, scholarship was viewed by academics as original and groundbreaking scholarly contributions to a particular field of study. As such, both the quantity and prestige of published research efforts was the measure used by most universities and departments to determine the scholarly value of professors. However, Boyer (1990) argued that the use of distinct areas of scholarship might better reflect the roles and contributions of scholars in the modern era. These four types of scholarship can provide students with a sense of the different types of research they will find when reviewing and synthesizing research:

- **Discovery**: This scholarship seeks to make an original research contribution to a field of study. It can involve landmark achievements, breakthrough scientific studies or revolutionary ideas. Such scholarship is at the heart of scholarly work, fueling innovation and inspiring the progress of knowledge for its own sake. Historical figures such as Marie Curie, Albert Einstein, and Ludwig Wittgenstein may be associated with this particular category.

- **Integration:** This scholarship attempts to synthesize or merge research-based ideas either within or between fields of study. Despite the high level of specialization found across fields of study today, some scholars work to find unique connections between ideas that would otherwise be viewed as completely separate or distinct. Such integration-based scholarship is an important part of scientific understanding that has the capacity to inform new breakthroughs and creative innovations.

- **Application:** This scholarship utilizes discovery and integration-based research to create new practical applications for use in real-world settings. It often involves finding how well new ideas and practices actually work for communities, cultures, and societies. It can also include scientific research that measures the usefulness of theoretical concepts in practical situations. Tremendous testing is involved in making the world a better place and application-based scholarship is at the forefront of the movement creating best-practices that improve the lives of people.

- **Teaching:** This scholarship is designed to improve the way information is disseminated and the manner in which education is conducted. It can include the research-based application of teaching methods, the measurement of learning processes, and the development of innovative pedagogies. This scholarship is largely guided by a desire to improve the best practices of teachers, but can also involve the examination of principles and styles of learners. In all such cases, this scholarship signifies the recognition that even the very best of ideas means little, if those ideas cannot be taught to and learned by others.

> What type of scholarship would include research studies that assess the relationship of first-year seminars with students' persistence to graduation?

CRITERIA FOR SCHOLARLY WORKS

While the categories of scholarship provide some sense of the types of research used by scholars, it does not provide any rules by which to distinguish scholarly from non-scholarly work. As mentioned previously, finding peer-reviewed or refereed sources is the single best method for making such distinctions. However, a set of assessment criteria has been developed that further clarifies the basic differences. According to Glassick, Huber, and Maeroff (2007), scholarly works include:

- Clear goals—The work includes an explicit statement of goals and objectives that are realistic, achievable, and stand in relation to other works in the field.

- Adequate preparation—The work includes references to other scholarly efforts, is relevant to the advancement of the field, and the author is a qualified expert.

- Appropriate methodology—The work evidences the use of scientific, critical, or statistical methods that are suitable to the intended goals of the research.

- Significant results—The work evidences an achievement of the intended goals that contributes to the advancement of the field of study.

- Effective presentation—The work exhibits, in both style and organization, a professional appearance that is published in an appropriate academic journal.
- Reflective critique—The work evidences critical thought on the part of the author, who uses the research process, appropriate results, and peer-reviewed feedback to inform the audience as to the benefits and limitations of the original concept.

UNDERGRADUATE RESEARCH

Most undergraduate students do not view themselves as researchers or scholars, as they do not have the credentials or experience by which to contribute to peer-reviewed publications. However, it is untrue in the sense that college students are fully expected to abide by the rules of scholarship. Writing research papers is a clear example of this expectation. Before college, very few students would have written a scholarly paper. By graduation, many students will have written numerous papers using guidelines that are every bit as scholarly as those published in peer-reviewed journals. In this respect, undergraduates are clearly expected to become scholarly researchers through the process of higher education.

Further more, national organizations such as the Association for American Colleges and Universities (AAC&U) are actively promoting the value of collaborative research between undergraduates and faculty. If this is an indication of the role undergraduates will come to play in scholarly research, then students will be publishing with faculty and staff more often as the years go by. However, for the time being, undergraduate research mostly takes place in the realm of typical class assignments and projects. Therefore, understanding how to write an effective college-level research paper is of primary importance.

PREPARING TO WRITE RESEARCH PAPERS

RESEARCH TOPICS AND QUESTIONS

Deciding on a topic is the most critical part of the research process. Considerable time and energy goes into researching and writing a typical college-level paper. A poor choice of topics—whether due to a lack of personal interest or deciding on a topic that is too narrow or too broad in scope—can make research very difficult. Many students become overly focused on simply getting the paper done, and as a result, rush through this part of the process. Being intentional when choosing a research topic can make the entire writing process much easier.

Consider using the following four steps as a guide when choosing a research topic:

1. *Brainstorming*

The purpose of brainstorming is to think of ideas and the process can take many different forms. Reviewing class materials, searching through databases or online information, or simply sitting down to free-write and create topic lists can aid in the process. When brainstorming ideas, asking certain questions can be of immense help:

- What is the range of topics available for the class?
- Is there some aspect of the class that is of particular interest to you?
- Do you have a personal issue, opinion, or goal that relates to that interest?
- How can exploring this topic expand your interest and build your knowledge?

BRAINSTORMING:
A mental process used to generate new ideas, develop creative solutions to problems, and access creative or spontaneous mental resources.

Using these four questions as a guide ensures that two things are accomplished:

a) the topic will align with the purpose of the class and
b) the topic will be something of personal interest.

Meeting both criteria is important in order to complete a meaningful research paper. Do not worry if the topic is overly general or broad at this point, because step two is designed to narrow a broad topic into a more manageable one.

2. *The Concept Tree*

Generating ideas for a topic can be pretty easy. Narrowing the possibilities down to a topic of choice can be difficult. When students claim that they do not know what to write about, this is typically not knowing how to narrow down their choices down to a single, well-refined topic, rather than having no ideas at all. A concept tree is a visual way to develop unique solutions to problems or to pare down a broad set of ideas into a more manageable form. It is a simple means of generating more specific sets of ideas in order to create a workable research question.

To begin, write down the general topic of interest at the top of your paper. Below it, develop a list of between three and five subtopics that relate to this general topic. Continue this process for each of these new topics, creating additional subtopics that branch out. It is also important to ask questions about personal interests related to each new subtopic in order to generate relevant ideas. This can go on as long as there are more specific concepts to explore, although a refined set of research options is typically established by the third or fourth set of subtopics.

It can also be used as a brainstorming tool that starts with the general topic of the class (e.g., US History), then narrows down using fairly broad parameters (e.g., time periods or populations of interest), then even more specific parameters (e.g., industrial advancements or cultural view of children), and so forth. The following is an example of a general topic-based concept tree (Figure 1.2.1).

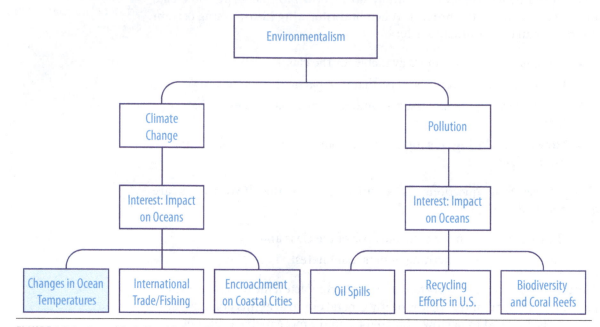

FIGURE 1.2.1: General Topic-Based Concept Tree

Source: Angela Vaughan and Brett Wilkinson

3. *Types of Research Papers*

Once a topic has been chosen, it is important to decide on the writing approach. Two major types of approaches are typically used: analytical and argumentative. The stylistic approach taken when writing a research paper depends on the choice of one or the other. The analytical style requires neutrality on the part of the writer while the argumentative style demands that the writer choose and support a particular position on the topic.

ANALYTICAL PAPER:

The neutral evaluation of a research topic that uses available evidence to analyze, explore, and provide an audience with balanced information on the thesis.

- *Analytical papers* involve the objective analysis of a topic. A research question is framed to explore aspects of the topic and a conclusion is drawn using the evidence provided. For example, say the topic is "recent changes in ocean temperature" as derived from the above concept tree. An analytical paper might break this topic down into three additional subtopics: possible causes, short-term effects, and long-term consequences. Providing an explanation of the reputable scientific data on each subtopic would thus be the larger purpose of the analytical paper. The writer lets the evidence speaks for itself.

- *Argumentative papers* involve taking a side on a debatable topic and then using logical arguments and support from source materials to persuade the audience towards one side of the debate. This requires modifying the climate question used previously by taking a position, such as whether or not recent changes in ocean temperature are due to human activities. An argumentative paper would choose a side before breaking the topic down into relevant subtopics. If the argument was that climate change is in fact due to human activities, the subtopics might include an examination of the scientific evidence, flaws in the arguments against the scientific evidence, and a discussion on the importance of taking that evidence seriously. The writer thus argues for the value of a position by using supporting evidence.

ARGUMENTATIVE PAPER: The subjective evaluation of a debatable research topic that uses available evidence to support a particular idea or position and persuade an audience to adopt the thesis.

Each style has its merits and the choice to use one or the other should be based on the expectations of course instructors, angles provided by the topic itself, and the writer's vested interests. However, both styles require a detailed evaluation of the topic and the use of legitimate source materials. Neither is easier or better than the other, although it might be more appropriate to use one or the other under a certain set of circumstances. For example, an argumentative paper on the benefits of abstinence from smoking cigarettes would be unreasonable as no one today argues that smoking is healthy. Because there would be no one to debate, an analytical paper on the challenges of addiction or the virtues of smoking cessation programs would be more appropriate.

Some students may view the analytical style as too objective or "dry" and decide to use the argumentative approach because they think it is easier to write about opinions. Sometimes this can be true, particularly if the writer has a significant amount of personal experience related to the topic. However, there are many times when analytical papers are simpler to write than argumentative ones because the analytical approach requires facts to be presented without bias. Personal opinions must be justified and supported with logical evidence, if they are to be taken seriously, and some argumentative positions are easier to justify than others. One has to keep in mind that a strong argumentative paper demands both sufficient logical evidence to support the argument and a good deal of forethought in preparing for the writing process.

4. *Thesis Statements*

Now that the general topic, specific subtopics, and writing style have all been chosen, it is time to develop a thesis statement. This is a single sentence that encapsulates the main ideas of the paper. It provides the reader with a snapshot of the topic being presented and serves as a guidepost for the writing process itself. Because research papers are meant to examine a topic from a certain point of view, a clear and concise statement of purpose gives the reader some sense of what to expect.

THESIS STATEMENT: A single sentence that summarizes the main themes or ideas of an essay or research paper.

Keeping in mind that thesis statements are created only after deciding the style, either analytical or argumentative, because its wording will change depending on which style is used. Also, there are two types of thesis statements: basic and dynamic. Basic thesis statements directly announce the purpose of a paper and are therefore easy for readers to identify. Dynamic thesis statements indirectly convey the purpose of a paper while providing a clear indication of what the reader can expect.

Some examples of basic analytical thesis statements include:

> "This paper seeks to provide evidence that _____ has an influence on _____."

> "The purpose of this paper is to investigate _____, _____, and _____ in relation to _____."

> "This paper will investigate the relationship between _____ and _____."

Some examples of basic argumentative thesis statement include:

> "This paper argues that _____ and _____ influence _____ despite evidence to the contrary."

> "The debate on _____ will be assessed in regards to the evidence for _____ and _____."

> "The purpose of this paper is to show that _____ is, in fact, a consequence of _____."

Two examples of dynamic thesis statement include:

> *"Future government healthcare initiatives would benefit from examining how the failed projects launched by previous U.S. administrations has directly influenced our modern interpretation of healthcare reform."*

> *"In a culture of widespread acceptance of pharmaceuticals, recent scientific evidence is beginning to shed light on the devastating social consequences of its misuse and abuse."*

RESEARCH STRATEGIES: FINDING SOURCES

Now that a well-defined research question and a clear thesis statement have been created, it is time to begin the research process. Although the research was started in the process of choosing a research topic, it was likely unfocused and general in nature. It is also likely that the thesis will need to be revisited and refined after finding relevant sources. A more formal approach is required from this point forward. College-level research papers always require strong documented evidence to support claims. Searching for this evidence is time consuming, so learning how to be efficient yet thorough is important. Below are some general steps used to improve research outcomes and create a strong foundation for future research.

Begin with the Research Question and Thesis Statement

Choosing the sources needed to support a research project requires keeping the so-called *goldilocks effect* in mind. Start off too broadly and there are too many sources to navigate, begin too narrowly and there are often too few sources to find what is needed. A thoughtful and step-wise approach to devising the research question is by brainstorming, using a concept tree, choosing a style, and developing a thesis statement—is very important. A solid thesis statement makes the research process easier by clearly identifying what is relevant and what is not. Whenever a question arises as to what is important for the paper, return to the original thesis statement and consider which sources make the most sense.

The search process appears daunting to many students. With so much information available, it can be a challenge to decide what is useful for a research paper. Furthermore, huge databases and vast number of published materials can make for a real headache. But with a strong thesis statement and a critical eye towards the larger purpose of a paper, finding useful resources is much easier. It requires using information technology efficiently, identifying the main ideas of a research paper, and choosing credible sources.

Using Information Technology

Almost all research begins with direct access to information technology. Online databases are the most efficient means of finding both print and digital source materials. However, there is a learning curve involved in using those databases well. Although online searches are efficient, one has to avoid accessing exclusively popular search results. It is often more effective in the long run for students to learn how to work with library databases. Most university library search engines include advanced features to include or exclude keywords, refine database search options, and navigate through specific catalogs used for different fields of study. A librarian can be of immense help in learning how to use these tools.

Identify Main Ideas

The main idea of a research paper should be the guide post for an effective search, whether reviewing print materials or weaving through online databases. The focal point in either case should be on using keywords related to the main topic and subtopics. With normal print materials, organize keyword searches using the table of contents and index. With online or library database engines, use keywords to refine the search and to narrow the field. It is extremely easy to get off topic in the research process. Always remember to recall the purpose of the search by referencing the main ideas from the thesis statement. Writing a short list of additional keywords is also highly effective in the search process and will help to sustain focus.

Choose Credible Sources

Determining the difference between credible and non-credible sources can be a tough task when specific criteria are not provided. This is made easier when professors specify what materials should be included or excluded from a research paper. If only peer-reviewed materials should be used, then the challenge is reduced to an ability to distinguish between peer-reviewed and non-peer-reviewed sources. If only original source materials are to be used, then the research process will always involve reading and citing the original source materials. In the absence of such specifications it is the responsibility of the student to decide what is to be considered. In academia, it is considered a "best practice" to use peer-reviewed and original source materials. One should check with their professor to determine what is acceptable for any given research paper and proceed accordingly.

RESEARCH STRATEGIES: EVALUATING SOURCES

Remember that not all sources are created equally. Thinking critically about source materials and making judgments about the relative value and credibility of each source is a vital aspect of information literacy. As discussed previously, many internet sources are unreliable as are non-scholarly works. However, there are also plenty of non-scholarly documents and books published on library databases and sitting on library shelves. Discerning the good from the bad is complicated, the following points can assist in making a thoughtful decision on what to include in your research paper.

Accuracy

Finding an accurate source means that the information can be verified elsewhere. Most credible sources will provide citations to verify accuracy, such as a reference list. Rather than accepting a statement, definition, or graph is correct because it has been published by a scholar or professional, one can cross-reference the materials. By verifying accuracy instead of assuming, it is also possible to learn more about the topic at hand. Few writers convey the same information in the exact same way and the differing perspectives often lead to new insights that improve understanding of the material.

Authority

Just because someone writes about an idea, it does not make them an authority on the matter. Determine the credentials of the author as well as the publication when reviewing the source materials. Is the author an expert in the field of study? Is the publication a peer-reviewed academic source? Sometimes these questions are easy to answer. Many peer-reviewed academic journal articles include the author credentials on the title page, and a quick trip to the publisher website can verify the credentials of a particular journal. As for books, checking author credentials can be as easy as reading the author biography provided on the first few pages.

Audience

Everyone writes for an intended audience. Students write papers for professors to grade, professors write scholarly papers for other professors to assess, and many professionals write non-scholarly books and articles for the general public. The intended audience is important for determining the credibility of a source. For the most part, college-level research papers require the use of academic sources rather than popular sources and original source materials are preferred over secondary sources. Many popular books include attention-grabbing ideas taken from academic sources without any clear reference to the original source materials. Additionally, popular magazine articles are often editorial or journalistic in style rather than scientific in nature.

Objectivity

Scientific evidence is meant to be objective and its documentation is impartial. Of course, this is not always the case in practice. Even the most virtuous of scientists can present data that supports their viewpoint while excluding evidence to the contrary. Although it can be difficult to assess for bias when doing research, it is still important to consider it. Cross-referencing the materials for accuracy and looking at credentials to ascertain authority can be helpful in this respect. At times when authors are quite clear in asserting their opinions, it is important to cite that information as opinion rather than fact. Objectivity also comes into question with popular books and articles that are meant for broader audiences.

Currency

The age of a source should always be considered when doing research. However, there are no clear lines to draw on the value of newer and older publications. Some old publications remain definitive and authoritative sources of information while others have not aged as well. Some newer publications have not been around long enough to determine their merit or verify their conclusions. It also depends on the field of study. Most of the classic texts cited in philosophy are extremely old whereas many of the social science fields prefer those references to newer scientific sources to be used for research papers (Figure 1.2.2).

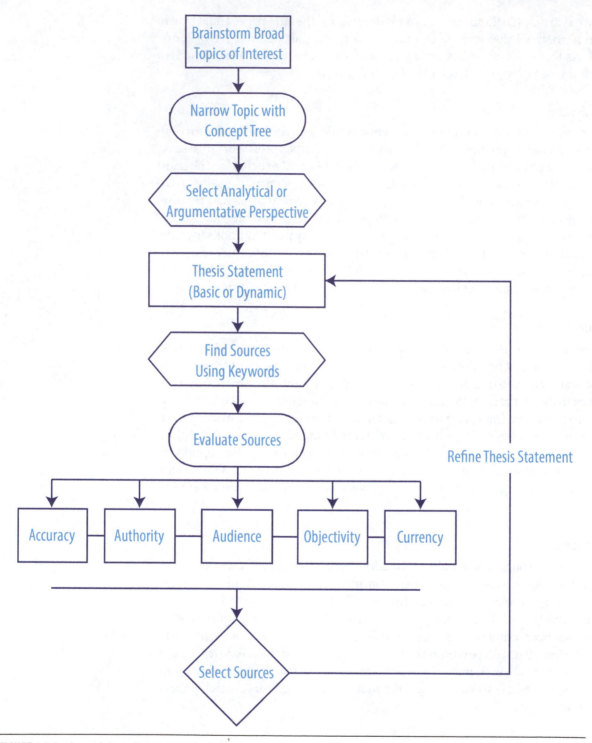

FIGURE 1.2.2: Research Paper Process

Source: Angela Vaughan and Brett Wilkinson

RESEARCH PROCESS, CITATIONS AND PLAGIARISM

ACADEMIC RESEARCH PAPERS: STRUCTURE

The typical published scientific research paper is divided into seven major sections. While there is some variation, these sections are used as a formal template in most scientific fields of study to ensure consistency in reporting research. It should also be noted that many conceptual, or theoretical papers as well as non-scientific papers in the humanities do not follow these general guidelines. The function of each is described below.

Title Page

For most research publications, this information is included on the same page as the abstract.

Abstract

In this section, a brief synopsis of the article that may include the general purpose, methods, results, and conclusions to be taken from the article is summarized. It can be used to quickly assess whether or not an article contains information that is pertinent to the reader. Most publications include reference information on the same page as the abstract, including the article title, author names and institutions, journal name, publication date, and other information to be used in a citation. The following is an example of an abstract for the article titled, First-Year Seminars: Supporting Male College Students' Long-Term Academic Success taken from the peer-reviewed journal, Journal of College Student Retention: Research, Theory & Practice.

Example Abstract:

Research has revealed a gender gap where male students have higher rates of academic difficulties and lower college enrollment and graduation rates compared with females. This study measured the relationship of male student (including first generation and minority students) participation in a first-year seminar and their first-term grade point average and first-year persistence for two cohorts (N=828; 683) and third-year persistence for one cohort. There were significant differences in first-term grade point average (as high as 0.7 grade points greater) and first- and third-year persistence for all participants (including subgroups) in both cohorts as compared with nonparticipants. There were strong statistical findings where the range of differences in persistence between all male participants and nonparticipants was as large as almost 25% (third-year persistence). For male minority students, this difference increased to 34%. The study presents compelling evidence for a three credit, academic-based first-year seminar to promote male student success over the short and long term (Swanson, Vaughan, & Wilkinson, 2015).

Introduction or Literature Review

The structure of this section changes depending on the type of research or publication. Some articles include both an introduction and a literature review while others use just one. The purpose of this section is to provide background information on other studies in the field that are relevant to the current article. It ensures that the article is understood in relation to the broader field of study and provides insight into the direction of the research (i.e., research purposes, questions or hypotheses). It also defines relevant terms and provides a broader synopsis of what is found in the article.

Methods or Procedures

This section explains the design and methods used to perform the research. It includes a description of the research participants, questionnaires or measures used, and any information on data collection (including procedures or descriptions of interventions). By providing details on how the research was conducted, other researchers can replicate the study in the future. It gives a clear explanation for what was done and how it was done.

Results

This section examines the data from the research. All statistics, graphs, and tables are provided so that readers can evaluate the merits of the research approach and determine whether or not certain conclusions should rightfully be drawn. Many people who read and use research articles are unfamiliar with the statistical processes. You should not panic if you do not understand the details included in this section. The next section will be more helpful.

Discussion

This section translates the results into a fuller and more practical explanation of the data. This section is intended for all audiences who are interested in the research. It includes a connection drawn between the hypothesis or purpose of the study, and the actual results. It also explores the potential ramifications of the research in terms of its impact on the field. It can also include a review of study limitations and ideas for future research based on the findings. After reading the Abstract, it is helpful to read the Discussion section next to get an overview of the article and its relevance to your project.

References

This section provides full and complete information on all of the citations used in the article, so that readers can cross reference source materials.

TABLE 1.2.1 ORGANIZATION OF JOURNAL ARTICLES

Section	Description
Abstract	Overview of the Study
Introduction/ Literature Review	Past Research Findings; Description of Concepts or Theories; Purpose of the Research; Research Questions or Hypotheses
Method	Participants; Procedures; Questionnaires/Surveys
Results	Statistical Findings
Discussion	Results in General Terms; Implications of the Research (Practical Importance); Limitations of the Study; Future Research
References	Listing of All Sources Used in the Article

ACADEMIC RESEARCH PAPERS: CITATIONS

All scholarly works require authors to appropriately cite sources. As previously noted, this ensures the credibility of the published work and gives due credit to other scholars in the field. However, there is not a universal approach to citations. Different professional organizations require different formats and rules. While all scholarly works include citations, these may vary depending on the citation style. The three major professional styles in use today are outlined below.

- *APA Style*—Created by the American Psychological Association, APA style formatting is widely used in the social sciences and sometimes used in the applied and natural sciences. It makes use of parenthetical references in the body of the text that include author names, dates of publication, and page numbers for quotes (e.g., Smith, 2016, p. 6). No footnotes or endnotes are included. The references page found at the end of APA articles tends to use the following format for other books and articles:

Books: Smith, A. (2016). *The big book of how to write in APA style.* New York: Freedom Press.

Articles: Smith, A. (2016). How to write in APA style. *The Journal of Excellence in Citations, 5*(8), 47–63.

- *MLA Style*—Created by the Modern Language Association, MLA style formatting is generally used in the humanities. It makes use of parenthetical references in the body of the text that include author names and page numbers (e.g., Smith 6). No publication dates, footnotes, or endnotes are included. The works cited page found at the end of MLA articles tends to use the following format for books and articles:

Books: Smith, Anna B. *The Big Book of How to Write in MLA Style.* Freedom Press, 2016.

Articles: Smith, Anna. "How to Write in MLA Style." *The Journal of Excellence in Citations,* no. 5, 2016, pp. 47–63.

- *Chicago Style*—Created by the University of Chicago Press, Chicago style formatting is primary used in the humanities, some social sciences, and many non-academic publications. It emphasizes the use of footnotes or endnotes in the body of the text. The bibliography page found at the end of Chicago style articles tends to use the following format for articles:

Books: Smith, Anna B. *The Big Book of How to Write in Chicago Style.* New York: Freedom Press, 2016.

Articles: Smith, Anna. "How to Write in Chicago Style." *The Journal of Excellence in Citations* 5 (2016): 47–63.

ACADEMIC RESEARCH PAPERS: PLAGIARISM

PLAGIARISM:
The unauthorized use, theft, or misrepresentation of another's original work as one's own.

There are few ethical issues of more egregious academic concern in higher education than plagiarism. Plagiarism is considered the unauthorized use, theft or illegal misrepresentation of a work. While issues of plagiarism extend well beyond the realm of education including issues such as copyright infringement and journalistic ethics. The topic of plagiarism is most often discussed in educational circles. For both students and professors, academic integrity is upheld as an ethical standard and charges of plagiarism can result in serious academic penalties, suspensions or even expulsions. In other words, it is in the best interest of every researcher to give credit where credit is due by accurately citing source materials.

Generally, any concept or idea that has been taken from published academic sources must be cited. Otherwise, it appears that an author is intentionally misrepresenting the work done by others as their own work. The only exception to this rule is related to *common knowledge* or information that is known by most people. This might include scientific facts such as the boiling point of water or historical facts such as George Washington being the first President of the United States. This information is factual, not discovered by a specific scholar, and is widely known to most people. However, very few ideas used in research papers are this obvious. When unsure, it is best to take the side of caution and cite a source.

The most serious violation involves intentionally copying text or quotes from an article or book verbatim and then acting as though it is an original concept. With the ability to copy and paste text, some students intentionally use the work of others as their own. Such blatant misrepresentations are unethical and, in some cases, illegal. Often at times students unintentionally plagiarize by failing to cite sources appropriately. There are numerous guides available online and provided by university writing centers to help students learn to avoid plagiarism. Accessing these resources is a good idea for every college student.

Avoiding plagiarism requires some diligence in the research process. Knowing when a citation is needed involves following general rules of academic integrity and keeping up with the sources for a research paper. When doing research, develop a habit of noting down author names, dates, titles, and publications for sources used during a study session. This can be extremely helpful in retracing steps to find original source materials. It may take extra time, effort, and organization to do it properly, but this sacrifice is minor considering the dramatic pitfalls of academic dishonesty.

Avoiding plagiarism is the responsibility of every individual student. Here are a few basic rules to keep in mind when it comes to plagiarism:

Rule #1: Always credit a source when the information used is not your own and is not considered common knowledge.

Rule #2: Always credit a source when using text verbatim in order to provide a quote.

Rule #3: Summarizing or paraphrasing the ideas of another author always requires a citation and the resulting interpretation must be significantly different from the original text.

Rule #4: Use of the following sources must include a citation: books, articles, magazines, newspapers, speeches, interviews, websites, personal letters or correspondences, radio or television references, audio or digital recordings, electronic databases, etc.

Rule #5: Use of the following formats must include citations: text, quotes, stories, images, videos, graphs, tables, statistics, etc.

Rule #6: Submitting the same research paper in multiple classes or for multiple publications is considered self-plagiarism, and is subject to the same rules and penalties used for plagiarizing the work of others.

A librarian or professor can be helpful for further questions in this sphere.

MODULE 1.2 SUMMARY

- Information literacy is a transferrable learning skill that can be improved through the experience of seeking, evaluating, and using research in college.
- Scholarly works are research-based articles published by credentialed experts in peer-reviewed or refereed journals.
- Four types of scholarly research approaches include discovery-based, integration-based, application-based, and teaching-based approaches.
- Scholarly works include: clear goals, adequate preparation, appropriate methodology, significant results, effective presentations, and reflective critiques.

- Four steps to preparing a research topic include: brainstorming, using a concept tree, choosing a writing style, and developing a thesis statement.
- When evaluating research, it is important to gauge the accuracy, authority, audience, objectivity, and currency of source materials.
- The structure of most scientific research papers includes seven sections: title page, abstract, introduction or literature review, methods or procedures, results, discussion, and references.
- Major citation formatting styles include APA style, MLA style, and Chicago style.
- Plagiarism refers to the unauthorized use of source materials and can be avoided by using appropriate citations for all sources referenced in a research paper.

KEY TERMS

- **Analytical Paper** – The neutral evaluation of a research topic that uses available evidence to analyze, explore, and provide an audience with balanced information on the thesis.
- **Argumentative Paper** – The subjective evaluation of a debatable research topic that uses available evidence to support a particular idea or position and persuade an audience to adopt the thesis.
- **Brainstorming** – A mental process used to generate new ideas, develop creative solutions to problems, and access creative or spontaneous mental resources.
- **Information Literacy** – An ability to both determine the need for additional information and to find, evaluate, and use that information appropriately.
- **Plagiarism** – The unauthorized use, theft or misrepresentation of another's original work as one's own.
- **Scholarly Sources** – Research-based articles written by credentialed experts that have been published in peer-reviewed or refereed journals.
- **Thesis Statement** – A single sentence that summarizes the main themes or ideas of an essay or research paper.

REFERENCES

American Library Association. (1989). *Presidential committee on information literacy: Final report.* Retrieved May 23, 2016 from http://www.ala.org/acrl/publications/whitepapers/presidential

Boyer, E. L. (1990). *Scholarship reconsidered: Priorities of the professoriate.* Princeton, NJ: Carnegie Foundation for the Advancement of Teaching.

Glassick, C. E., Huber, M. R., & Maeroff, G. I. (1997). *Scholarship assessed: Evaluation of the professoriate.* San Francisco, CA: Jossey–Bass.

Swanson, N. M., Vaughan, A. L., & Wilkinson, B. D. (2015). First-year seminars: Supporting male college students' long-term academic success. *Journal of College Student Retention: Research, Theory & Practice.* doi: 10.1177/1521025115604811

ADDITIONAL READINGS

Bikson, T. A. (1996). Educating a globally prepared workforce: New research on college and corporate perspectives. *Liberal Education, 82*(2), 12–19.

Brew, A. (2012). Teaching and research: New relationships and their implications for inquiry-based teaching and learning in higher education. *Higher Education Research & Development, 31*(1), 101–114.

Gibaldi, J., & Modern Language Association of America. (2009). *MLA handbook for writers of research papers* (7th ed.). New York: Modern Language Association of America.

Harper, R. D. (2010). *The Chicago manual of style* (16th ed.). Chicago: The University of Chicago Press.

Johnston, B., & Webber, S. (2003). Information literacy in higher education: A review and case study. *Studies in Higher Education, 28*(3), 335–352.

Publication Manual of the American Psychological Association (6th ed.). (2010). Washington, DC: American Psychological Association.

Kaiser, B., Mishler, D., Peoples, W., & Wells, A. (2014). Undergraduate research and a liberal arts education: Similar goals, similar solutions. *Journal of College Science Teaching, 43*(5), 48–54.

Roth, M. S. (2014). *Beyond the university: Why liberal education matters.* New Haven, CT: Yale University Press.

Zilvinskis, J. (2019). Measuring quality in high-impact practices. Higher Education, 1–23. doi: 10.1007/s10734-019-00365-9

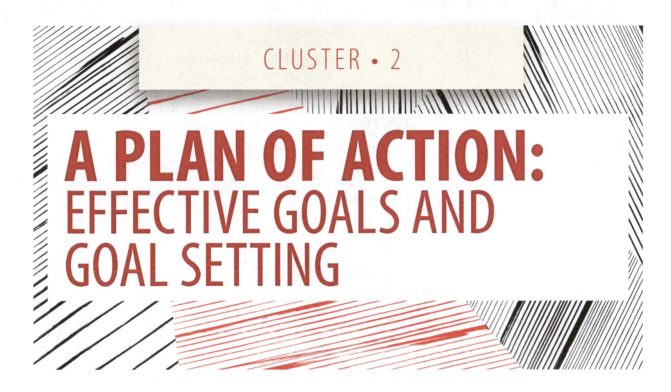

A PLAN OF ACTION:
EFFECTIVE GOALS AND GOAL SETTING

CASE STUDY

Derrick is a first-semester freshman. Going to college has been a goal of his since elementary school. Now that he is here, he is very excited and is eager to do well. However, after three weeks of classes, some of the excitement has turned to feelings of stress and anxiety. He is starting to feel overwhelmed. Because he still wants to do well his first semester, he begins the next week, by telling himself he'll study more, be better organized and manage his time more effectively. Yet, by the end of the week, not much has changed. In fact, he has taken exams in two of his classes and made a 63 and 68%. He is starting to question whether coming to college was mistake and wonders if he belongs here.

QUESTIONS

1. Has Derrick set goals for his first semester? Do they include characteristics that will be useful and help him be successful? Why or why not?

2. Do you think Derrick's exam results reflect his potential in these classes? Why or why not?

3. What would you recommend to Derrick to help him focus his efforts and to achieve better performance?

My Goals: Financial, Attitude, Artistic, Education, Pleasure, Public Service, Career, Family

CLUSTER OVERVIEW

"Because judgments and actions are partly self-determined, people can effect change in themselves and their situations through their own efforts" (Bandura, 1989, p. 1175).

Goals provide the foundation for motivation by directing behaviors and focusing efforts. Although most people have a sense of the things they would like to accomplish in their lives from day to day, the most successful people use goals and goal setting in intentional ways. Yet, not all goals are equally helpful or useful, and effective goal setting is not based on simply writing down your goals.

As such, the first module will discuss the characteristics and types of useful goals, the qualities of goal setting that drive action, and the empirical evidence that connects goal setting with achievement. The second module will provide more details about incorporating these elements in your educational experiences as well as provide specific examples and plans of action.

CLUSTER OBJECTIVES

- Describe the relationship between values, goals, and goal commitment.
- Describe the characteristics of a useful goal.
- Describe the types of goals - short-term, long-term, and enabling goals - and their relationship to directing behavior.
- Describe the characteristics of effective goal setting.
- Formulate beginning goals and associated goal plans using goal-setting techniques.

UNDERSTANDING GOALS AND GOAL SETTING

CLUSTER 2 OBJECTIVES COVERED IN THIS MODULE

☐ **OBJECTIVE:** Describe the relationship between values, goals and goal commitment.

☐ **OBJECTIVE:** Describe the characteristics of a useful goal.

☐ **OBJECTIVE:** Describe the types of goals - short-term, long-term and enabling goals - and their relationship to directing behavior.

☐ **OBJECTIVE:** Describe the characteristics of effective goal setting.

GOALS AND GOAL SETTING

Many people have been told from an early age that they should have goals. It is likely you have already heard of SMART goals or some other acronym that highlights the characteristics of effective goals. Because there is strong, consistent research that connects specific goal characteristics and types, and intentional goal setting with achievement, the intent of this module is to provide an in-depth discussion of the theories and achievement research around goals.

GOAL SETTING AND ACHIEVEMENT

Why should you set goals? Decades of consistent research show that setting effective goals is a developed life skill that can potentially impact your academic, personal, and professional lives (Koestner et al., 2002; Locke & Latham, 2002; Morisano, Hirsh, Peterson, Pihl, & Shore, 2010). Although much of the research is related to attaining specific outcomes, other research also suggests that people who set goals, irrespective of whether they are achieved, will potentially have increased positive affect, or positive feelings, from the experience (Emmons & Diener, 1986). In other words, the act of

POSITIVE AFFECT:
Experiencing positive moods such as joy, happiness and interest.

setting goals that are personally meaningful can lead to feelings of happiness, even if you do not necessarily achieve your goals.

Being happy is important, but most students also want to feel confident that their efforts will lead to tangible outcomes. Here the research is clear. Using effective, intentional goal-setting techniques leads to increased effort and persistence, motivation, higher GPAs, greater course loads, and more adaptive learning strategies (Adriessen, Phalet, & Lens, 2006; Bandura & Schunk, 1981; Fryer, Ginns, & Walker, 2014; Koestner et al., 2002; Locke & Latham, 2002; Morisano et al., 2010). The following will first describe the characteristics of useful goals and then describe how to incorporate these goals into a goal-setting technique that produces results.

USEFUL GOALS

REFLECTION: Have you set a goal to do well in college? How do you define "well"? Have you thought about *how* you will achieve this goal?

VALUES, COMMITMENT, AND OWNERSHIP

Where do your goals come from? It may seem that the obvious answer is your own wants and needs. Both goal and motivation theories suggest that goals and purposes that are "personally meaningful" (La Guardia, 2009, p. 92) will lead to greater benefits, health, and well-being (Deci & Ryan, 2002). Personally meaningful goals or self-concordant goals are also related to significantly "greater goal progress" (Koestner, Lekes, Powers, & Chicoine, 2002, p. 236). Despite this, especially for adolescents transitioning to adulthood, goals can also be established or shaped by others (La Guardia, 2009). This may appear as parents encouraging or even insisting on a particular major or college choice for their child. This can also happen in relationships when someone's partner wants him or her to eat healthy or to exercise more. Typically, when people are in these situations, they may begin with high levels of motivation; however, over time, if these goals are not part of their own value system, their ability to persevere past challenges and to maintain motivation becomes difficult or even impossible.

SELF-CONCORDANT GOALS: Goals that are personally meaningful.

Alternatively, goals that you set based on your own values and beliefs will lead to greater levels of motivation and commitment. In other words, "persons develop and maintain commitment to goals that are important to them" (Austin & Vancouver, 1996, p. 343). Ideally, relational partners will also support and nurture these choices, which then further strengthen the connection between values, goals and motivation (Deci & Ryan, 2002; La Guardia, 2009). Therefore, the first and most critical goal characteristic is whether you *own* your goals. As you set goals in different areas of your life, determining the basis for each of your goals will help establish your commitment and ability to achieve your goals. The following section will discuss other essential characteristics of useful goals.

What are some behaviors or choices that might signal that a person does not own his or her goals?

CHARACTERISTICS OF USEFUL GOALS

Specific and Measurable ⁄

Researchers, motivational speakers, and textbooks on college success almost always recommend that goals be *specific* and/or *measurable* (Bandura & Schunk, 1981; Cuseo, Thompson, Campagna, & Fecas, 2013; Doran, 1981; Gore, Leuwerke, & Metz, 2016; Harrington, 2013; Locke, 1968; Locke & Latham, 1990; 2002; Nist & Hoschuh, 2000; Weinstein, Woodruff, & Await, 2004). For example, consider the following two goals:

- I would like to do well this semester.
- I would like to earn a 3.0 GPA this semester.

The second goal is more helpful because it evaluates your progress towards the goal, it is clearly defined, and it is more likely to direct your efforts towards goal-relevant activities versus goal-irrelevant activities (Locke & Latham, 2002). The research also suggests that specific goals lead to greater effort. In the 1960s, Locke (1968) did an extensive review of the literature and found consistent results (i.e., more than 10 separate studies) where specific goals produced higher levels of performance as compared to circumstances where the subjects were only encouraged to do their best. These results have been replicated in the decades since (Locke & Latham, 2002; Smith, Locke, & Barry, 1990). Additionally, specific and clear goals increase persistence and promote the use of effective and appropriate strategies (Locke & Latham, 2002).

Challenging ⁄

Another suggested characteristic is that goals should be *challenging* (Weinstein, Woodruff, & Await, 2004). However, many of the recommendations do not include challenging and only list achievable or realistic. Locke and Latham (1990; 2002) found that goals that are moderately difficult or challenging produced the highest levels of effort. Goals that are too easy or too hard produced significantly less effort. In other words, a reasonably challenging goal raises the bar for what is considered "realistic" and makes the goal-seeking process more rewarding. It is very important to strike a balance between the two. Achievable or realistic goals tend to promote increased self-efficacy or the belief that you can accomplish the task (Bandura, 1995); while challenging goals tend to support one's innate need for developing skills and building competence and lead to higher levels of motivation (Deci & Ryan, 2002; see Cluster 6 for a more detailed discussion on self-efficacy and innate needs). Alternatively, goals that are too hard could lead to decisions to not try at all. Consider the following goals:

- I will earn a 100% on all of my exams this semester.
- I will earn at least an 80% on my first chemistry exam.

SPECIFIC AND MEASURABLE GOALS: Goals that include details and criteria such that goal attainment can be clearly determined.

A goal is specific if you can answer the question, "Did you achieve your goal?" with a definitive yes or no. Using the goal examples: Did you do well this semester? I think so, maybe, um, depends. Versus: Did you earn a 3.0 GPA this semester? Yes, I earned a 3.25.

CHALLENGING AND REALISTIC GOALS: Goals that can be achieved with higher levels of effort.

The first goal is likely unrealistic and too hard for most students. If you did not believe you could accomplish the goal, it is unlikely that this goal would direct any behaviors or increase motivation for the task. Why study, if you are not going to succeed? The second goal may or may not be challenging or realistic. This decision would depend on the student (it is here that self-awareness is most important).

Timeframe

Another common characteristic is *time related* (Cuseo et al., 2013; Doran, 1981; Gore et al., 2016; Weinstein et al., 2004). Setting specific timeframe guidelines allows you to evaluate your progress, tells you what to do and when, and sometimes, more importantly, when you are done. Consider Ray's following goal:

- For the next month, I will work out for an hour three times a week.

This goal includes several timeframes. First, by stating "the next month," this allows Ray the opportunity to evaluate his progress and decide if he should continue or if he should make any changes. Stating "an hour three times a week," tells him exactly what to do. He can also feel a sense of accomplishment by following his specified plan and not feel "guilty" because he did not work out more.

How do these characteristics help hold you accountable to your goals?

Other Characteristics

In 1981, Doran was the first to propose SMART (specific, measurable, assignable, realistic, and time-related) goals. His audiences at the time were corporate leaders and managers who were trying to increase productivity and effectiveness in their organizations. Since that time, SMART goals have been adapted to other contexts, especially in education. The acronym has also changed to reflect these other contexts and includes the characteristics described previously. Other goal characteristics have also been suggested, including relevant (Gore et al., 2016), actionable (Cuseo et al., 2013), and desirable and believable (Nist & Hoschuh, 2000). The following table summarizes the different goal recommendations.

TABLE 2.1.1 SUMMARY OF RECOMMENDED GOAL CHARACTERISTICS

Weinstein, Woodruff, & Await (2004)	Harrington (2013)	Nist & Hoschuh (2000)	Doran (1981)	Gore, Leuwerke, & Metz (2016)	Cuseo, Thompson, Campagna, & Fecas (2013)
Specific	Specific	Believable *(Belief that you can achieve the goal)*	Specific	Specific	Specific
Measurable	Measurable	Measurable	Measurable	Measurable	Measurable
Challenging	Challenging	Desirable *(How much do you want the goal?)*	Assignable	Achievable	Actionable *(Identifies the specific behaviors to achieve the goal)*
Realistic	Realistic	Realistic	Realistic	Relevant *(Important to you and your values)*	Realistic
Time-Related			Time-Related	Time-Related	Time-Related

For the remaining discussions, useful goals are defined as being specific and measurable, realistic and challenging, and include a timeframe. Using this definition, the following illustrates some examples of vague goals that have been modified to include these more useful characteristics.

USEFUL GOALS:
Goals that include the characteristics of specific and measurable, realistic and challenging, and include a timeframe.

TABLE 2.1.2 EXAMPLES OF MODIFIED GOALS

Goal	Useful Goal
I will study more.	I will study one hour, five days a week for each of my courses.
I will be more organized.	Every Sunday, I will plan my weekly goals based on the syllabi of each of my classes.
I will eat healthier.	Every day, I will eat fruits and/or vegetables at every meal.
I will get more involved on campus.	By the end of the month, I will go to meetings for at least two clubs related to my major.
I will make more friends.	Every day at lunch, I will introduce myself to someone new at the dining hall.

TYPES OF GOALS

SHORT-TERM GOALS:
Goals achieved in a relatively short timeframe such as within days, weeks, or months.

LONG-TERM GOALS:
Goals achieved over a long period of time such as a semester or even years.

ENABLING GOALS:
Short-term goals that directly help a person achieve other long-term goals.

There are several types of goals related to timeframes. These include: short-term and long-term goals. Although the actual time defined for short and long term is unimportant, the idea of proximity is important. Typically, short-term goals are considered more immediate, such as the next several days, weeks, or months. Long-term goals can be defined as a semester or even the next 10 years.

Despite this, the research strongly suggests that having proximal subgoals or enabling goals (short-term goals that lead to attainment of long-term goals) are necessary to maintain high levels of motivation (Bandura & Schunk, 1981). Enabling goals affect our motivation in multiple ways. First, consider Anna's long-term goal of, "I will earn my college degree in nursing in four years." This goal has all three characteristics of a useful goal; however, because of the four-year timeframe, her motivation may be diminished as obstacles and challenges appear from day to day. In fact, with this length of time, keeping a focus on goal-relevant activities may feel impossible. Without enabling goals, Anna, as a freshman student, may evaluate her current first-semester performance, skills and abilities against the future standard of graduating (Bandura & Schunk, 1981). This evaluation may be more discouraging rather than motivating.

Now consider that Anna has set several enabling goals that will eventually lead to her long-term goal of graduation. For example, one of these enabling goals may be, "I will earn at least an 85% on all of my reading quizzes in chemistry." Now, Anna can evaluate her performance against an immediate outcome and then make any adjustments if necessary. Additionally, because this enabling goal is short term, it provides immediate "guides for performance" and can "effectively mobilize effort" (Bandura & Schunk, 1981, p. 587). If Anna accomplishes this enabling goal, her self-efficacy or belief in her abilities in chemistry will increase as well as her feelings of competence. Repeated success can lead to strengthening of Anna's interest in her coursework (Vallerand & Ratelle, 2002). With heightened feelings of competence and interest, it is also more likely that Anna will seek other challenging tasks within this domain.

As in the example above, effective goal setting will combine some short- and long-term goals, and should also include associated enabling goals.

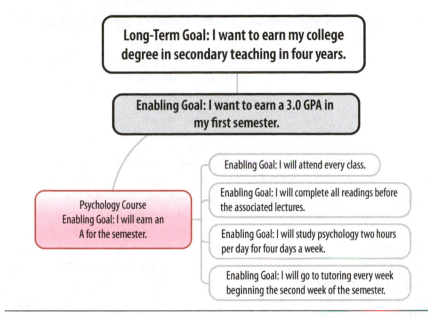

FIGURE 2.1.1: A Long-Term Goal with Enabling Goals   *Source: Angela Vaughan and Brett Wilkinson*

Other types of goals related to commitment, effort, and motivation include achievement goals. For a detailed discussion of achievement goals, see Cluster 6.

GOAL SETTING

In addition to setting *useful* goals, there are several other characteristics that should be incorporated to gain the most for your efforts. The following summarizes effective goal-setting characteristics based on the research:

- Set useful goals that are specific and measurable, realistic and challenging, include a timeframe (Weinstein et al., 2004), and that are personally meaningful (Koestner et al., 2002)
- Set a combination of short- and long-term goals with associated enabling or proximal subgoals (Bandura & Schunk, 1981)
- Create detailed implementation plans or action plans (Gollwotzer & Brandstätter, 1997; Koestner et al., 2002; Morisano et al., 2010)

- Share your goals with friends and family and make your goals public (Hayes et al., 1985)
- Write a future narrative that describes how you will feel and how your life will look like if you attain your goals (Bandura, 1977; Morisano et al., 2010; Oettingen, Pak, & Schnetter 2011; Schunk 1991)

IMPLEMENTATION PLANS

Once useful goals are defined, detailed implementation or action plans are needed to help maintain commitment and to focus your efforts on specific goal-relevant activities (Gollwotzer & Brandstätter, 1997; Koestner et al., 2002; Morisano et al., 2010). Action steps or means should also include the same characteristics of useful goals. In many ways, action steps are essentially smaller, very short-term enabling goals. For example, consider the two following action steps listed to achieve the goal of, "I will earn an 85% on my next exam in sociology:"

- Action Step 1: I will study more before my next exam.
- Action Step 2: During the next two weeks before my exam, I will study one hour per day for six days a week.

Action Step 2 provides clear instructions to guide behaviors before the exam. Research also indicates that identifying multiple means or actions steps, leads to greater goal commitment and progress while reducing perceived difficulty in goal attainment (Kruglanski, Pierro, & Sheveland, 2011). For the same goal, multiple action steps or means could look like:

GOAL: I WILL EARN AN 85% ON MY NEXT EXAM IN SOCIOLOGY.

Two weeks before the exam,…

- Action Step 1: I will study one hour per day for six days a week.
- Action Step 2: I will meet an additional time each week with my study group (i.e., twice a week).
- Action Step 3: By the end of each week, I will meet with my sociology professor and ask any questions that emerged during studying.
- Action Step 4: By the end of the first week, I will create a graphic organizer and flash cards for each of the chapters so that I can study throughout each day during short breaks and off times.

Each of these action steps include characteristics of useful goals and provides clear directions on behaviors to take when preparing for the exam.

As part of a detailed plan, identifying potential obstacles and steps to overcome them is also critical (Morisano et al., 2010). Researchers have described these action steps as "if-then" implementation intentions (Oettingen & Gollwitzer, 2010). In other words, "if this event happens, then I will do this behavior." Cluster 7 further discusses these implementation intentions as part of a self-regulatory process that leads to greater persistence and goal attainment.

When considering potential obstacles, it is also helpful to consider action steps in two ways: proactive and reactive. A proactive action step is a step taken to avoid a known, likely obstacle, whereas a reactive action step is a step used when an obstacle actually occurs (i.e., if this occurs, then I will do this). For example, in the goal above, a possible and likely obstacle could be the student being distracted by his or her peers. A proactive action step could be:

- During my study times, I will study in the library (not my dorm room) and I will turn off all electronics while studying.

Another potential obstacle might be that the student gets called into work for extra shifts. A reactive action step could be:

- Any study times missed due to work, I will study on my off day to make up the time.

Although it is unlikely that you will be able to predict all the obstacles that may occur, taking the time to identify more common obstacles and associated action steps will empower you and help build the confidence needed to be successful.

PUBLIC GOALS

Another helpful characteristic of goal setting is to make your goals public (Hayes et al., 1985). In Hayes et al.'s (1985) study, the researchers found that, "the effects of public goal setting were relatively strong, long lasting, and highly consistent across students" (p. 210). In fact, the experimental group's (i.e., group who set public goals) achievement on the academic post-test were more than double to those who only set private goals or the control group who did not set any goals. By sharing your goals with friends, family members, or other people close to you, it is more likely that your goals will be "effective in modifying behavior" (p. 211). Using your social context bolsters your ability to self-reinforce necessary behaviors and actions that can eventually lead to attaining your goals.

FUTURE NARRATIVE

The last characteristic is writing a future narrative. After analyzing the results of their study on goal setting and academic achievement, Morisano et al. (2010) suggested that reflecting on an "ideal future" may be one of the "intervention's most valuable components" (p. 260). Setting a specific goal tells you what you want to achieve; however, reflecting on your future tells you how the goal will impact your life. Achieving a "3.0 semester GPA" has

PROACTIVE ACTION STEP:
An action step that is identified to avoid a known, likely obstacle.

REACTIVE ACTION STEP:
An action step that is identified for potential obstacles that may or may not occur.

Who would be the first person you would share your goals with?

no meaning unless it is tied to the consequences and effects on someone's life. For example, a student with this GPA first-semester goal may write the following:

> Achieving this GPA goal will give me increased confidence going into my second semester. As such, it will be easier to select courses and know that I am capable of completing them successfully. Letting my parents know that I achieved this goal will be exciting, because I know they will be very proud of me. I will also know that the money spent on this semester was worthwhile and not wasted. I'll be able to enjoy my winter break with little stress and then be excited to return to classes once the break is over. I will also know that I am one step closer to my long-term goal of graduating.

Thinking about your goals, what are you looking forward to the most in achieving them?

Reflecting on these possibilities and attempting to "feel" these emotions can help maintain commitment and focus on required goal activities.

The next module will guide you in this goal-setting process and include specific examples within several domains.

MODULE 2.1 SUMMARY

- Goal setting is strongly related to positive outcomes including affect, motivation, and academic achievement.
- Setting goals based on personal values and beliefs is a critical characteristic for attaining goals.
- Useful goals include the characteristics of specific and measurable, realistic and challenging, and include a timeframe.
- An enabling goal is a short-term goal that helps a person achieve another long-term goal. Setting enabling goals is essential in achieving these long-term goals.
- Characteristics of effective goal setting include forming useful goals, creating detailed implementation plans, making goals public, and writing future narratives.

KEY TERMS

- **Challenging and Realistic Goals** – Goals that can be achieved with higher levels of effort.
- **Enabling Goals or Proximal Subgoals** – Short-term goals that directly helps a person achieve other long-term goals.
- **Long-Term Goals** – Goals achieved over a long period of time such as a semester or even years.
- **Positive Affect** – Experiencing positive moods such as joy, happiness, and interest.

- **Proactive Action Step** – An action step that is identified to avoid a known, likely obstacle.
- **Reactive Action Step** – An action step that is identified for potential obstacles that may or may not occur.
- **Self-Concordant Goals** – Set goals that are personally meaningful.
- **Short-Term Goals** – Goals achieved in a relatively short timeframe such as within days, weeks, or months.
- **Specific and Measurable Goals** – Goals that include details and criteria such that goal attainment can be clearly determined.
- **Useful Goals** – Goals that include the characteristics of specific and measurable, realistic and challenging, and include a timeframe.

REFERENCES

Adriessen, I., Phalet, K., & Lens, W. (2006). Future goal setting, task motivation and learning of minority and non-minority students in Dutch schools. *British Journal of Educational Psychology, 76,* 827–850.

Austin, J. T., & Vancouver, J. B. (1996). Goal constructs in psychology: Structure, process, and content. *Psychological Bulletin, 120*(3), 338–375.

Bandura, A. (1977). Self-efficacy: Toward a unifying theory of behavioral change. *Psychological Review, 84,* 191–215.

Bandura, A. (1989). Human agency in social cognitive theory. *American Psychologist, 44*(9), 1175–1184.

Bandura, A. (1995). *Self-Efficacy in changing societies.* Cambridge University Press.

Bandura, A., & Schunk, D. H. (1981). Cultivating competence, self-efficacy, and intrinsic interest through proximal self-motivation. *Journal of Personality and Social Psychology, 41*(3), 586–598.

Cuseo, J. B., Thompson, A., Campagna, M., & Sox Fecas, V. (2013). *Thriving in college and beyond. Research-based strategies for academic success and personal development.* Dubuque, IA: Kendall Hunt.

Deci, E. L., & Ryan, R. M. (Eds.). (2002). *Handbook of self-determination research.* Rochester: University of Rochester Press.

Doran, G. T. (1981). There's a SMART way to write management's goals and objectives. *Management Review, 70*(11), 35–36.

Emmons, R. A., & Diener, E. (1986). A goal-affect analysis of everyday situational choices. *Journal of Research in Personality, 20,* 309–326.

Fryer, L. K., Ginns, P., & Walker, R. (2014). Between students' instrumental goals and how they learn: Goal content is the gap to mind. *British Journal of Educational Psychology, 84*, 612–630.

Gollwitzer, P. M., & Brandstätter, V. (1997). Implementation intentions and effective goal pursuit. *Journal of Personality and Social Psychology, 73*(1), 186–199.

Gore, P. A., Leuwerke, W., & Metz, A. J. (2016). *Connections. Empowering college and career success.* Boston, MA: Bedford/ St. Martin's.

Harrington, C. (2013). *Student success in college: Doing what works!* Boston, MA: Cengage Learning.

Hayes, S. C., Rosenfarb, I., Wulfert, E., Munt, E. D., Korn, Z., & Zettle, R. D. (1985). Self-reinforcement effects: An artifact of social standard setting? *Journal of Applied Behavior Analysis, 18*(3), 201–214.

Koestner, R., Lekes, N., Powers, T. A., & Chicoine, E. (2002). Attaining personal goals: Self-concordance plus implementation intentions equals success. *Journal of Personality and Social Psychology, 83*(1), 231–244.

Kruglanski, A. W., Pierro, A., & Sheveland, A. (2011). How many roads lead to Rome? Equifinality set-size and commitment to goals and means. *European Journal of Social Psychology, 41*, 344–352.

La Guardia, J. G. (2009). Developing who I am: A self-determination theory approach to the establishment of healthy identities. *Educational Psychologist, 44*(2), 90–104.

Locke, E. A. (1968). Toward a theory of task motivation and incentives. *Organizational Behavior and Human Performances, 3*, 157–189.

Locke, E. A., & Latham, G. P. (1990). *A theory of goal setting and task performance.* Englewood Cliffs, NJ: Prentice Hall.

Locke, E. A., & Latham, G. P. (2002). Building a practically useful theory of goal setting and task motivation. A 35-year odyssey. *American Psychologist, 57*(9), 705–717.

Morisano, D., Hirsh, J. B., Peterson, J. B., Pihl, R. O., & Shore, B. M. (2010). Setting, elaborating, and reflecting on personal goals improves academic performance. *Journal of Applied Psychology, 95*(2), 255–264.

Nist, S., & Holschuh, J. (1999). *Active learning. Strategies for college success.* Boston: Allyn & Bacon.

Oettingen, G., & Gollwitzer, P. M. (2010). Strategies of setting and implementing goals. In J. E. Maddux & J. P. Tangney (Eds.), *Social psychological foundations of clinical psychology* (pp. 114–135). New York: Guilford.

Oettingen, G., Pak, H., & Schnetter, K. (2001). Self-regulation of goal-setting: Turning free fantasies about the future in binding goals. *Journal of Personality and Social Psychology, 77*, 623–630.

Schunk, D. H. (1991). Self-efficacy and academic motivation. *Educational Psychologist, 26*, 207–231.

Smith, K., Locke, E., & Barry, D. (1990). Goal setting, planning and organizational performance: An experimental simulation. *Organizational Behavior and Human Decision Processes, 46*, 118–134.

Vallerand, R. J., & Ratelle, C. F. (2002). Intrinsic and extrinsic motivation: A hierarchical model. In E. L. Deci & R. M. Ryan (Eds.), *Handbook of self-determination research* (pp. 37–63). Rochester, NY: The University of Rochester Press.

Weinstein, C., Woodruff, A., & Await, C. (2004). Motivation module. In C. Weinstein, A. Woodruff, & C. Await, *Becoming a strategic learner: LASSI instructional module*. Clearwater, FL: H & H.

MODULE 2.2

DEVELOPING A PLAN OF ACTION

This module will help you to formulate goals in three domains: academic, personal, and social. Within each of these domains, a detailed example will be shared and then it will be your turn to set a goal. Specific questions for reflection are included to guide you in this process.

In addition to setting outcome goals, there are other ways that goals can be incorporated and used to support your academic success. These are explained further in Clusters 3 and 4.

AN ACADEMIC GOAL

REFLECTION: Are there any particular areas of your academics or specific courses that are becoming more difficult or harder to stay motivated? Consider these as you begin setting goals.

The first domain is academics. Notice that the example includes all of the characteristics of effective goal setting:

- Set useful goals that are personally meaningful, specific and measurable, realistic and challenging, and include a timeframe
- Set a combination of short- and long-term goals with associated enabling or proximal subgoals
- Create detailed implementation plans or action plans
- Share your goals with friends and family and make your goals public
- Write a future narrative that describes how you will feel and how your life will look like if you attain your goals

TABLE 2.2.1 ACADEMIC GOAL EXAMPLE USING EFFECTIVE GOAL SETTING TECHNIQUES

	Academic Goal	Notes
Long-Term Goal	I want to earn my degree in business marketing in four years.	Specific & Measurable: Earn a degree in business marketing Realistic and Challenging: Earning a degree requires hard work but many students accomplish this goal Timeframe: Four years
Long-Term Semester Goal	I want to earn a 3.0 this semester.	Specific & Measurable: 3.0 GPA Realistic and Challenging: College is harder but this student has had some academic success so with effort he or she should be able to achieve this goal Timeframe: This semester
Enabling Goal for Semester GPA	I want to earn a B+ in my calculus course this semester.	Specific & Measurable: B+ in calculus Realistic and Challenging: Math is challenging for the student but by seeking out additional support he or she should be able to achieve this goal Timeframe: This semester
Action Steps (Short-Term Enabling Goals)		**Notes**
Over the course of the semester,… 1. I will go to tutoring once a week beginning when the center opens in the second week. 2. I will study 90 minutes per day, five days a week (four class days plus Sunday). 3. I will read and attempt any textbook examples prior to each lecture and I will bring any questions to class. 4. I will complete my calculus homework on the day it is assigned. 5. Beginning in the first week, I will partner with a classmate and discuss our notes immediately after each class. 6. During the second week, I will form a study group and we will meet at least once a week throughout the semester. 7. During the week of any exam, I will visit the professor and ask any remaining questions.		Each of the action steps states what the student will do (e.g., go to tutoring), how often he or she will do it (e.g., once a week), and when (e.g., when it opens in the second week and then throughout the semester).

Obstacles		Notes
There are no tutoring appointments available.		It can be helpful to use your action steps to generate any potential obstacles towards completing them. The proactive and reactive steps are still very specific and tell the student exactly what to do and when.
Proactive Step: I will schedule my appointment for the following week when I leave my current appointment.	**Reactive Step**: I will still use this time as an additional study time and try to meet with either a classmate or my study group.	
Homework problems take longer than expected.		
Proactive Step: If twice I am unable to complete my homework on the day it is assigned, then I will change my schedule and increase my daily study time.	**Reactive Step**: I will complete the homework the following day.	
I will get distracted by my peers.		
Proactive Step: I will share my study schedule with my dorm mate. I will study in the library and I will turn off electronics while I am studying.	**Reactive Step**: I will remind myself of my goal, why I want to achieve the goal and revisit my future narrative.	Some obstacles require an honest self-assessment of your own temptations and things that typically put you off course.

Sharing Goals	Notes
I will share my class goals as well as my progress with my parents and my calculus study group.	In addition to sharing your goals with the people you care about, consider sharing your goals with people who will help hold you accountable. A study group can help you prepare but it can also help remind you of the commitment you have made to yourself and to the people in the group.

Future Narrative	Notes
I have always been a little nervous about math so earning a B+ will give me more confidence. This class also will set the foundation for my other required math classes and so this will help me be more competent and successful in these other classes. Earning a B+ will make it easier to earn my 3.0 this semester so that I can keep my scholarship and continue school. My parents will be proud and I will be proud of myself and know that the hard work was worth it.	A future narrative can go further and link feelings and outcomes that are related to the long-term goals associated with this enabling goal, such as, earning the degree.

Now it's your turn. Use the template below to complete a detailed implementation plan for one of your academic goals.

Academic Goal

Begin by reflecting on why you are here at college. How does going to college align with your values, beliefs, strengths, etc.? In other words, why is it important to you?

Now list a long-term goal, a long-term semester goal, and at least one enabling goal that aligns with your reflection above. Be sure all of them are specific and measurable, realistic and challenging and include a timeframe.

Long-Term Goal:

Long-Term Semester Goal:

Enabling Goal:

Action Steps (Short-Term Enabling Goals)

List action steps you will take to achieve your enabling goal. It would be helpful to treat this as a brainstorming activity and list as many steps as you can think of. Afterwards, you can eliminate any that are not realistic or maybe will not be helpful. If necessary, rewrite any action steps so that they specifically state what you should do, how often you should do it and when.

1.

Obstacles

Similar to the action steps, try brainstorming obstacles. Use your action steps to help generate any possible obstacles. Once you have your obstacles written, determine the proactive and reactive action steps you will use (again, be very specific about what to do and when).

Obstacle:	Proactive Step:	Reactive Step:
Obstacle:	Proactive Step:	Reactive Step:
Obstacle:	Proactive Step:	Reactive Step:

Sharing Goals

Now list who you will share this goal with. Consider both the people who care about you as well as those who will be helpful in holding you accountable.

Future Narrative

Reflect on potential feelings you will have when achieving the goal. You can also describe any realized outcomes from either achieving this goal or the related long-term goals. Be as descriptive as possible. Revisiting your future narrative can be a source of recommitment when needed.

A PERSONAL GOAL

The next example includes a personal goal. Notice that the steps and characteristics are still the same, although the domain has changed.

TABLE 2.2.2 PERSONAL GOAL EXAMPLE USING EFFECTIVE GOAL SETTING TECHNIQUES

Personal Goal		Notes
Long-Term Goal	I want to become a runner and run a marathon within two years.	Specific & Measurable: Run a marathon Realistic and Challenging: Training requires hard work but many people are successful runners Timeframe: Two years
Enabling Goal	I will run my first 5k in 12 weeks.	Specific & Measurable: Run my first 5k Realistic and Challenging: This is a relatively short distance that can be achieved with some effort Timeframe: 12 weeks

Action Steps (Short-Term Enabling Goals)	Notes
1. Tomorrow I will find a training plan that will get me ready for a race within the 12 weeks and I will follow the plan. 2. Once I have a training plan, I will sign-up and pay for a race by the end of the first week. 3. During the first week, I will visit a runner's store and purchase any necessary equipment. 4. On Sundays, I will make my schedule for the week and incorporate my training days and times.	These action steps are the same as before and state what the person will do (e.g., make my schedule), how often he or she will do it (e.g., weekly), and when (e.g., on Sundays).

Obstacles		Notes
I may get sick.		It can be helpful to use your action steps to generate any potential obstacles towards completing them. The proactive and reactive steps are still very specific and tell the student exactly what to do and when.
Proactive Step: I will follow a healthy diet (55–65% complex carbohydrates; fruits and vegetables at every meal) that supports my training program and get at least 7–8 hours of sleep per night.	**Reactive Step**: I will rest and recover and then adjust my schedule if possible to include the missed runs. If that is not possible, I will pick up where I left off.	
Bad weather may interfere with a training run.		
Proactive Step: The first week, I will find a place that is available with a treadmill that I can access if needed.	**Reactive Step**: I will complete my training run on the treadmill.	
I may feel too busy to do a scheduled run.		
Proactive Step: On really busy weeks, I will create my schedule so that I run first thing in the morning before I do anything else. This way I won't get distracted by other activities.	**Reactive Step**: I will remind myself of my goal, why I want to achieve the goal and revisit my future narrative. I'll also call my best friend and ask for a "pep talk".	Another example of an honest self-assessment.

Sharing Goals	Notes
I will share my race goals with my best friend and my parents and ask them to come to the race to cheer me on.	In addition to sharing your goals, sometimes there is an opportunity to include them in the outcome, which will also bolster your accountability.

Future Narrative	Notes
I have always wanted to be a runner. By finishing the 5k, I will be proud of my accomplishment. By following my training plan, I know I will feel excited at the race and feel good when I'm done. This will lead to signing up for more races and moving towards my long-term goal. Because I will be training, I will also boost my health and will feel more energetic. I'll be able to tackle more things I want to accomplish because I have the energy. I know by creating a habit and becoming a runner, I will also add years to my life.	This narrative focuses on feelings and then some potential outcomes such as increased energy, better health, and longer life.

Now it's your turn. Use the template below to complete a detailed implementation plan for one of your personal goals.

Personal Goal

Begin by reflecting on areas of personal development or growth. Are there things that you have wanted to accomplish for yourself? Why are these important to you? Are there role models or mentors that you look up to?

Now list a long-term goal and at least one enabling goal that aligns with your reflection above. Be sure all of them are specific and measurable, realistic and challenging and include a timeframe.

Long-Term Goal:

Enabling Goal:

Action Steps (Short-Term Enabling Goals)

List action steps you will take to achieve your enabling goal. It would be helpful to treat this as a brainstorming activity and list as many steps as you can think of. Afterwards, you can eliminate any that are not realistic or maybe will not be helpful. If necessary, rewrite any action steps so that they specifically state what you should do, how often you should do it and when.

1.

Obstacles

Similar to the action steps, try brainstorming obstacles. Use your action steps to help generate any possible obstacles. Once you have your obstacles written, determine the proactive and reactive action steps you will use (again, be very specific about what to do and when).

Obstacle:	Proactive Step:	Reactive Step:
Obstacle:	Proactive Step:	Reactive Step:
Obstacle:	Proactive Step:	Reactive Step:

Sharing Goals

Now list who you will share this goal with. Consider both the people who care about you as well as those who will be helpful in holding you accountable.

Future Narrative

Reflect on your potential feelings you will have when achieving the goal. You can also describe any realized outcomes from either achieving this goal or the related long-term goals. Be as descriptive as possible. Revisiting your future narrative can be a source of recommitment when needed.

A SOCIAL GOAL

The next example includes a social goal. With social goals, it is sometimes more difficult to set them to be specific and measurable; however, this can be done by reflecting on what you are hoping to accomplish. If the goal you are pursuing is not possible in terms of being specific and measurable, the action steps can be.

TABLE 2.2.3 SOCIAL GOAL EXAMPLE USING EFFECTIVE GOAL SETTING TECHNIQUES

Social Goal		Notes
Long-Term Goal	I want a social support network at school that I can turn to beginning my first year and lasting through graduation.	**Specific & Measurable**: Social support network **Realistic and Challenging**: People typically can make friends with some effort **Timeframe**: First year and then through graduation
Enabling Goal	I will develop a close relationship with at least one new person this semester in my major.	**Specific & Measurable**: Close relationship with at least one person in my major **Realistic and Challenging**: Because the person will most likely be very busy in this first semester, this realistically balances social activities and academics **Timeframe**: This semester

Action Steps (Short-Term Enabling Goals)	Notes
1. This week, I will contact Student Activities and research clubs that are related to my major. 2. After finding out which clubs are available, I will immediately email the contact persons and find out when the next meetings are and attend. 3. In my classes starting this week, I will sit next to someone new each week and introduce myself. 4. Within two weeks of meeting people in my major, I will invite them to do something on campus such as lunch, a sporting event, etc.	These action steps are the same as before and state what the person will do (e.g., sit next to someone new), how often he or she will do it (e.g., weekly), and when (e.g., starting this week).

Obstacles	Notes
Sometimes I get a little shy and going to a meeting where I don't know anyone could be intimidating.	
Proactive Step: I will ask the contact person if he or she would meet me a few minutes before the meeting so I don't have to go in alone.	**Reactive Step:** I will remind myself that everyone was new at one point and went through these same experiences.	
There may not be people in my classes who are in my major.	
Reactive Step: I will focus on meeting people at the related clubs and other events in my department to meet people in my major; however, I will adjust my goal such that I am still making at least one close friend on campus with the major not being as important.	In this example, who is enrolled in this student's classes is not within his or her control. However, being aware of the possibility and deciding on some action steps can still be helpful.

Sharing Goals	Notes
I will share my goals with my roommate. Potentially, we could help each other with meeting new people.	This is similar to the personal goal where you can include them in the outcome, which will also bolster your accountability.

Future Narrative	Notes
With the strong support of my network, I know I will be able to face new challenges. I will be able to share in both the triumphs as well as the disappointments with my friends. They will celebrate with me and help pick me back up if needed. I will be able to do the same for them. As we continue in our education, I know our bonds will grow and I will be able to go into the world confidently bolstered by their support.	

Now it's your turn. Use the template below to complete a detailed implementation plan for one of your social goals.

ACTIVITY 2.2.3 SOCIAL GOAL TEMPLATE USING EFFECTIVE GOAL SETTING TECHNIQUES

Social Goal

Begin by reflecting on your social environment. What does friendship and community mean to you? Is it important for your wellbeing? Why or why not?

Now list a long-term goal and at least one enabling goal that aligns with your reflection above. Be sure both of them are specific and measurable, realistic and challenging, and include a timeframe.

Long-Term Goal:

Enabling Goal:

Action Steps (Short-Term Enabling Goals)

List action steps you will take to achieve your enabling goal. It would be helpful to treat this as a brainstorming activity and list as many steps as you can think of. Afterwards, you can eliminate any that are not realistic or maybe will not be helpful. If necessary, rewrite any action steps so that they specifically state what you should do, how often you should do it and when.

1.

Obstacles

Similar to the action steps, try brainstorming obstacles. Use your action steps to help generate any possible obstacles. Once you have your obstacles written, determine the proactive and reactive action steps you will use (again, be very specific and what to do and when).

Obstacle:	Proactive Step:	Reactive Step:
Obstacle:	Proactive Step:	Reactive Step:
Obstacle:	Proactive Step:	Reactive Step:

Sharing Goals

Now list who you will share this goal with. Consider both the people who care about you as well as those who will be helpful in holding you accountable.

Future Narrative

Reflect on your potential feelings you will have when achieving the goal. You can also describe any realized outcomes from either achieving this goal or the related long-term goals. Be as descriptive as possible. Revisiting your future narrative can be a source of recommitment when needed.

MODULE 2.2 SUMMARY

- Goal-setting characteristics include useful goals, long-term and enabling goals, detailed implementation plans, public goals, and future narratives.
- Effective goal-setting techniques can be used in multiple life domains including academic, personal, and social.

CASE STUDY

Derrick is a first-semester freshman. Going to college has been a goal of his since elementary school. Now that he is here, he is very excited and is eager to do well. However, after three weeks of classes, some of the excitement has turned to feelings of stress and anxiety. He is starting to feel overwhelmed. Because he still wants to do well his first semester, he begins the next week, by telling himself he'll study more, be better organized and manage his time more effectively. Yet, by the end of the week, not much has changed. In fact, he has taken exams in two of his classes and made a 63 and 68%. He's starting to question whether coming to college was mistake and wonders if he does belong here.

QUESTIONS

1. Has Derrick set goals for his first semester? Do they include characteristics that will be useful and help him be successful? Why or why not?

2. Do you think Derrick's exam results reflect his potential in these classes? Why or why not?

3. What would you recommend to Derrick to help him focus his efforts and to achieve better performance?

POTENTIAL RESPONSES

1. Derrick has set goals for the semester. He wants to do well his first semester, study more, be better organized, and manage his time more effectively. Each of these goals are very vague and do not include all of the characteristics of useful goals. Words such as "well," "more," and "better" are not clearly defined and would be difficult to measure or to evaluate his progress. Each of these goals is likely realistic and challenging; however, without defined timeframes, they would also be difficult to effectively focus Derrick's efforts.

2. If Derrick has not given a fully concentrated amount of effort on helpful goal-relevant activities, it is doubtful that these scores reflect his true potential.

3. Derrick should set some long-term semester goals, with useful characteristics, for each of his courses and then associated short-term enabling goals that will help direct his efforts. He should also include the following aspects of goal setting:

- He should create a detailed implementation plan that identifies multiple action steps for any goals as well as any possible obstacles.
- He should share his goals with his close friends and his family. He will gain their support and it will increase his sense of accountability.
- He should write a future narrative and describe how he will feel and what his life will look like after a successful first semester. He can revisit this narrative to reinforce his commitment when he faces obstacles.

ADDITIONAL READINGS

Acee, T. W., Cho, Y., Kim, J., & Weinstein C. E. (2012). Relationships among properties of college students' self-set academic goals and academic achievement. *Educational Psychology*, *32*(6), 681–698.

Davis, W. E., Kelley, N. J., Kim, J., Tang, D., & Hicks, J. A. (2015). Motivating the academic mind: High-level construal of academic goals enhances goal meaningfulness, motivation, and self-concordance. *Motivation and Emotion*. Advanced online publication. doi: 10.1007/s11031-015-9522-x

Ferguson, Y. L., & Sheldon, K. M. (2010). Should goal-strivers think about "why" or "how" to strive? It depends on their skill level. *Motivation and Emotion*, *34*, 253–265.

Gollwitzer, P. M. (2014). Weakness of the will: Is a quick fix possible? *Motivation and Emotion*, *38*, 305–322.

Krause, K., & Freund, A. M. (2016). It's in the means: Process focus helps against procrastination in the academic context. *Motivation and Emotion*. Advanced online publication. doi: 10.1007/s11031-016-9541-2

Sheldon, K. M., & Houser-Marko, L. (2001). Self-concordance, goal attainment, and the pursuit of happiness: Can there be an upward spiral? *Journal of Personality and Social Psychology*, *80*(1), 152–165.

Sheldon, K. M., Ryan, R. M., Deci, E. L., & Kasser, T. (2004). The independent effects of goal contents and motives on well-being: It's both what you pursue and why you pursue it. *Personality and Social Psychology Bulletin*, *30*(4), 475–486.

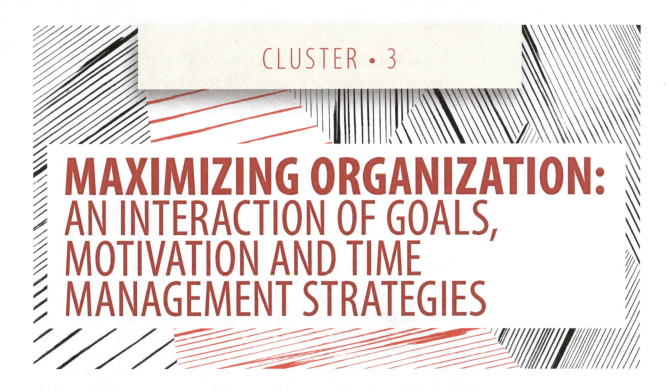

MAXIMIZING ORGANIZATION:
AN INTERACTION OF GOALS, MOTIVATION AND TIME MANAGEMENT STRATEGIES

CASE STUDY

Eli is a first-semester college freshman. His parents and high school teachers had told him that managing his time would be much different in college. In fact, they warned him that many new students become overwhelmed and do poorly their first year due to inadequate time management skills. At first, he did not understand what the big deal was. He had all his free time and none of his professors assigned homework or even took attendance. Because his first exams were not until the fifth week of school, he did not always go to classes nor do the readings before lectures. He figured that he would read and study the week of his exams just like he did in high school, *and* do well. However, when he started to study that week, he had not realized that there would be so much material to cover. Although he stayed up all night cramming for his first exam, he barely did more than read and skim over the material. As a result, he failed the exam.

He knew going forward that he would have to do better; however, he continued to struggle. Every time he sat down to read and study, he felt overwhelmed with the amount of material and continued to push it off until later. This led to more cramming with no results. By mid-semester, he was missing more classes because he was embarrassed about his performance. The stress and anxiety continued to build and he started to have trouble sleeping. And even though he spent time with friends to make himself feel better, there was always this nagging guilt that he should be doing something else. By the end of the semester, Eli thought to himself, "I have always been a good student. I do not understand. What happened?"

1. What are some of Eli's time management problems?
2. How much time should Eli spend outside of class to prepare for exams? When should he start preparing?
3. What time management strategies can Eli use to minimize his procrastination and to make the material feel less overwhelming?
4. What time management strategies can he use to create a balance between academics and leisure?

CLUSTER OVERVIEW

For students everywhere, time management is usually one of the biggest areas of concern. This is especially true for freshmen students transitioning to college. Unfortunately, for many students starting college, the first few weeks are deceptive. As compared to the structures of high school and student schedules being managed primarily by others, college can initially feel undemanding, and even easy. Over the course of the week, you only go to class for 15 hours (rather than almost 40 in high school), parents are typically not there telling you what to do and even some professors do not seem to care if you show up for class. This is a deception. Balancing the academic requirements needed to be successful while still achieving personal and social goals becomes more difficult—and its importance more readily apparent—as the semester progresses. However, by developing awareness about your ability to manage your attention and time and incorporating strategies early in the semester, you can avoid the common missteps and difficulties that students tend to face.

The first module is intended to help you develop awareness by describing theories about time and attention management, prioritizing, and procrastination. The second module provides specific examples of tools to help with planning and establishing routines, and the last module provides over 30 strategies intended to increase focus, motivation, and efficiency.

CLUSTER OBJECTIVES

- Describe the different approaches to setting priorities and understanding habits.
- Describe how perceived time control influences the experience of both stress and time management efforts.
- Describe how the theories of procrastination can explain decision-making, and how underlying psychological factors can influence chronic procrastination.

- Construct a master calendar that supports short-, mid-, and long-range planning.

- Establish a weekly schedule that supports academic and personal goals.

- Describe time management strategies and how they are related to improving focus and motivation.

- Identify multiple strategies that will help improve personal time management difficulties.

TIME MANAGEMENT THEORIES, MODELS, AND TECHNIQUES

CLUSTER 3 OBJECTIVES COVERED IN THIS MODULE

☐ **OBJECTIVE:** Describe the different approaches to setting priorities and understanding habits.

☐ **OBJECTIVE:** Describe how perceived time control influences the experience of both stress and time management efforts.

☐ **OBJECTIVE:** Describe how the theories of procrastination can explain decision-making, and how underlying psychological factors can influence chronic procrastination.

REFLECTION: What does it mean to manage your time more effectively? Have you found that to-do lists, schedule books, and calendars can be difficult to maintain? If so, what might explain this difficulty? Do you find yourself stuck with bad habits, poor attention control, or a tendency to procrastinate despite your very best intentions? If so, how much energy and effort are you willing to dedicate to overcome these challenges?

TIME MANAGEMENT VERSUS ATTENTION MANAGEMENT

The idea that time can be managed is something of a misnomer. People do not really manage their time so much as their priorities, effort, and attention. In other words, time management is primarily a matter of effective planning and scheduling. It involves the ability to productively plan and efficiently manage important tasks. When you schedule priorities or develop concrete plans of action you are managing your efforts and energies first, which then influence your time.

TIME MANAGEMENT:
The productive and organized use of time to accomplish tasks and complete activities.

ATTENTION MANAGEMENT:
Ability to maintain focus and self-control in order to accomplish tasks and complete activities.

Attention management has to do with how well you harness your focus and eliminate distractions when completing a task. It also has to do with your ability to complete tasks that you have decided are important. Managing attention is actually a far more difficult prospect than managing schedules. For example, it takes relatively little effort to schedule a three-hour study session in your schedule book and to plan your general study approach. It can be more difficult to follow through on the plan, stave off distractions and stay on task for the full three hours. Creating and scheduling a plan of action are typically far easier than successfully completing it.

Managing your attention within a time frame can be challenging for any student. It is natural to prefer fun and enjoyable activities over challenging or unpleasant ones. The problem is that so many of the tasks you have to complete in life—class assignments, work projects, laundry, taxes—are not necessarily pleasurable. Attention management becomes far more difficult in the face of such tasks because your natural tendency is to seek out enjoyable activities. Whether hanging out with friends, watching online videos, scanning social media, or simply daydreaming about other things you might be doing, there are countless opportunities for distraction that make managing your attention and energies difficult.

What are some distractions that you deal with on a regular basis?

It is not that you do not want to succeed. It is that the path to success is riddled with less than pleasurable obstacles. So what is an intelligent and aspiring college student such as yourself to do in the face of all these distractions? The purpose of this module is to provide you with some of the knowledge and skills to tackle this challenge. Psychologists, economists, philosophers, and neuroscientists have been studying time and attention management for many years. While there are no easy answers, there are many valuable ideas that can frame your approach to improving your attention and organization. By equipping yourself with these tools and taking the time to consider your priorities, habits, methods of self-control, and typical behavioral patterns, you will position yourself to make constructive changes that can lead to greater productivity and academic success.

PRIORITIES

Making the most effective use of your time requires knowing your priorities. While certain priorities may change from day-to-day, there are always overarching priorities that remain steadfast in their importance. To get the very most out of your time and effort, finding ways to establish both short-term and long-term priorities are crucial. A more detailed discussion of short-term and long-term goals can be found in Cluster 2. This module focuses on methods you can use to determine which goals are priorities and which are not at any given time. Two different models can be used to analyze your priorities: the ABCDE method and the Eisenhower method.

ABCDE METHOD

This method for determining your priorities is very straightforward (Wexley & Baldwin, 1986). It involves creating a list of tasks and placing them into one of five categories based on their relative importance. The value in this method is its directness. You can start with a to-do list that includes everything that needs to be accomplished in the near future. Then, you rank those tasks in one of the following categories:

- **A: Very important.** These tasks must be done and are considered of the highest priority. If these tasks are not accomplished, then you will face serious consequences.
- **B: Important.** These tasks should be done but are not of the highest priority. If these tasks are not accomplished, then you will face minor negative consequences.
- **C: Nice to do.** These tasks are optional and are considered low priority. If these tasks are not accomplished there will be no negative consequences.
- **D: Delegate.** These tasks can be assigned to other people who can get the job done.
- **E: Eliminate.** These tasks should be eliminated from to-do lists. By choosing to eliminate unnecessary tasks from your list, you can ensure time is not wasted on trivial matters.

The intent with this method is that you complete "A" tasks before beginning "B" tasks and so on.

EISENHOWER METHOD

This method hinges on the idea that there is a distinction between *urgent* and *important* tasks (Jovanovich, Fiorillo, & Rossler, 2015). Just because something is important does not automatically mean it is urgent, and vice versa. Urgent tasks require immediate action and attention. Important tasks align with personal goals or values but do not necessarily require immediate action. The combination of these two categories can help you determine your major priorities and evaluate how you are allocating your time. By assessing the relative value of tasks in your life, you will be in a better position to make choices that reflect what you want and who you want to be.

Sometimes students get the categories confused, believing that urgent tasks are always important, or ignoring important tasks that do not feel urgent. There are probably times when you have been incredibly busy, but, at the end of the day, felt as though you did not accomplish anything of great merit. This is often a result of confusing urgent tasks for important tasks. On the other hand, individuals often recognize the importance of tasks such as regular exercise but do not follow through due to a lack of urgency. The following descriptions of the four quadrants clarify how the value of tasks can be evaluated in terms of urgency and importance.

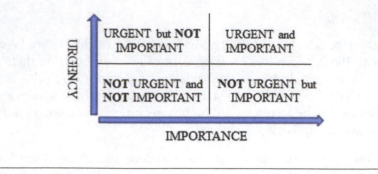

FIGURE 3.1.1 Eisenhower Method   *Source: Angela Vaughan and Brett Wilkinson*

- *Urgent and important*: These tasks should be done immediately. This may include emergency situations and upcoming deadlines that are personally relevant to your well-being.

- *Urgent but not important*: These tasks should be dealt with quickly and efficiently in order to move on to more important tasks. These tasks can quickly steal your time and energy because they feel urgent but do not help you progress toward accomplishing important goals.

- *Not urgent but important*: These tasks should be emphasized and respected. These tasks are the building blocks for developing a successful, productive, and well-rounded life. They are often overlooked and underappreciated due to a lack of urgency, but most of your valuable time should be spent on these tasks.

- *Not urgent and not important*: These tasks should only be done at a time when there are no tasks in the previous three categories. These tasks do not help you accomplish goals and are generally time-wasters.

TABLE 3.1.1 SUMMARY OF PRIORITIZING METHODS

	Approach	**Benefit**
ABCDE method	Determines priority by assigning a value to each item on the to-do list. A items are the most important and E items should be eliminated.	Most simplistic way to analyze priorities and can be used on both daily and weekly to-do lists.
Eisenhower method	Determines priority by creating a 2 × 2 matrix of urgency and importance.	Also incorporates urgency as a means to determine priority.

REINFORCEMENT AND HABITS

According to the behaviorist view in psychology, human behaviors are the result of conditioning. One type of conditioned response occurs when behaviors are repeatedly paired with neutral stimuli. For example, Pavlov trained a dog to salivate to the ringing of a bell rather than food. To accomplish this, he would ring the bell every time he gave the dog food. After a period of time, the dog associated the bell with food and thus would salivate upon hearing the bell ring, regardless of whether or not any food was provided. This process is called classical conditioning.

Individuals experience classically conditioned responses on a daily basis, and perhaps far more often than you would like to admit. For example, marketing agencies rely heavily on such conditioning to manipulate your thoughts, feelings, and attitudes via advertisements and television commercials (Stuart, Shimp, & Engle, 1987). However, classical conditioning is only one aspect of the behaviorist method. Operant conditioning is the other. According to operant conditioning principles, learning occurs through either the reinforcement or punishment of behaviors. When a behavior is followed by a reinforcement, it is more likely to occur again in the future. However, when a behavior is followed by punishment, it is less likely to occur.

So what does this have to do with time management? Everything in this module is designed to help you understand how to increase desired behaviors and reduce undesired behaviors. As mentioned previously, the term "time management" is something of a misnomer. What you really need to focus on is managing your organization, effort, and attention. It can be helpful to recognize that many of the choices you make every day are conditioned rather than intentional. Simply becoming aware of this fact can help you learn to identify whether it might be beneficial to retrain, or recondition, yourself in certain areas.

In daily life, this learning process is generally discussed in terms of habits rather than conditioned responses. Habits are the direct result of conditioning. When you repeat a procedure over and over again, eventually the brain will automatically respond to environmental cues that trigger the procedure (Verplanken & Aarts, 1999). Habits are learned and automatic responses to environmental cues. Through sheer repetition, certain sequences of behavior are connected in your associative memory when an environmental cue takes place. Such routines are the foundation for a great deal of human behavior and require little effort or conscious control.

Some habits are clearly beneficial, like the routine of brushing your teeth before bed to prevent tooth decay and gum disease. Other habits are detrimental, such as smoking despite the possibility of developing lung cancer. In both cases, enacting the habitual behavior requires very little forethought. For better or for worse, habits are central to our lives. There are three major models for explaining habit formation in the contemporary

CONDITIONING:
Psychological process by which a regular and predictable behavioral response occurs as a result of reinforcement.

REINFORCEMENT:
Strengthening of specific behavioral responses through the use of rewards.

PUNISHMENT:
Weakening of specific behavioral responses through the use of negative consequences.

HABITS:
Unconscious behavioral patterns that form as a result of conditioned or reinforced routines.

psychology literature. These include direct-context cueing, implicit goals, and motivated context models. All three models view habits as an association between goals and actions that are triggered by contextual, or environmental, cues. However, each model views the mechanisms underlying habits in a unique way.

DIRECT-CONTEXT CUEING

According to this model, habits form independently of goals. In other words, the association your memory creates between a situation and a response automatically forms a habit if repeated consistently over time (Neal, Wood, & Quinn, 2006). The primary idea is that you do not need goals, rewards, or punishments to form habits. Instead, repeated exposure to a certain context (e.g., turning on your computer) can trigger a habitual response (e.g., checking your email before doing anything else) regardless of whether or not you want to respond in that way. The context directly and automatically triggers the habit through the power of sheer repetition.

Can you identify three positive habits and three negative habits in your own life?

A major take away from this model is the idea that by changing the environmental context of a habit you can significantly increase the likelihood of eliminating bad habits. Public health experts who promote smoking cessation programs have touted this notion for years, suggesting that the removal of environmental triggers (e.g., throwing out ashtrays and avoiding smoke breaks with friends at work) is the single most powerful way to ensure smoking abstinence. The same concept applies to academic activities, such as removing habitual distractions from your study environment to increase your ability to stay on task, or sitting on the opposite side of the classroom from your best friend to increase your focus during class.

IMPLICIT GOALS

According to this model, habits form as a result of goal pursuit. This means that habits are created indirectly, as opposed to the direct connection formed according to the direct-context cueing model. When repeatedly trying to accomplish goals, your behavior and the environmental context just happen to become associated with a particular goal. Studies indicate that many habits are not activated unless a relevant goal has been considered (Aarts & Dijksterhuis, 2000). For example, a student who consistently chooses not to study might rely on their ability to spend entire nights "cramming" right before big exams. This habit of cramming is goal-oriented, since the behavior (e.g., cramming) and the environmental context (e.g., night of the exam) would not occur without the student having formed an implicit goal (e.g., a desire to avoid failing the class).

An important point to take from this model is the value of goal reminders and persistence. Because habits form as a byproduct of goal pursuit, creating a positive habit requires you to be dedicated in accomplishing your goal.

Otherwise, the link between your goal-oriented behavior and the context remains weak. Finding unique ways to remind yourself about particular goals can help you activate habitual patterns. If you want to start a regular exercise routine, place sticky notes around your house, keep your workout equipment accessible and in plain sight, or set daily goal notifications on your phone. Such goal reminders can activate behavioral patterns that might otherwise be ignored.

MOTIVATED CONTEXT

According to this model, habits form due to the presence of rewards. Similar to the implicit goals model, habits are indirectly created. However, it is the motivating effect of past rewards rather than the pursuit of implicit goals that drives this model. Simply experiencing a reward (e.g., positive encouragement) as a result of a behavior (e.g., correctly answering a question) in an environmental context (e.g., your freshman biology class) will increase your likelihood of repeating that behavior again, in that context, in the future. Repeated rewards serve to enhance the habitual association because you are motivated to attain the mood-elevating effects of dopamine released in your brain (Schultz, Dayan, & Montague, 1997).

The most practical consideration with this model is the importance of creating powerful reward systems to build positive habits. From stickers on your first grade homework assignments to good grades and accolades in college, reward systems form the motivational basis of most educational systems. Although intrinsic motivation is a more effective means of sustaining interest and effort in the long run (see Cluster 6), extrinsic motivators can also be powerful tools for supporting the short-term patterns that lead to habit formation (Lally & Gardner, 2013). Selected behaviors can flourish when the right reward systems—either intrinsic or extrinsic—are in place. By actively deciding what habits you want to grow and finding rewards that will entice you to pursue those behaviors, it is possible to create lasting habits that improve your life.

How could you reward yourself this weekend for accomplishing all of your goals for this week?

TABLE 3.1.2 SUMMARY OF MODELS TO SUPPORT POSITIVE HABITS

Model	Mechanism	Action	Example
Direct-context cueing	Repeated exposure = habits	Change environmental context and cues to support positive responses	I will sit in the center seat in the front row of each classroom.
Implicit goals	Goals = habits	Set and then remind yourself of specific goals that support completing tasks	I will review each of my course goals and evaluate my progress when I complete my weekly to-do planning.
Motivated context	Rewards = habits	Include rewards for successful completion of tasks	Every Friday night when I have completed all of my weekly goals and to-dos, I will go out with my friends. Otherwise, I will stay home and finish my to-dos.

PERCEIVED TIME CONTROL AND STRESS

PERCEIVED TIME CONTROL:
Subjective experience of viewing time as a variable that is either within or outside of personal control.

Another approach to understanding time management focuses on the perception of control over time. From this point of view, the broader purpose of time management is to reduce stress and increase productive outcomes. However, time management practices such as planning, goal-setting, and organization only reduce stress and increase productivity if these practices enhance your sense of control over time. If not, then time management strategies alone are not sufficient to overcome stress. Empirical evidence dating back to the 1990s heavily supports this position, indicating that time management strategies must first alter your relationship to time if they are to improve performance-related outcomes (Claessens, van Eerd, Rutte, & Roe, 2004; Haffner & Stock, 2010; Macan, 1994).

Regardless of how much training you receive on time management strategies, they will only help if you believe the practices enhance your time control. This is a subtle but important distinction. In effect, it supports the idea that attention management is the most critical aspect of productivity. When you feel in control of your time, your stress levels tend to remain low and your attention is focused. While there are innumerable ways to create the conditions for this sense of time control, they all work to build your feeling of mastery and thereby increase your ability to concentrate on the task at hand.

AN APPLIED THOUGHT EXPERIMENT

To understand what this means in practice, imagine yourself sitting down for a one-hour study session. As you review your notes and cross-reference your textbook, your attention shifts continuously. At one moment you are fully engaged and the next your mind wanders to a random conversation from earlier in the day. As this extraneous thought creeps up time and time again, you can feel the stress and frustration building. Your final exam is in two days and you still have to finish writing a paper for another class. To combat this distraction and reign in your focus, you decide to implement a strategy. Pulling out a piece of paper, you write down three major study goals to be implemented in the next hour. As you briefly review the goals and return to your work for the next hour, you find that your attention has drastically improved.

What happened in this process that worked for you? On one hand, it could be claimed that setting goals directly influences attention because it is a motivating force. When you know exactly what needs to be done, you are just more likely to follow through and do it. On the other hand, it could be claimed that setting goals provides a sense of perceived control over time itself. When you know that there is one hour in which to study and three major objectives that need to be accomplished, a sense of time-oriented mastery arises. Your confidence increases, your stress level decreases, and your ability to pay attention are enhanced as a result.

Have you ever set study session goals or objectives in the past?

While this is indeed a subtle difference, it has major repercussions. The strategy of "writing down specific study goals" serves only as a catalyst for your larger sense of mastery. The same thing applies to using a schedule book, keeping to-do lists, or organizing class notes. Implementing such time management strategies can increase your sense of control over time and thereby relieve some of your stress. However, you can use every strategy imaginable and experience no reduction in stress if you still perceive your time as uncontrollable. In other words, finding ways to readjust your perception of time is critical if you want to relieve the pressure that accompanies a busy schedule.

THE POMODORO TECHNIQUE

One method that can be effective in readjusting both your sense of time control and your attention is the Pomodoro exercise (Cirillo, 2013). It involves the use of a timer, a study task, a scratch piece of paper, and a reasonable degree of self-control. The premise is simple: choose a study task, set your timer for 15 minutes, and then study until the timer goes off. This is one Pomodoro. When the timer rings, put a checkmark on your scratch piece of paper, take a five-minute break, and then start the timer again. If you complete four consecutive Pomodoros, take a 15-minute break and choose whether or not it would be beneficial to restart the process and continue to work.

Now here is the caveat. To keep tabs on wandering thoughts during the exercise, briefly write something down on the scratch paper about any distraction that crosses your mind. As distractions accumulate, you can make an intentional decision to abandon the exercise but only after completing the current Pomodoro. Whether distractions are your own thoughts or incoming phone calls, any significant amount of time taken away from the Pomodoro-based task means you have to start over again. By taking the task at hand seriously and avoiding distractions, you can earn not only a 15- to 30-minute break after completing four sets but also a sense of pride in your enhanced ability to focus.

Have you ever sat down to study for a "while"? How long is a "while"? Sometimes the undefined can feel like forever or worse, never enough. The defined promotes intentionality and feelings of control.

The value of this technique is that it provides a time-oriented sense of attentional training. Knowing that you only have 10 minutes left in your set, for example, can relieve some of the internal, psychological pressure that often accompanies distractions (Gobbo & Vaccari, 2008). During the five-minute break, you can decide whether or not it would be beneficial to start a new task, return to your original task, or abandon the process altogether. In any case, the Pomodoro exercise is a unique way to increase your sense of control over time by training yourself to stay on task in short and regular intervals.

PROCRASTINATION

There is no doubt that everyone feels the need to procrastinate at some time or another. Whether it involves a preference to hang out with friends rather than study or watch a movie rather than exercise, the allure of pleasurable activities often tends to overshadow the importance of less pleasurable ones. Research on college campuses has found that somewhere between 80% and 95% of students procrastinate and nearly 75% define themselves as procrastinators (Steel, 2007). According to O'Brien (2002), more than 95% of people who regularly procrastinate view it as a harmful pattern that should be reduced or eliminated.

PROCRASTINATION:
The irrational delay or postponement of a task or activity.

Yet procrastination is not something that needs to be completely eradicated. It really needs only to be more effectively managed. Finding ways to manage your own procrastination tendencies is an important task that includes elements found throughout this book. This section is designed to provide a foundation for understanding how procrastination works and for grasping some of the psychological barriers to overcoming it. Although the ideas in this section are based on a theoretical framing of procrastination, translating them into real world practices is not as difficult as you might think.

If your future self could talk to you right now about an upcoming task or project, what do you think your future self would tell you?.

The real key to overcoming procrastination in your own life is to consider the relationship between your present self and your future self (Oettingen, 2000). Your future self will reap the rewards and experience the value of accomplishments. Your present self is typically more interested in enjoying the present moment. Bridging the gap between the two requires a commitment made by your present self for the betterment of your future self. In each of the following points on procrastination, taking the time to think about long-term rewards and to consider their value is extremely important.

Furthermore, examining your own ability to formulate well-crafted goals (see Cluster 2) and stimulate your own motivation (see Cluster 6) will help in overcoming impulsiveness. By putting in the time and effort to consider your own habits and priorities, you will be in a much better position to make thoughtful decisions about your time and attention management.

HYPERBOLIC DISCOUNTING

Despite the fact that it sounds complex, the term *hyperbolic discounting* refers to a very simple concept: people tend to choose smaller rewards in the near future over larger rewards in the more distant future (Laibson, 1997). For example, you would probably prefer that someone give you 50 dollars right now rather than 100 dollars sometime next year. Of course, this preference also depends on the timeframe. You would probably be willing to wait a week or two to get that 100 dollars, but the allure of the reward diminishes the longer you have to wait. The term "hyperbolic" simply refers to the mathematical wave function that predicts this motivational difference between long- and short-term decision making.

The point is that people are typically more interested in short-term rewards than long-term ones. It turns out that this principle explains much of human behavior. For example, even though saving money for retirement is an important long-term financial consideration, most young professionals put very little, if any, of their hard earned money into a retirement account. This appears to be a hardwired human tendency despite the fact that it is an illogical decision (Kable & Glimcher, 2007). Whether it is the financial decision to buy a new television rather than put that money in a savings account, or the choice made to watch a movie rather than study for an exam that is still three weeks away, hyperbolic discounting exerts a lot of influence on procrastination tendencies.

EXPECTANCY THEORY

According to expectancy theory, people tend to behave according to the pleasure–pain principle. Our most basic desire is to increase pleasure and minimize pain. Procrastination is guided by this principle because it involves consciously choosing more pleasurable activities over less pleasurable ones (Vroom, 1964). The value of expectancy theory is that it also pinpoints the conditions under which you determine how much more pleasurable one activity is compared to another (Magidson, Roberts, Collado-Rodriguez, & Lejuez, 2014). It is not that some activities are inherently more or less pleasurable than others. For example, whereas you might despise doing calculus homework, other people happily spend their entire lives completing differential equations.

What qualifies as a pleasurable task is a matter of perspective. In other words, your expectations guide the relative value you attribute to different activities. These expectations are indeed relative, based on your own sets of preferences and interests. However, such expectations are also heavily tied to your belief that you will achieve a certain outcome. People who excel at calculus to the point that they can make a career as a theoretical physicist tend to believe in

HYPERBOLIC DISCOUNTING: The tendency to choose immediate smaller rewards rather than wait for larger rewards in the future.

How do you think hyperbolic discounting is related to the effectiveness of enabling goals (or proximal subgoals)?

Is there an activity you enjoy that many other people do not? How much does your effectiveness at the activity guide your interest and time-investment?

their ability to achieve their long-term goals by working out complex mathematical equations. When you have little faith in your ability to complete your calculus homework assignment, it is hard to get excited about putting in the necessary time and effort.

This is one-part self-efficacy (see Module 6.2), one-part motivation (see Module 6.1), and one-part goal formation (see Cluster 2). To better understand how procrastination works, the following describes how these ideas relate to expectancy theory. This theory suggests that three factors come together to determine why you choose one activity instead of another: expectancy, instrumentality, and valence. *Expectancy* is the belief that your efforts will lead to an outcome that you want. *Instrumentality* is the belief that achieving that outcome will lead to a reward that you want. *Valence* is the value that you attribute to getting that reward. In combination, expectancy theory suggests that you exert more effort when you believe it will lead to a rewarding outcome that you value.

The equation guiding this theory has been extremely successful in measuring how people make decisions and commit to a course of action:

TABLE 3.1.3 EXPECTANCY THEORY EQUATION AND MOTIVATION EXAMPLES

Equation: Motivation = Expectancy × Instrumentality × Valence

Equation Defined: Motivation = Expected Outcome × Desired Reward × Value of Reward

High Motivation	Motivation = I can effectively study for my Calculus exam (**high outcome**) × High exam grade (**high reward**) × Calculus is required for my degree (**high value**)
Low Motivation	Motivation = I don't know how to study for my Calculus exam (**low outcome**) × Low exam grade (**low reward**) × Calculus is required for my degree (**high value**)
Low Motivation	Motivation = I can complete my required readings for my psychology class (**high outcome**) × None of the readings were on the first exam (**low reward**) × Psychology is required for my degree (**high value**)

For tasks that you enjoy and feel capable, as described previously, it is easy to see how this equation leads to higher motivation and action.

UNDERLYING CAUSES OF PROCRASTINATION

While problems with time management alone can account for procrastination issues, there can also be underlying psychological causes. Chronic procrastination may be a sign that one or more of the tendencies outlined below are influencing your decision-making. Identifying patterns of behavior in light of these psychological causes can be an important step toward over-coming procrastination.

- **Perfectionism**: Setting unrealistically high standards for performance leads some people to delay or avoid completing a task rather than to risk doing it less than perfectly. Perfectionism is actually a multidimensional trait, meaning that it includes other factors such as fear of failure, high levels of self-criticism, concerns about the perceptions of others, and the need for order and organization (Flett, Blankstein, Hewitt, & Koledin, 1992). In combination, these factors can severely hinder your ability to overcome self-imposed obstacles in order to get things done. For example, setting an ideal standard for a class presentation can actually lead the perfectionist to avoid or even abandon the project when it appears the ideal might not be met. Overcoming such tendencies requires being more flexible about your own expectations and setting more realistic performance standards (Steel, 2007).

- **Indecisiveness**: Simply making decisions related to starting, continuing, or completing tasks can be a challenge for some people. While lack of motivation is a typical culprit in such situations, indecisiveness can also be a contributing factor. In terms of chronic procrastination, the effect of indecisiveness can range from frustrating to paralyzing when the amount of energy spent making basic decisions prevents you from getting any real work done (Ferrari & Dovidio, 2000). For example, writing term papers can become increasingly time consuming and extremely demoralizing when you change your mind several times during the semester about the topic, style, or highlights of the essay.

- **Over-doing**: The phrase "biting off more than you can chew" is probably the simplest way to grasp the idea of over-doing. There are so many tasks and activities that a college student has to complete in order to be successful that the mere thought can sometimes be overwhelming. When excessive workloads become too much to handle, it can seem easier to avoid tasks altogether in order to relieve stress. However, being thoughtful and selective in prioritizing can significantly reduce both your workload and stress level. There are only so many hours in a day, so learning to say "no" to less important activities can be a valuable time management skill (Brown, 1992). On the other hand, over-doing can also result from a desire to avoid less enjoyable tasks. If you find that your daily schedule is full but the important tasks are not getting done, ask yourself what you might be trying to avoid by overloading your schedule.

- **Self-handicapping**: Placing obstacles in your own way in order to cope with poor performances or potential failures is called self-handicapping. It is a way to protect self-esteem by creating an external excuse for negative outcomes (Steel, 2007). For example, by choosing not to study until the night before an exam, you can rationalize getting a "C" on the test and even tell yourself that you did a good job under the circumstances. The question is whether or not this procrastination–rationalization cycle is a pattern. If so, you may be self-handicapping in an effort to protect your self-esteem.

Similar to over-doing, many times students also feel overwhelmed by the perceived size of an academic task. Knowing that you have to read 100 pages of difficult text or write a 20-page research paper can make students feel as if the "job is too big" even if due dates are well into the future for these tasks. For example, the result is that students continue to delay starting on these tasks because they do not want to write 20 pages. However, there are strategies that can help students successfully overcome these obstacles and others. The next two modules will talk about these specific strategies.

MODULE 3.1 SUMMARY

- Effective task completion requires both time management and attention management.
- Two effective ways to define priorities include the ABCDE method and the Eisenhower method.
- Three models for understanding habit formation include direct-context cueing, implicit goals, and motivated contexts.
- Perceived time control is one of the most important factors in managing time and stress.
- Three models that explain procrastination include hyperbolic discounting, expectancy theory, and temporal motivation theory.
- Chronic procrastination can also be related to underlying psychological factors such as perfectionism, indecisiveness, over-doing, and self-handicapping.

KEY TERMS

- **Attention Management** – Ability to maintain focus and self-control in order to accomplish tasks and complete activities.
- **Conditioning** – Psychological process by which a regular and predictable behavioral response occurs as a result of reinforcement.
- **Expectancy** – Belief that your efforts will lead to desired outcomes.
- **Habits** – Unconscious behavioral patterns formed as a result of conditioned and reinforced routines.
- **Hyperbolic Discounting** – The tendency to choose immediate smaller rewards rather than wait for larger rewards in the future.
- **Instrumentality** – Belief that achieving outcomes will lead to desired rewards.
- **Perceived Time Control** – Subjective experience of viewing time as a variable that is either within or outside of personal control.
- **Procrastination** – The irrational delay or postponement of a task or activity.
- **Punishment** – Weakening of specific behavioral responses through the use of negative consequences.

- **Reinforcement** – Strengthening of specific behavioral responses through the use of rewards.
- **Time Management** – The productive and organized use of time to accomplish tasks and complete activities.
- **Valence** – The value that someone places on an achieved reward.

REFERENCES

Aarts, H., & Dijksterhuis, A. (2000). Habits as knowledge structures: automaticity in goal-directed behavior. *Journal of Personality and Social Psychology, 78*(1), 53–63.

Brown, R. T. (1992). Helping students confront and deal with stress and procrastination. *Journal of College Student Psychotherapy, 6*(2), 87–102.

Cirillo, F. (2013). *The pomodoro technique.* Raleigh, NC: Lulu Press.

Claessens, B. J. C., van Eerde, V., Rutte, C. G., & Roe, R. A. (2004). Planning behavior and perceived control of time at work. *Journal of Organizational Behavior, 25*(8), 937–950.

Ferrari, J. R., & Dovidio, J. F. (2000). Examining behavioral processes in indecision: Decisional procrastination and decision-making style. *Journal of Research in Personality, 34*(1), 127–137.

Flett, G. L., Blankstein, K. R., Hewitt, P. L., & Koledin, S. (1992). Components of perfectionism and procrastination in college students. *Social Behavior and Personality: An International Journal, 20*(2), 85–94.

Gobbo, F., & Vaccari, M. (2008). The pomodoro technique for sustainable pace in extreme programming teams. In A. Sillitti, O. Hazzan, E. Bache, & X. Albaladejo (Eds.), *Agile processes in software engineering and extreme programming* (pp. 180–184). Berlin: Springer.

Haffner, A., & Stock, A. (2010). Time management training and perceived control of time at work. *The Journal of Psychology, 144*(5), 429–447.

Jovanovich, N., Fiorillo, A., & Rossler, W. (2015). Managing self: Time, priorities, and well-being. In A. Fiorillo, U. Volpe, & D. Bhugra (Eds.), *Psychiatry in practice: Education, experience and expertise* (pp. 33–44). Oxford, England: Oxford University Press.

Kable, J. W., & Glimcher, P. W. (2007). The neural correlates of subjective value during intertemporal choice. *Nature Neuroscience, 10*(12), 1625–1633.

Laibson, D. (1997). Golden eggs and hyperbolic discounting. *The Quarterly Journal of Economics, 112*(2), 443–477.

Lally, P., & Gardner, B. (2013). Promoting habit formation. *Health Psychology Review, 7*(1), 137–158.

Macan, T. H. (1994). Time management: Test of a process model. *Journal of Applied Psychology, 79*(3), 381–391.

Magidson, J. F., Roberts, B. W., Collado-Rodriguez, A., & Lejuez, C. W. (2014). Theory-driven intervention for changing personality: Expectancy value theory, behavioral activation, and conscientiousness. *Developmental Psychology, 50*(5), 1442.

Neal, D. T., Wood, W., & Quinn, J. M. (2006). Habits: A repeat performance. *Current Directions in Psychological Science, 15*(4), 198–202.

O'Brien, W. K. (2002). *Applying the transtheoretical model to academic procrastination.* Unpublished doctoral dissertation, University of Houston, Houston, TX.

Oettingen, G. (2000). Expectancy effects on behavior depend on self-regulatory thought. *Social Cognition, 18*, 101–129.

Schultz, W., Dayan, P., & Montague, P. R. (1997). A neural substrate of prediction and reward. *Science, 275*(5306), 1593–1599.

Steel, P. (2007). The nature of procrastination. *Psychological Bulletin, 133*(1), 65–94.

Steel, P., & König, C. J. (2006). Integrating theories of motivation. *Academy of Management Review, 31*(4), 889–913.

Stuart, E. W., Shimp, T. A., & Engle, R. W. (1987). Classical conditioning of consumer attitudes: Four experiments in an advertising context. *Journal of Consumer Research, 14*(3), 334–349.

Verplanken, B., & Aarts, H. (1999) Habit, attitude, and planned behaviour: Is habit an empty construct or an interesting case of goal-directed automaticity? *European Review of Social Psychology, 10*(1), 101–134.

Vroom, V. H. (1964). *Work and motivation.* Oxford, England: Wiley.

Wexley, K. N., & Baldwin, T. T. (1986). Post-training strategies for facilitating positive transfer: An empirical exploration. *The Academy of Management Journal, 29*(3), 503–520.

THE IDEAL SCHEDULE— CREATING BALANCE AND GETTING IT DONE

CLUSTER 3 OBJECTIVES COVERED IN THIS MODULE

☐ **OBJECTIVE:** Construct a master calendar that supports short-, mid-, and long-range planning.

☐ **OBJECTIVE:** Establish a weekly schedule that supports academic and personal goals.

OVERVIEW: STRATEGIES AND ACADEMIC ACHIEVEMENT

Module 3.1 provided the theoretical foundations for understanding time and attention management as well as procrastination. This module and the next will focus more specifically on tools and strategies that support prioritization, habit formation, taking control of time, and minimizing procrastination tendencies. Although some of these strategies will be new or have not been needed until now, the good news is that time management is similar to other learning tasks. The more you incorporate these strategies and practice these skills, the more effective you will become.

The other good news is that the research is consistent about the relationship between incorporating time management strategies and higher academic achievement (Britton & Tesser, 1991; Wintre et al., 2011). In fact, in Britton and Tesser's (1991) research, they found the use of time management strategies accounted for more variance in students' four-year cumulative college GPA than students' entering SAT scores. What does this mean? It means that regardless of entering academic preparation or skill level (i.e., as represented by a student's SAT score), students who were able to learn and gain time management skills were able to perform academically at a higher level over the long-term. Additionally, Wintre et al.'s (2011) study provided evidence that students were more likely to maintain their high school achievement levels in their first year of college by incorporating time management strategies. In both studies, it is clear that students can learn to take control of their time and enhance their academic achievement.

To begin, this module will focus on establishing routines and effective tools for short- and long-term planning.

ROUTINES AND PLANNING

REFLECTION: Have you ever wondered how some people earn good grades and still manage to have a social life? Do you feel you are currently achieving this balance?

To achieve balance while still accomplishing your goals, establishing routines and ongoing planning are essential. Routines and planning promote a mindset of, "this is what I do" and influence motivation by telling you exactly what to do and when. As a result, you are more efficient, which allows you to spend less time and cognitive resources on continuous decision making. Consider the example shared previously: brushing your teeth. It is something you do without much thought and you do it every day (hopefully, anyways!). It is routine, and does not require a large amount of energy or thought. It is just something you do. You can create other routines that will also allow you to maximize efficiencies and reduce the use of cognitive resources.

Some students fear that scheduling everything will create too much "structure" and they will not be able to enjoy everything the college experience has to offer. In fact, the opposite occurs. Routines and planning result in *less* stress and *more* time for the things that students want to accomplish and enjoy. Students who do not have routines and do not continuously plan typically experience more stress, have less time to enjoy leisure activities, and still do not accomplish their goals.

Additionally, routines and planning generate more flexibility for students and support their ability to adapt to setbacks and any unexpected life events. Consider the following:

> Carmen has a chemistry exam next Monday. Currently, her routine is to study chemistry five days a week (Sunday, Monday, Tuesday, Wednesday, and Thursday). She also has some FLEX time built into her schedule (on Friday afternoons) she can use if she does not quite get everything done. Unfortunately, she gets called into work on Thursday and she misses her time to study. As a result, she uses her FLEX time on Friday and gets back on track for her exam preparation.

By having a routine where Carmen is studying chemistry on a regular basis, she only has to make up the one to two hours to get back on track. Now consider Li:

Li has his first psychology exam on Friday. He has been putting off reading and studying but he knows he does not have anything planned on Wednesday or Thursday night. So, he plans to read and study for his exam on those two nights. However, Li is called into work on Wednesday night. He has class all day on Thursday and is not able to start studying until after dinner. The result is he must cram on Thursday night for his exam. He stays up all night and barely accomplishes more than reading the material.

Have you ever had to stay up all night studying? What decisions led to that situation? Do you think this resulted in your best work?

By not establishing a routine and not studying psychology on a regular basis, Li's unexpected setback creates anxiety and stress (i.e., pulling an all-nighter) that leads to poor academic outcomes.

Finally, any plans or routines established should be based on set goals. What are you trying to accomplish this semester? This includes goals in each domain of your life (i.e., academics, social, and personal). When goals provide the foundation for your planning and decision-making, it becomes much easier to prioritize tasks according to the things that are most important to you.

ESTABLISHING A PLAN

MASTER CALENDAR

One of the differences and major benefits of classes at the college level versus high school is the availability of your syllabi. Unlike high school, many of your syllabi will give you a semester schedule that includes major due dates and exam dates. Unfortunately, many students do not take advantage of this information. Your syllabi coupled with a "Master Calendar" will allow you to establish short-, mid-, and long-range plans to successfully accomplish each of your goals this semester.

A master calendar is a one-page planning tool that will help give you an overview of your responsibilities. It includes all due dates listed on your syllabi as well as any other important commitments or events over the course of the semester. The master calendar is used *with* your other planners and/or planning tools. It does not replace these other tools. As one page, it provides an accessible and convenient way to view your schedule at a glance. Completing a master calendar now will help you in two major ways. First, it allows you to do your weekly and daily planning based on what is pending without flipping through multiple course packets and syllabi (and potentially missing something). Second, it allows you to identify and prevent any surprises. If you have two papers and two exams in week 11, you can see it now and plan accordingly. One recommendation is to start each week (e.g., Sunday evenings) by planning your goals and to-do lists for the week based on the upcoming tasks found on your master calendar. Then, each evening, plan your next day based on your weekly plan. A planner can be helpful in listing these weekly and daily goals and to-dos. Using your master calendar will also allow you to break-up major projects and papers into smaller parts and to set due dates for these accordingly. Breaking efforts into smaller parts promotes greater focus and higher motivation (see Module 3.3).

To complete the master calendar, include all important dates that impact your schedule and planning. The following lists any potential dates you may want to include:

1. Using each of your syllabi, list the due dates for any papers, projects, exams, weekly homework assignments or quizzes, labs, etc.

2. For any large projects or papers, determine if you need to add your own due dates for items such as selecting a topic, completing drafts, and visiting the writing center.

3. Are there any special holidays, university or family events that could potentially impact your schedule and ability to work on academics (e.g., Homecoming, Spring Break, and a wedding)? List these and any associated travel.

4. Are you involved in any extracurricular activities? List these commitments and any associated travel or events.

> A master calendar allows you to identify those "Not Urgent but Important" tasks and incorporate some to-dos each week to help accomplish them well before they become "Urgent and Important."

Some students will use colors to highlight different classes or obligations. Figure 3.2.1 is an example of a master calendar. This student is taking 16 credits: English, Biology, Psychology, First Year Seminar, and History.

FIGURE 3.2.1 MASTER CALENDAR EXAMPLE

Fall Semester Example

	Sun	Mon	Tue	Wed	Thurs	Fri	Sat
1		**22- Aug Classes Begin**	23-Aug	24-Aug	25-Aug	26-Aug	27-Aug
2	28-Aug	**29-Aug**	30-Aug	31-Aug	1-Sep **BIO: Quiz 1**	2- Sep	3-Sep
3	4-Sep	5- Sep **Labor Day (University closed)**	6-Sep **BIO: LAB HW**	7- Sep **FYS: Quiz 1**	8- Sep **BIO: Quiz 2**	9-Sep **FYS: Goals Paper** **ENG: JNL 1**	10-Sep
4	11-Sep	12-Sep **ENG: PERS Paper**	13-Sep **BIO: LAB HW**	14-Sep	15-Sep **HIST: Exam 1** **BIO: Exam 1**	16-Sep **FYS: Time Use Chart** **ENG: JNL 2**	17-Sep
5	18-Sep	19-Sep	20-Sep **BIO: LAB HW**	21-Sep **FYS: Quiz 2**	22-Sep **BIO: Quiz 3**	23-Sep **PSY: Exam 1** **ENG: JNL 3**	24-Sep

6	25-Sep	26-Sep	27-Sep BIO: LAB HW	28-Sep	29-Sep BIO: Quiz 4	30-Sep ENG: JNL 4	1-Oct
7	2-Oct	3-Oct	4-Oct BIO: LAB HW	5-Oct FYS: Quiz 3 ENG: ARG Paper	6-Oct BIO: Exam 2	7-Oct ENG: JNL 5 Go home for Mom's birthday.	8-Oct Mom's party
8	9-Oct Get home late.	10-Oct FYS: Midterm Exam	11-Oct BIO: Lab Project 1	12-Oct	13-Oct HIST: Exam 2 BIO: Quiz 5	14-Oct ENG: JNL 6	15-Oct
9	16-Oct	17-Oct PSY: Exam 2	18-Oct BIO: LAB HW	19-Oct FYS: Quiz 4	20-Oct BIO: Quiz 6	21-Oct FYS: Draft Paper ENG: JNL 7	22-Oct Homecoming
	Spirit Week						
10	23-Oct	24-Oct ENG: CRIT Paper	25-Oct BIO: LAB HW	26-Oct FYS: Quiz 5	27-Oct BIO: Exam 3	28-Oct FYS: 4-YR Plan ENG: JNL 8	29-Oct
11	30-Oct	31-Oct	1-Nov BIO: LAB HW	2-Nov	3-Nov BIO: Quiz 7	4-Nov ENG: JNL 9	5-Nov
12	6-Nov	7-Nov	8-Nov BIO: LAB HW	9-Nov	10-Nov HIST: Exam 3 BIO: Quiz 8	11-Nov FYS: Final Paper PSY: Exam 3 ENG: JNL 10	12-Nov
13	13-Nov	14-Nov ENG: ANALYSIS Paper	15-Nov BIO: LAB HW	16-Nov FYS: Research Poster	17-Nov BIO: Exam 4	18-Nov HIST: Paper ENG: JNL 11	19-Nov Leave for home.
14	20-Nov	21-Nov	22-Nov	23-Nov Thanksgiving	24-Nov Thanksgiving	25-Nov Thanksgiving	26-Nov
	Thanksgiving						
15	27-Nov Get home late.	28-Nov	29-Nov BIO: Lab Project 2	30-Nov	1-Dec	2-Dec PSY: Paper	3-Dec
16	4-Dec	5-Dec (Finals) ENG: Final Paper	6-Dec (Finals) PSY: Final	7-Dec (Finals) BIO: Final	8-Dec (Finals) HIST: Final FYS: Final	9-Dec (Finals)	10-Dec

When examining this calendar, notice the following:

- In her fourth week, she has a paper and two exams. Both are her first exams in biology and history and they are on the same day.

- In the eighth week, she has a mid-term on Monday, a major lab project due on Tuesday, and her second history exam on Thursday. She has already promised her Mom to go home the weekend before and will not get home until late on Sunday evening. The only way she will successfully manage this week's tasks is if she plans ahead and gets some work done early.

- The following week will also be impacted by spirit week and Homecoming. This will also require some planning and discipline so that she can still focus on her academics but also enjoy some of the activities that week.

- Weeks 12 and 13 are also busy weeks with several major due dates and will require some advanced planning.

Although this calendar may seem to have some crazy weeks, it can be very similar to what students encounter on a regular basis. By using a master calendar, this student already knows where her schedule is more hectic and can be proactive and plan for these weeks; therefore, balancing her academic and personal goals for the semester.

It is easy to create a master calendar using either a word processing program (e.g., Microsoft Word) or spreadsheet program (e.g., Microsoft Excel). Figure 3.2.2 is a blank template of a sample calendar for a 16-week semester.

How do you think using a Master Calendar can promote higher levels of perceived time control?

FIGURE 3.2.2 MASTER CALENDAR TEMPLATE: 16-WEEK SEMESTER

Week	Sun	Mon	Tue	Wed	Thurs	Fri	Sat
1							
2							
3							
4							
5							
6							
7							
8							
9							
10							
11							
12							
13							
14							
15							
16							

As a final reminder, refer to this calendar when you plan your days and weeks. Last minute surprises can wreak havoc on a busy schedule, so use your master calendar to plan ahead. The next section will provide details about creating the ideal week that will build routines and support your short-range plans.

ANALYZING YOUR TIME

One of the first steps in creating a routine and schedule is gaining a keen awareness of how you spend your time. Do you think you can answer each of these questions accurately?

- How much time do you study outside of class per week for each of your courses?
- How much sleep do you get?
- How much time are you spending on social media?
- How much time do you spend getting ready, eating, etc.?

The next set of activities is to help you gain this understanding and then to establish a routine that aligns with your personal and academic goals. Using Activities 3.2.1 and 3.2.2, complete the following:

1. Begin by predicting the amount of time that you spend on various activities and complete column (1) in the Time Analysis Chart (Activity 3.2.1). Remember there are 168 hours in a week.

2. Using the Time Log Chart (Activity 3.2.2), log all of your activities for one week. Be as accurate as possible. If you are taking a shower and getting ready, hanging out drinking a cup of coffee, or attending class, be sure to log this information. When you are studying for particular courses, identify the specific course in the log. You can either complete this log here or create a blank template (e.g., Microsoft Word or Excel) and carry it with you over the course of the next week.

3. After you have stopped logging your information, total the number of hours for your activities and complete column (2) in the Time Analysis Chart (Activity 3.2.1).

4. Before completing columns (3) and (4), reflect on the following questions:

   - How accurate were your predictions?
   - Were there any surprises?
   - Are you spending too much time on any particular activities?
   - Should you be spending more time on other activities?
   - Are there any changes you need to make to better support your goals?

5. Now complete columns (3) and (4). Remember the recommendation for time spent studying outside of class is one to three hours per hour spent in class (e.g., a three-hour course would require three to nine hours of studying outside of class per week).

	(1) **Predict** the number of hours in a week that you:	(2) How many hours **did you:**	(3) How many hours **should** you:	(4) How many hours **will you:**
Sleep				
Attend class				
Study				
Eat				
Get ready				
Commute				
Work				
Watch TV				
Socialize				
Talk on the phone/text				
Social Media				
Play video games				
Exercise/workout				
Attend sports practice				
List any others:				
Total hours				

ACTIVITY 3.2.2 TIME LOG CHART

	Sun	Mon	Tues	Wed	Thurs	Fri	Sat
7am							
8am							
9am							
10am							
11am							
12pm							
1pm							
2pm							
3pm							
4pm							
5pm							
6pm							
7pm							
8pm							
9pm							
10pm							
11pm							
12am							

WEEKLY SCHEDULE

The next step is to use the information you gained from the previous activities and create an ideal schedule. The following are some advantages to setting a schedule:

1. You start to establish routines.
2. You may begin to view going to school as your full-time job that deserves your ongoing time and effort.
3. You can share your schedules with roommates and friends so that they can support your efforts and goals.
4. You can take advantage of your strengths and adjust for your limitations.
5. You can maximize the time you have to fully support both academic and social activities.

How does an established schedule and routines relate to direct-context cueing?

The following includes some examples of an ideal schedule.

Slow in the Mornings—Example 1

In this first example (Figure 3.2.3), Mia knows that she is not very productive in the morning. In fact, she knows that the only thing that will motivate her to get up is going to class. She is taking 16 credits (English, Biology, Psychology, First Year Seminar, and History). When determining the amount of time to study outside of class, she considers which classes will be her hardest and require the most time. She also remembers the recommendation of studying outside of class one to three hours per hour of class time. She decides that she will study the following hours and *then will reevaluate after two weeks*:

- Study Plan—ENG (four hours), BIO (eight hours), PSY (five hours), FYS (three hours), and HIST (four hours)

FIGURE 3.2.3 MIA'S WEEKLY SCHEDULE

	Sun	Mon	Tue	Wed	Thurs	Fri	Sat
6–630			BREAKFAST GET READY				
630–7							
7–730			BIO LAB				
730–8							
8–830							
830–9							
9–930		BREAKFAST GET READY		BREAKFAST GET READY	BREAKFAST GET READY	BREAKFAST GET READY	
930–10							
10–1030		ENG	HIST	ENG	HIST	ENG	
1030–11							
11–1130		GYM		GYM		GYM	
1130–12			HIST - WORK (1.5HRS)		HIST - WORK (1.5HRS)		
12–1230		LUNCH		LUNCH		LUNCH	
1230–1							
1–130			LUNCH		LUNCH		
130–2		FYS		FYS		FYS	
2–230			BIO		BIO		
230-3		FYS - WORK (1HR)		FYS - WORK (1HR)		FYS - WORK (1HR)	
3-330							
330-4		PSY	BIO - TUTOR (1HR)	PSY	BIO - TUTOR (1HR)	PSY	
4-430							
430-5	DINNER	PSY - WORK (1HR)	BIO - WORK (1HR)	PSY - WORK (1HR)	BIO - WORK (1HR)	PSY - WORK (1HR)	
5-530							
530-6	PLANNING	DINNER	DINNER	DINNER	DINNER	DINNER	
6-630	BIO - WORK (2HRS)						
630-7		FLEX	FLEX	FLEX	FLEX	FLEX	
7-730							
730-8		BIO - WORK (1HR)	PSY - WORK (1HR)	BIO - WORK (1HR)	PSY - WORK (1HR)		
8-830	HIST - WORK (1HR)						
830-9		ENG - WORK (1HR)	ENG - WORK (1HR)	ENG - WORK (1HR)	ENG - WORK (1HR)		
9-930							
930-10		PLANNING	PLANNING	PLANNING	PLANNING		

Within this example, there are several elements to notice:

- Mia is working a 40-hour work week. School is her full-time job where she goes to class for 16 hours and studies for 24 hours.

- Mia has late starts the majority of mornings (i.e., 9am alarm with 10am class).

- She is more effective in the evenings and is comfortable with studying at that time; however, she is still done every evening by 9:30pm (10pm with planning). This leaves her several hours to socialize with friends, watch television, etc.

- She has two lengthy breaks (i.e., two and a half hours gym/lunch and two hours for dinner/FLEX) that allow her to re-energize during the day.

- Gym time is a priority and is planned three days a week.

- Friday nights, all day Saturday, and Sundays until 5:30pm are completely open. This time can be used for social wants or possible job commitments. This can also be additional FLEX time if Mia needs to complete unfinished weekly goals.

- Planned study time is based on the needs of the courses. Biology is the hardest course for Mia so more time is planned. Additionally, she either goes to class or studies biology five days out of seven. Constantly, revisiting the material on an almost daily basis is an effective strategy to ensure deeper learning (see Cluster 4).

- Tutoring is built in as a regular part of her schedule.

- Mia enjoys her English class and so finishes each day with this study time. It is easier for her and so doing it during the last part of the day is not a problem. She begins biology earlier when she is fresher and can maintain concentration better.

- FLEX time is included, which can be used on weeks where additional study time is needed (e.g., exam weeks). If this time is not needed, then she can use it however she likes. On a normal week, she can take a longer dinner and break if she likes or she can start her other studying earlier.

- Planning is also a normal part of her routine. On Sunday, before the week starts, she uses her Master Calendar to plan her weekly goals and to-dos and then plans her specific goals for Monday. Then each night, she reviews her progress on her weekly goals and plans her specific goals for the next day.

The Early Riser—Example 2

In the next example (Figure 3.2.4), Ellie likes to get up early and then finish early. She is also taking the same 16 credits (ENG, BIO, PSY, FYS, and HIST) and follows the same study plan:

- Study Plan—ENG (four hours), BIO (eight hours), PSY (five hours), FYS (three hours), and HIST (four hours)

FIGURE 3.2.4 ELLIE'S WEEKLY SCHEDULE

	Sun	Mon	Tue	Wed	Thurs	Fri	Sat
6–630			BREAKFAST GET READY				
630–7							
7–730		GYM	BIO LAB	GYM	GYM	GYM	
730–8							
8–830		BREAKFAST GET READY		BREAKFAST GET READY	BREAKFAST GET READY	BREAKFAST GET READY	
830–9							
9–930		BIO - WORK (1HR)		BIO - WORK (1HR)	BIO - WORK (1HR)	BIO - WORK (1HR)	
930–10							
10–1030		ENG	HIST	ENG	HIST	ENG	
1030–11							
11–1130		ENG - WORK (1.5HRS)	HIST - WORK (1.5HRS)	ENG - WORK (1.5HRS)	HIST - WORK (1.5HRS)	ENG - WORK (1.5HRS)	
1130–12							
12–1230							
1230–1		LUNCH		LUNCH		LUNCH	
1–130			LUNCH		LUNCH		
130–2		FYS		FYS		FYS	
2–230			BIO		BIO		
230–3		FYS - WORK (1HR)		FYS - WORK (1HR)		FYS - WORK (1HR)	
3–330							
330–4	PLANNING	PSY	BIO - TUTOR (1HR)	PSY	BIO - TUTOR (1HR)	PSY	
4–430	BIO - WORK (2HRS)						
430–5		PSY - STUDY GROUP (1HR)	PSY - WORK (1HR)	PSY - WORK (1HR)	PSY - WORK (1HR)	PSY - WORK (1HR)	
5–530							
530–6		DINNER	DINNER	DINNER	DINNER	DINNER	
6–630	HIST - WORK (1HR)						
630–7		FLEX/PLANNING	FLEX/PLANNING	FLEX/PLANNING	FLEX/PLANNING	FLEX/PLANNING	
7–730	DINNER						
730–8							
8–830							
830–9							

Within this example, there are several elements to notice:

- Ellie is working a 40-hour week. School is her full-time job where she goes to class for 16 hours and studies for 24 hours.
- Ellie is more effective during the day and does not mind getting up early. She is done every day by 5:30 pm. This easily allows for a part-time job, or extra-curricular and social activities.
- Gym time is still a priority and is planned four days a week.
- Friday nights, all day Saturday, and Sundays until 3:30pm are completely open. This time can also be used for social wants or possible job commitments. This can also be additional FLEX time if Ellie needs to complete unfinished weekly goals.
- Planned study time is based on the needs of the courses. Biology is also the hardest course for Ellie, so more time is planned. Additionally, she either goes to class or studies biology six days out of seven.
- Tutoring and study group are built in as a regular part of her schedule.
- FLEX time is included, which can be used on weeks where additional study time is needed (e.g., exam weeks).
- Planning is also a normal part of her routine. On Sunday, before the week starts, she uses her Master Calendar to plan her weekly goals and to-dos and then plans her specific goals for Monday. Then each night, she reviews her progress on her weekly goals and plans her specific goals for the next day.

Although both of these examples specify the subject being studied, some people prefer scheduling blocks of regular study time and then assign the subjects and tasks during that time as part of their weekly planning (See Figure 3.2.5).

> Does the thought of studying for 24 hours outside of class worry you? Do you imagine long hours of reading and re-reading? Cluster 4 will discuss more effective and motivating learning strategies that will allow you to use this time productively.

> Do you feel like you have the same amount of leisure time *and* accomplish this amount of studying on a weekly basis as in these examples?

FIGURE 3.2.5 GENERIC STUDY TIME EXAMPLE

	Sun	Mon	Tue	Wed	Thurs	Fri	Sat
10–1030		ENG	HiST	ENG	HiST	ENG	
1030–11							
11–1130		STUDY (1.5HRS)		STUDY (1.5HRS)		STUDY (1.5HRS)	
1130–12			STUDY (1.5HRS)		STUDY (1.5HRS)		
12–1230							
1230–1		LUNCH		LUNCH		LUNCH	
1–130			LUNCH		LUNCH		
130–2		FYS		FYS		FYS	
2–230			BIO		BIO		
230–3		STUDY (1HR)		STUDY (1HR)		STUDY (1HR)	
3–330							
330–4		PSY	BIO - TUTOR (1HR)	PSY	BIO - TUTOR (1HR)	PSY	
4–430							
430–5		PSY - STUDY GROUP (1HR)	STUDY (1HR)	STUDY (1HR)	STUDY (1HR)	STUDY (1HR)	
5–530							

The Football Player—Example 3

In this last example (Figure 3.2.6), Angelo is a student athlete and plays football. He is taking 13 credits (English; Psychology; Mathematics; and First Year Seminar). Several aspects of his schedule are set for him due to his commitments as a student athlete including film study, practice and study hall. To effectively manage all of his commitments, it becomes even more critical for him to establish a routine and begin studying for his courses on a regular basis. There is very little time or opportunity to "cram." He starts with the following study plan:

- Study Plan—ENG (five hours), PSY (six hours), MATH (six hours), and FYS (three hours).

FIGURE 3.2.6 ANGELO'S WEEKLY SCHEDULE

	Sun	Mon	Tue	Wed	Thurs	Fri	Sat
6–630		WORKOUTS					FOOTBALL/ POTENTIAL TRAVEL
630–7							
7–730		SHOWER/BREAKFAST					
730–8							
8–830		MATH	MATH	MATH	ENG – TUTOR (1 HR)	MATH	
830–9							
9–930		ENG	PSY – WORK (0.5 HR)	ENG	PSY – WORK (0.5 HR)	ENG	
930–10			PSY		PSY		
10–1030		ENG – WORK (1HR)		ENG – WORK (1HR)		ENG – WORK (1HR)	
1030–11							
11–1130		FYS	PSY – WORK (1 HR)	FYS	PSY – WORK (1 HR)	FYS	
1130–12							
12–1230		LUNCH					
1230–1							
1–130							
130–2		FILM STUDY					
2–230							
230–3		GET READY FOR PRACTICE					
3–330		WARM–UP					
330–4		PRACTICE					
4–430							
430–5							
5–530							
530–6		SHOWER					
6–630		DINNER					
630–7							
7–730		STUDY HALL •Math •ENG •Planning	STUDY HALL •Math Tutor •PSY •Planning	STUDY HALL •Math •FYS •Planning	STUDY HALL •FYS •PSY •Planning	STUDY HALL •Math Tutor •FYS •Planning	POTENTIAL TRAVEL
730–8							
8–830							
830–9							
9–930							
930–10							

Within this example, there are several elements to notice:

- With both of his academic and athletic commitments, Angelo is working more than a 40-hour work week. School and athletics are a full-time job where he goes to class for 13 hours, studies for 20 hours, and then potentially travels and plays football.
- Friday nights and all day Saturday are completely open for travel and games. During travel (or the times he does not have to travel), he can use this as additional FLEX time if Angelo needs to complete unfinished weekly goals.
- All day Sunday (until 7:00pm) is completely open. This can be used for social activities or additional FLEX time if needed.
- Tutoring is built in as a regular part of his schedule.
- Planning is also a normal part of his routine.

Although there is not as much free time included in this schedule as the other examples, this is the trade-off that successful student athletes tend to make to achieve both their academic and athletic goals.

Hopefully, what is clear about all three examples is that *there are* enough hours in the week to effectively balance academic requirements and personal wants, *if* you are intentional! The following gives suggestions on how to build your own weekly schedule.

Your Weekly Schedule

This is an exciting opportunity! Many working adults will tell you that their weekly schedule is largely determined by others. This is the time in your life where you get to make many of the decisions that will impact your schedule. You have the control! What do you want it to look like? Do you want to work on the weekends? Or take the weekends off? Do you want to spend Wednesday afternoons playing intramurals with friends or Monday evenings watching Monday Night Football? As you go through the process listed, think carefully about your schedule and how it will best support all of your goals (i.e., academic and social).

As suggested before, you can use either a word processing program (e.g., Microsoft Word), spreadsheet program (e.g., Microsoft Excel), or other available online program to create your schedule. Figure 3.2.7 is a blank template of a sample weekly schedule. Once you have established a schedule, be sure to print it and keep it with you (or have access to it on your phone). It will be difficult to follow your schedule, if you do not know what is on it. Additionally, you should review your schedule regularly and determine if it is still meeting your needs. If you are continuously changing it, then adjustments should be made.

Use the following guidelines to create your schedule:

1. Block and label the hours, Monday–Friday that you have scheduled classes.

2. Block and label the hours, Monday–Sunday that you have scheduled for any part-time work.

3. Block and label any other times for activities that you are committed to each week. **Do not forget to include your study time!** Remember, not all of your classes are created equal. Some will be more difficult, some will be harder to maintain focus, and some will be personally enjoyable. Consider this as you decide how much time you should devote to each class and *when you* will study each one. In terms of deep learning and processing, the more difficult the class, the more time you should invest over multiple days during the week. For example, if chemistry is your most difficult class, then you should devote the maximum amount of time, eight to nine hours per week outside of class, over several days during the week (five to six days per week). It is more effective to study for shorter amounts of time over multiple days than to engage in long study sessions over one to two days.

   > Which subjects are the easiest and most enjoyable for you? Which are your hardest?

4. If you have other weekly activities—sports practice, religious services, clubs, and meetings, etc., fill them in, too.

5. Review your time log that you completed. What other activities did you do every day? Block and label those times as well as when you typically eat, exercise, watch a little TV, and hang out with your friends.

6. Consider other detractors in your schedule and account for them. If nap time after lunch is necessary to refresh yourself for the afternoon, then schedule this in as a normal part of your routine. This is more helpful then scheduling study time and then you *still* take a nap and now you are behind on your day's goals and to dos (as well as feeling guilty because you took a nap). By knowing yourself and your needs, it allows you to plan for both, as in this example, a nap and *still* completing your studying.

   > What are some of your indulgences that you need to plan for?

FIGURE 3.2.7 BLANK WEEKLY SCHEDULE TEMPLATE

	Sun	Mon	Tue	Wed	Thurs	Fri	Sat
6–630							
630–7							
7–730							
730–8							
8–830							
830–9							
9–930							
930–10							
10–1030							
1030–11							
11–1130							
1130–12							
12–1230							
1230–1							
1–130							
130–2							
2–230							
230-3							
3-330							
330-4							
4-430							
430-5							
5-530							
530-6							
6-630							
630-7							
7-730							
730-8							
8-830							
830-9							

Continuously planning and establishing routines allows you to control your time and schedule versus your schedule controlling you. Using a master calendar to develop short-, mid-, and long-range plans and a weekly schedule to establish routines are two of your most powerful tools to diminish procrastination and to accomplish your goals. The other important benefit of using these tools is the resulting opportunity to relax and take *true* breaks. Have you ever gone out with friends but were not really able to enjoy yourself because of the nagging thoughts such as "I should have studied more or I should be studying right now"? When you are intentional with your schedule and your planning, you know that you have accounted for your responsibilities, you have a plan in place, and you are achieving your goals. Hanging out and enjoying time with friends and family is all part of your plan, and you deserve it. The next module will describe additional strategies that are effective in helping you take control of your schedule.

MODULE 3.2 SUMMARY

- Ongoing planning and routines are critical to feeling in control of your time.
- A master calendar is a one-page planning tool that includes all of the semester's due dates and events that helps with short-, mid-, and long-range planning.
- A weekly schedule should be set to help establish routines and create balance between social, personal, and academic goals.

REFERENCES

Britton, B. K., & Tesser, A. (1991). Effects of time-management practices on college grades. *Journal of Educational Psychology, 83*(3), 405–410.

Wintre, M. G., Dilouya, B., Pancer, S. M., Pratt, M. W., Birnie-Lefcovitch, S., Polivy, J., & Adams, G. (2011). Academic achievement in first-year University: Who maintains their high school average. *Higher Education, 62*, 467–481.

STRATEGIES—INCREASING FOCUS, MOTIVATION AND EFFICIENCIES

MODULE
3.3

CLUSTER 3 OBJECTIVES COVERED IN THIS MODULE

☐ **OBJECTIVE:** Describe time management strategies and how they are related to improving focus and motivation.

☐ **OBJECTIVE:** Identify multiple strategies that will help improve personal time management difficulties.

OVERVIEW

"Eat a live frog first thing in the morning and nothing worse will happen to you the rest of the day."—Mark Twain

The purpose of this module is to offer many time management strategies that are related to improving focus, motivation, and efficiencies. This module is organized a bit differently than the others. It is divided into many small sections that suggest and then describe time management strategies. At the end of the module, all of these strategies are listed (including strategies suggested earlier) within a single table. It is recommended that you read through the descriptions and then select one or two strategies that seem to target your particular areas of difficulty. Try these strategies over the next week and assess their effectiveness. Questions to reflect on include:

- Were the strategies effective?
- If not, should I make minor changes to implementing the strategies to make them more effective?
- Should I abandon these strategies and select others to try?

Once you feel confident about using these strategies, return to the list and select one or two more. Avoid trying to incorporate every strategy at once. You are building new skills. This requires time and practice; however, these newly adopted strategies will eventually become a normal part of your routine, improving not only your educational experience but your future professional life.

REFLECTION: In what ways do you struggle with your time and attention management? How willing are you to try something new in an attempt to improve this area?

STRATEGIES NO. 1 TO 3

1. Get adequate sleep.
2. Support physical health with exercise.
3. Avoid skipping meals.

These strategies fit into a theme. It is difficult to be your most effective and efficient if you are not at your peak physically. Even more alarming is the fact that research has found that sleep deprivation can affect performance similarly to alcohol intoxication (Williamson & Feyer, 2000)! There is a reason that sleep is the first strategy recommended. When you are tired, you are not efficient. You tend to make more mistakes, and it becomes more and more difficult to focus on the task at hand. Many students understand the importance of regular exercise; however, sleep and exercise are usually the first two activities sacrificed when students get busy. The next time you are extremely busy and so inclined to sleep less or abandon exercise, try to shift your perspective. Instead of thinking about how sleep and exercise are impeding your studies, remind yourself that sleep and exercise actively *contribute* to your studies. A similar recommended strategy is to use physical activity as a break (e.g., taking a walk, shooting hoops, etc.) between study sessions. A short 10- to 15-minute physical break can bring you back to the task refreshed, focused, and ready to start again.

Finally, staying up all night and cramming is rarely effective. Without sleep, it is unlikely you will learn or be able to recall anything during this type of cramming session. Worse, when you get to the exam, it is likely that the sleep deprivation will prevent you from recalling the things that you did know!

STRATEGY NO. 4

4. When eating a frog is on your to-do list, eat the frog first.

Brian Tracy (2007), a motivational speaker and author, has written books about "eating the frog." His recommendation is inspired by Mark Twain's quote shared at the beginning of this module. The idea is simple: once you have completed your most horrible and disgusting (or boring and difficult) task on your to-do list, everything else should be easy. The reverse is also true. If you leave the frog for later, it drains your energy and motivation because you will continue to work knowing this task still remains. It can distract your efforts to complete other tasks and, many times, cause you to abandon this aversive task altogether. Instead, eat the frog, build momentum, and avoid procrastination.

5. Plan smaller study sessions for subjects across the week and/or day rather than in large blocks.

6. Schedule readings in smaller blocks across the week rather than reading for long periods at a time.

7. Break large assignments into smaller pieces.

8. Divide study sessions by types of activities and/or subjects.

9. Plan for breaks and mini-rewards throughout the day.

These strategies are related to maintaining focus, increasing motivation, and allowing for deeper processing of information (Cluster 4 will describe more in-depth the reasons behind the effectiveness of these strategies). The overall theme for these strategies: shorter and more frequent is better. From a motivational perspective, each of these strategies influences your self-efficacy (your belief in your ability to complete a task). Consider the following example:

> *Emma went to three classes today and then went to her part-time job. She gets home about 10 pm, eats dinner and then starts her reading for history, which is due the next morning. She is supposed to read 75 pages. Understandably, Emma is tired from the long day and does not believe she can finish the readings, much less retain the information. She decides not to read any of it and goes to bed.*

Does this example sound familiar? Many times, especially, when fatigued and faced with large or overwhelming tasks, students make the decision not to complete the task at all. For some, it just does not seem worth reading 10 pages when 75 are required. Now consider the next example:

> *Maria went to three classes today and then went to her part-time job. She gets home about 10pm, eats dinner and then starts her reading for history, which is due the next morning. She has been reading 10 pages per night and only has the last 10 pages to go. She knows she can easily read 10 pages so she completes the reading and then goes to bed.*

Maria's self-efficacy is higher simply because of the smaller task at hand. By scheduling her reading this way she is incorporating strategies 5 to 7. This works similarly for other tasks. Imagine having to write a 20-page research paper. This would likely seem overwhelming and difficult to start; however, by planning to complete this project in multiple steps, your self-efficacy and motivation to begin the task increase. Now imagine that you must find two sources to use in your paper or that you need to write one page. Each of these tasks are smaller and more manageable, leading to a higher probability of starting and completing them.

How is the Pomodoro Technique related to these strategies?

These strategies are also effective in other ways. Scheduling your reading and study sessions throughout the week allows you to revisit the materials, ideas, and concepts multiple times. In Maria's example of reading 10 pages per night, she begins by reading 10 pages the first night. On the second night, she quickly reviews the first 10 pages and then begins the second 10 pages. She continues this each subsequent night. By the time she has completed the readings, she will have reviewed much of the content several times. This allows for deeper processing and also works when completing other academic tasks. Remember in the weekly schedule examples that were shared, both students studied biology either five or six days a week. This is related to the strategy of "shorter and more frequent is better." Studying one hour per day over five days is far more effective than marathon sessions conducted over one or two days.

Strategies 8 and 9 are directly related to maintaining focus and attention. It is helpful to switch between tasks and subjects. For example, a student could complete 15 calculus problems, then read 10 pages of psychology, and then write an introduction for an English paper. Additionally, taking breaks and giving yourself mini-rewards (e.g., 10 minutes on social media, an ice cream break etc.), allows you to come back refreshed and ready to start again. Many students will also feel better able to remain focused and follow through if they plan to study for 30 minutes and then take a break, as compared to sitting down and studying for two hours or more at one time.

Each of these strategies support intentional planning and will help you feel like you are in control of your time. At times, reading and studying can feel unending. However, with these strategies you will know exactly how much to do, when to do it, and (more importantly), when you are done.

STRATEGIES NO. 10 TO 14

10. Pack items for the day the night before.
11. Study in areas where there are no distractions.
12. Turn-off electronics when studying or sleeping.
13. Carry study aids for on the run (e.g., flashcards and graphic organizers).
14. Share your schedule, especially study times, with your friends, family and roommates, and *ask for their support.*

Although important, these strategies should be self-explanatory. Packing items, carrying study aids, turning off electronics, and studying in appropriate areas helps ensure you have all of your materials and can focus on the tasks at hand. Although slightly different than the others, strategy 14 also helps ensure distractions are diminished. Your friends, family, and roommates want to support you and one of the easiest ways to help them do this is to tell them how. If your routine is to spend Tuesday evenings studying from 7 to 9pm, then your friend should wait until 9pm to start texting you; however, he or she will not know this unless you share your schedule.

15. Plan study time to support long-term information processing rather than just completing assignments or studying for an examination.

16. Create test plans.

One key difference between high school and college is the nature of "homework." In high school, your teachers would assign you homework, you would go home and complete it, and then you would turn it in. In college, many classes do not include homework or assignments. You are expected to attend class, take notes, study, and prepare for exams. You have to create your own homework. This is why it is recommended to plan regular study sessions over the course of the week for each of your classes. You are not completing an assignment, but trying to learn the material as deeply as possible. Due to the typical volume of material, it is nearly impossible to learn, process, and retain all of the information in a couple of study sessions prior to an exam. Therefore, once you start a new unit, you are preparing for the next exam. Regular, ongoing study sessions help ensure successful processing of information.

Creating a test plan is specific to additional tasks, strategies, and time that you want to invest in the one to two weeks prior to an exam. This can include additional times meeting with your study group or tutor, planning visits with your professors, adding strategies (e.g., writing practice exam questions), and including extra review time to your normal routine. Combining ongoing studying and preparation with a specific test plan will help you build confidence going into your exam. Additionally, this type of continuous preparation helps promote long-term learning rather than just earning a grade on an exam.

STRATEGIES NO. 17 AND 18

17. Start assignments once you have all of the information (i.e., instructions and materials) rather than waiting to the last possible moment.

18. Finish assignments early.

These last two strategies rely on reinforcement to build positive habits and help minimize procrastination. Strategy 17 shifts the perspective that many students tend to take about assignments and preparation. Have you ever said to yourself, "When is the last possible moment I can start something and still complete it?" This strategy recommends changing this question to, "When is the earliest possible moment that I can start and complete this task?" These actions lead to strategy 18: finish assignments early.

Consider an essay assignment. Once your professor has given you all of the assignment's instructions, all of the necessary topics in the course have been covered, and there is nothing left to do but start, then start. Several things happen when you use this strategy. First, it allows you to produce your best work by allowing you to revisit the task, avoid technical problems, get feedback from

Have you ever done an assignment at the last moment, late at night, and suddenly realized you did not understand one of the requirements?

peers and professors, and ask any necessary questions. When the task is done early, reinforcement plays a part by creating feelings of relief and eliminating stress. This is especially true when you watch your peers frantically try to complete the assignment at the last moment and you are already done. The more often tasks are completed early and are reinforced with positive feelings (and better grades), the more likely you will continue this habit.

MODULE 3.3 SUMMARY

The following summary table also includes strategies that were described in previous modules.

Time management strategies	Notes/examples	Strategies tried
1. Get adequate sleep	Long-term lack of sleep can be the equivalent to being intoxicated	
2. Support physical health with exercise	Physical health supports peak mental performance	
3. Avoid skipping meals	Supports physical health and peak mental performance	
4. When eating a frog is on your to-do list, eat the frog first	By completing the hardest and/or most boring tasks first, everything else is easier	
5. Plan smaller study sessions for subjects across the week and/or day rather than large blocks	One hour per day over five days; one hour in the morning and one hour in the evening	
6. Schedule readings in smaller blocks across the week rather than sitting down and reading long periods/pages at a time	100 pages over five days, 20 pages per day	
7. Break large assignments into smaller pieces	10-page paper, one page per day	
8. Divide study sessions by types of activities and/or subjects	Switching between writing, reading, doing math problems, etc.	
9. Plan for breaks and mini-rewards throughout the day	45 minutes focused study, then 15 minutes Facebook/texting	
10. Pack items for the day the night before	Avoids forgetting important items and then wasting time during the day to retrieve needed items	
11. Study in areas where there are no distractions	Library, study halls, etc.	

12. Turn-off electronics when studying or sleeping	Phone and social media	
13. Carry study aids for on the run	Flashcards, graphic organizers, etc.	
14. Share your schedule, especially study times, with your friends and roommates and ask for their support	Allows your friends and family opportunities to reach out to you without interfering with your academic goals	
15. Plan study time to support long-term information processing rather than just completing assignments or studying for an examination	Reduces stress and allows for efficient studying versus cramming (i.e., you are always preparing for an examination)	
16. Create test plans	Plan studying and tasks over the course of weeks and plan specifics (e.g., amount of study time and tasks) during examination weeks	
17. Start assignments once you have all of the information (i.e., instructions and materials) rather than waiting to the last possible moment.	"What is the earliest date I can start?" versus "What is the last possible date I can start and still get done?"	
18. Finish assignments early	Allows you to produce your best work by allowing you to revisit tasks, avoid technical problems, get feedback from peers and professors, and ask questions	
Other Strategies		
Set study session to dos/goals	E.g., In the next hour, I will read 10 pages, create 10 flashcards for vocabulary words, etc.	
Use master calendar to plan weekly to dos/ goals	Module 3.2	
Using your master calendar, set short-term deadlines for long-term projects	Draft paper due date for end-of-semester research paper	
Plan weekly goals/to dos at the beginning of the week (e.g., Sunday night)	Module 3.2	
Each night, plan the next days to dos/goals based on weekly goals	Adjust as tasks and goals are completed throughout the week	
Prioritize to dos and weekly goals	ABCDE and Eisenhower methods	

Set-up routines and use your ideal schedule	Module 3.2	
Set time for household chores	Laundry, shopping, etc.	
Make tutoring and study groups a normal part of your weekly schedule/routine	Module 3.2	
Start with hardest subjects when fully refreshed	Module 3.2	
Finish with easier more enjoyable subjects when more tired, less focused	Module 3.2	
Base your schedule on realistic expectations of your periods of focus, distraction, etc.	If you are not a morning person, do not schedule study time first thing in the morning	
Build social and leisure times into your schedule	Allows you to get real breaks and then be fully focused for work and school tasks	
Build FLEX time into your schedule	Allows for extra time needed during examination weeks without destroying your routines/schedule	
Study time outside of class should be one to three hours per credit hour of class	A three credit class = three to nine hours of study time outside of class; all classes are not equal, base study time on level of difficulty	
Set real rewards for achieving weekly goals	Module 3.1—Motivated Context	
Set real consequences/plans of action when not achieving weekly goals	"I won't do anything else on Saturday morning until weekly goals are complete"	
Adapt schedule, if needed, to be more realistic as you learn more about yourself and your schedule	Module 3.2	

REFERENCES

Williamson, A. M., & Feyer, A. (2000). Moderate sleep deprivation produces impairments in cognitive and motor performance equivalent to legally prescribed levels of alcohol intoxication. *Occupational and Environmental Medicine, 57*(10), 649–655.

CASE STUDY

Eli is a first-semester college freshman. His parents and high school teachers had told him that managing his time would be much different in college. In fact, they warned him that many new students become overwhelmed and do poorly their first year due to inadequate time management skills. At first, he did not understand what the big deal was. He had all this free time and none of his professors assigned homework or even took attendance. Because his first exams were not until the fifth week of school, he did not always go to classes nor do the readings before lectures. He figured that he would read and study the week of his exams just like he did in high school, *and* do well. However, when he started to study that week, he had not realized there would be so much material to cover. Although he stayed up all night cramming for his first exam, he barely did more than read and skim over the material. As a result, he failed the exam.

He knew going forward that he would have to do better; however, he continued to struggle. Every time he sat down to read and study, he felt overwhelmed with the amount of material and continued to push it off until later. This led to more cramming with no results. By mid-semester, he was missing more classes because he was embarrassed about his performance. The stress and anxiety continued to build and he started to have trouble sleeping. And even though he spent time with friends to make himself feel better, there was always this nagging guilt that he should be doing something else. By the end of the semester, Eli thought to himself, "I have always been a good student. I do not understand. What happened?!"

QUESTIONS

1. What are some of Eli's time management problems?
2. How much time should Eli spend outside of class to prepare for exams? When should he start preparing?
3. What time management strategies can Eli use to minimize his procrastination and to make the material feel less overwhelming?
4. What time management strategies can he use to create a balance between academics and leisure?

POTENTIAL RESPONSES

1. Eli has not been going to class or maintaining any study routines. The result is that he continuously has to cram, which has led to poor outcomes.
2. Eli should be doing ongoing, consistent studying outside of class each week for one to three hours per hour in class (i.e., approximately three to nine hours each week per class). Once a new unit starts, Eli's work outside of class is in preparation for the next exam. Once the exam gets closer, Eli should establish a test plan to add any additional time, tasks or strategies.

3. Although many of the strategies will help Eli, the following strategies specifically address making tasks seem more manageable and less overwhelming:

- Plan smaller study sessions for subjects across the week and/or day rather than in large blocks.
- Schedule readings in smaller blocks across the week rather than reading for long periods at a time.
- Break large assignments into smaller pieces.

4. If Eli were to use a master calendar and a weekly schedule, he could plan out his short- and long-term requirements, which would allow him to balance his time during the week for both academic tasks and social wants. He can also set his weekly schedule and routine so that it includes his leisure activities that are important to him while still leaving adequate time for his studying.

ADDITIONAL READINGS

Bieling, P. J., Israeli, A. L., & Antony, M. M. (2004). Is perfectionism good, bad, or both? Examining models of the perfectionism construct. *Personality and Individual Differences, 36*(6), 1373–1385.

Hensley, L. C., & Cutshall, J. L. (2018). Procrastinating in college: Students' readiness and resistance to change. *Journal of College Student Development, 59*(4), 498–504.

Katz, I., Eilot, K., & Nevo, N. (2014). "I'll do it later": Type of motivation, self-efficacy and homework procrastination. *Motivation and Emotion, 38*(1), 111–119.

Krause, K., & Freund, A. M. (2014). How to beat procrastination. *European Psychologist, 19*(2), 132–144.

Macan, T. H., Shahani, C., Dipboye, R. L., & Phillips, A. P. (1990). College students' time management: Correlations with academic performance and stress. *Journal of Educational Psychology, 82*(4), 760–768.

Matute, H., Vadillo, M. A., Vegas, S., & Blanco, F. (2006). Illusion of control in Internet users and college students. *CyberPsychology & Behavior, 10*(2), 176–181.

Misra, R., & McKean, M. (2000). College students' academic stress and its relation to their anxiety, time management, and leisure satisfaction. *American Journal of Health Studies, 16*(1), 41–51.

Steel, P., & Klingsieck, K. B. (2016). Academic procrastination: Psychological antecedents revisited. *Australian Psychologist, 51*(1), 36–46.

Urdan, T., & Midgley, C. (2001). Academic self-handicapping: What we know, what more there is to learn. *Educational Psychology Review, 13*(2), 115–138.

UNDERSTANDING MEMORY:
INFORMATION PROCESSING FOR THE LONG TERM

CASE STUDY

Desiree had always done very well in high school. To prepare for her high school exams, she would read her textbooks carefully and take notes. She would complete all of her assigned homework and she would use flashcards to help her with any vocabulary words. Right before exams, she would re-read her textbook and notes. These strategies worked well, and she was satisfied with her grades.

Desiree is now in college, and after her first round of exams, she is beginning to worry. She tried using the same approach as before, and has continued to use the same learning strategies; however, she earned less than 70% on each of her exams. She thought maybe she needed to read and review her text more, but there was so much material, this strategy just felt overwhelming and not very effective. She was starting to think maybe college was too hard for her.

1. What are some reasons Desiree's learning strategies may no longer be effective at the college level?

2. What are potential approaches and learning strategies Desiree could use to help her encode, store and retrieve the information when needed?

3. Who are the people Desiree could easily reach out to for help?

CLUSTER OVERVIEW

Learning and processing information effectively is a developed skill that requires time, effort, and practice. Despite this, students often fall back on learning strategies they have been using since they first started studying for exams; for some, this may have been as early as middle school. Unfortunately, for most of these same students, they were not taught "how to learn." This results in a limited toolbox of learning strategies that includes reading and re-reading, maybe using some flashcards, and taking notes. At the college level and in professional careers, these strategies are usually ineffective and can stifle deep, long-term learning. In the worst-case scenario, such strategies are not even sufficient for students to earn passing grades.

However, because all people have a capacity to learn, learning *how to learn* is also possible. With effort and a willingness to practice new strategies, students can gain proficiency in this ability and achieve the results they want. This cluster provides the foundation for learning how to learn by describing memory and information processing, as well as how to apply this knowledge in order to improve personal learning strategies. There are also many examples of these techniques and strategies throughout the cluster.

CLUSTER OBJECTIVES

- Describe how the components of memory contribute to storing, encoding, and retrieving information.
- Describe how the memory continuum is related to processing information.
- Compare rehearsal and elaboration strategies, and their relationship to processing information.
- Describe learning strategies that use visual imagery to process information.
- Describe how active reading and note-taking are related to processing information into long-term memory.
- Describe the processes used in implementing active reading and creating effective lecture notes.

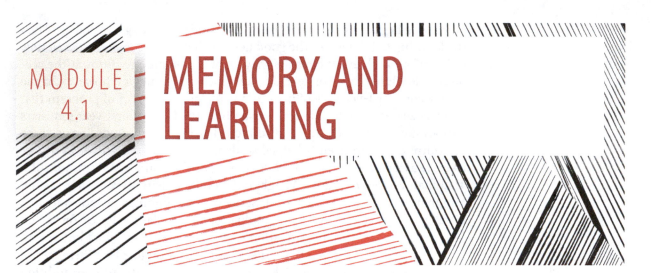

MEMORY AND LEARNING

CLUSTER 4 OBJECTIVES COVERED IN THIS MODULE

☐ **OBJECTIVE:** Describe how the components of memory contribute to storing, encoding, and retrieving information.

☐ **OBJECTIVE:** Describe how the memory continuum is related to processing information.

☐ **OBJECTIVE:** Compare rehearsal and elaboration strategies, and their relationship to processing information.

OVERVIEW

"It is better to know how to learn than to know"—Dr. Seuss

There is a distinction between learning and memory. Learning is acquiring new knowledge and skills, and memory is the ability to retrieve information that has been previously learned. However, these constructs also intertwine, and determine your ability to retrieve and use relevant information when you want. Therefore, the purpose of this module is to set the foundation for *how* you learn. Learning *how to learn* more effectively begins with understanding memory and how your brain processes information. In the end, this knowledge will expand your toolbox of learning strategies, develop your ability to create optimal learning strategies, and achieve the learning outcomes you desire.

LEARNING:
Acquiring new knowledge and skills.

MEMORY:
Retrieving information that has been previously learned.

LEARNING HOW TO LEARN

REFLECTION: Have you ever studied several hours for a test, only to take the test and not be able to remember the information you studied?

Although all students have a capacity to learn, many struggle with learning effectively. In the K–12 educational systems, some students do well academically, as measured by their earning grades and then graduating. Despite this promising beginning, many of these same students struggle in college when the learning tasks change. The good news is that *all* students can "learn how to learn" and achieve the results they want. There are programs at the secondary level that focus on learning and learning strategies; however, at the post-secondary level, 95% of institutions include some sort of program that emphasizes learning how to learn, usually in the form of first-year seminars (Goodman & Pascarella, 2006). By directly teaching learning strategies, these programs have consistently helped students achieve and graduate at higher levels (Pascarella & Terenzini, 1998; Swanson, Vaughan, & Wilkinson, 2015; Tuckman & Kennedy, 2011; Vaughan, Lalonde, & Jenkins-Guarnieri, 2014; Vaughan, Parra, & Lalonde, 2014). Some of these findings include 5 to 15% differences in overall four-year graduation rates (Pascarella & Terenzini, 1998), 50% differences in graduation rates for students who had initial academic difficulty (Tuckman & Kennedy, 2011), and up to 34% differences in fourth-year persistence for at-risk students (Swanson et al., 2015). In addition to these studies, many others show significant differences in GPAs, as well as persistence (Tuckman & Kennedy, 2011; Vaughan, Lalonde, & Jenkins-Guarnieri, 2014; Vaughan et al., 2014). For example, Vaughan et al.'s (2014) study showed significantly higher GPAs (on average 0.71 points higher on a 4-point scale) for first-generation students who participated in the seminar, as compared to non-participants.

Again, the research provides strong, consistent evidence that all students can improve and develop the skills to learn effectively, regardless of previous academic performance. The following describes existing memory theories and how memory is structured.

MEMORY

Theorists have proposed a number of memory models over the past century (Ashcraft & Radvansky, 2010; Atkinson & Shiffrin, 1968; James, 1890; Sternberg & Sternberg, 2012). Although there are some nuanced distinctions between the models, most reference three major components of memory. The earliest model by William James (1890) proposed these components to be an after-image, a primary memory and a secondary memory. Since then, other models have proposed these components to be the sensory register, short-term or working memory, and long-term memory (Ashcraft & Radvansky, 2010; Atkinson & Shiffrin, 1968; Sternberg & Sternberg, 2012). The most prominent of these include the duel-store and the information processing models. These models differ in the style of interaction between the components; but overall, there are more similarities than differences between the two.

Information processing models are primarily concerned with the process of storing, encoding, and retrieving information. Neuropsychologists are also interested in the physical aspects of cognition, determining which areas of the brain are activated in the processing and retrieval of information. Although brain structure is an important focus of modern science, the purpose of this module is to illuminate the information processing capabilities of the brain in terms of memory functions, rather than to explore its physical form.

MEMORY TERMINOLOGY

Earlier, the reflection question asked if you have ever "forgotten" information that was requested on an exam. If you answered yes, then you have struggled with retrieval. As a learner and a student, who is trying to earn good grades, retrieving information when you want it, is a primary goal for success. Hopefully, as a learner and future professional, your goal is also to process information deeply, to store it for the long-term, and to be able to use the information later in your career. In its simplest terms, memory is the process of storing, encoding, and retrieving. Storing is the process of putting new information into your memory. Encoding is the process of changing the information in a meaningful way so that it can be stored into long-term memory. Retrieving is the process of finding the information in your memory when it is needed. Table 4.1.1 provides examples of each of these terms.

STORING:
The process of putting new information into memory.

ENCODING:
The process of meaningfully changing information so that it can be stored in long-term memory.

RETRIEVING:
The process of finding information in your memory when needed.

TABLE 4.1.1 MEMORY TERMINOLOGY		
Term	**Definition**	**Example**
Storing	The process of putting new information into memory	You read the following fact in your American History class and put it into short-term memory: Pearl Harbor was attacked on December 7, 1941.
Encoding	The process of meaningfully changing information so that it can be stored in long-term memory	You create a timeline that connects this date and fact, with other important dates and facts of World War II.
Retrieving	The process of finding information in your memory when needed	You are able to correctly answer the examination question: When was Pearl Harbor attacked?

So how does storing, encoding, and retrieving relate to the memory models described earlier? The following describes how these are related.

MEMORY COMPONENTS

Sensory Register

According to the information processing model, there are three components of memory: sensory register, short-term or working memory, and long-term memory. Information first enters your brain through your senses (i.e., sight, smell, hearing, taste and touch), and passes into your sensory register. The amount of information that enters through your senses is thought to be unlimited. In fact, almost everything in your environment enters into the sensory register. Consider the amount of light in the room, the feel of the air on your skin, the sounds you hear, the feel of your shirt on your back or the shoes on your feet. Most of this information enters the sensory register without your conscious knowledge. This information has not been processed,

SENSORY REGISTER:
The memory component where information from the environment enters through the senses.

and is quickly forgotten as a result. The capacity of your sensory register is very large but its duration is very short, lasting only a few seconds. Although the brain is capable of receiving vast amounts of sensory information, it does not have the capacity to process this much information without becoming overloaded (Sternberg & Sternberg, 2012). As such, the mechanism of *attention* acts as a sort of mental filter for determining what information will be processed and what information will be ignored.

SHORT-TERM OR WORKING MEMORY:
The memory component where information is briefly stored until it is either encoded or lost.

Short-Term or Working Memory

What happens next? What information do you pay attention to? Right now, you are likely attending to the words on this page. If you are taking notes, then you are attending to the words you are writing down. If your roommate interrupts you, then you are attending to what your roommate is saying. Attention not only filters out unwanted or extraneous sensory information, but it also funnels the information you are paying attention to, from sensory register into short-term or working memory. Your short-term memory is where information is briefly held or stored until it can be processed. Earlier, it was mentioned that some theorists have further distinguished this component of memory with working memory. Baddeley (2001) has described working memory as being the central executive of your memory, meaning that it directs attention, combines information from long-term memory, and produces responses to this content. For example, working memory is engaged when you are deciding what information is important to include in your notes.

A person's capacity to pay attention to multiple stimuli is very limited (Pashler, 1992; Sternberg & Sternberg, 2012); therefore, short-term or working memory is also limited. Early experiments by George Miller (1956) provided evidence that people remembered approximately seven units of information plus or minus two units (i.e., a range of five to nine units of information) and the number of units could be increased if they were chunked, such as a telephone number.

- 5839452267 is easier to remember as (583)945-2267 or
- SNFMSXCNOBNC is easier to remember as MSN CNN FOX CBS

However, the ability to remember this particular number of units specifically refers to discrete items. Many times, the information you are paying attention to, is not an individual or discrete item; yet the overall point is still the same. Your short-term or working memory has a limited capacity, and it is lost from memory unless the information is further encoded.

The duration of short-term memory, is also short, as the name implies. Some experiments provide evidence that storage for new information lasts approximately 5 to 20 seconds (Baddeley, 2001; Peterson & Peterson, 1959). Although this is true in many instances—especially in a laboratory setting while working with discrete units of information—consider how often you are exposed to new information within one day. For example, sitting in your class, you learn a new piece of information at the beginning of the lecture. Your professor asks you a question about this information towards the end of the lecture. It is likely that you will be able to recall this information after such a short span of time, regardless of whether you only listened to the lecture or wrote down key points in your notes. However, if you do not review or engage with the information again after the class is over, it will most likely be lost in the near future. Remember, short-term or working memory has a small capacity and a short duration. As such, short-term memory is not helpful for long-term learning and memory goals. So how is information moved into long-term memory?

Long-Term Memory

REFLECTION: Have you ever heard something in a lecture that seemed simple (for example, useful goals have three characteristics) and then decided not to write it down because the information was so easy to understand? Have you also found that, several weeks later, you could not recall this simple information? "Easy to understand" does not necessarily equal "easy to remember".

For information to move into long-term memory, it must be actively encoded or processed. This encoding of information occurs in working memory. Unfortunately, due to the limited capacity and duration of working memory, this process can be slow, occurring over longer periods of time. Think of all of the information you have attended to, while in school. How much of this information has been effectively stored in your long-term memory? This is typically where students, who were successful in high school, start to struggle at the college level. The sheer volume of information that must be attended to, and then processed, overwhelms their memory systems (the following modules in this cluster will give more information about making this process more effective). On the positive side, long-term memory is believed to be unlimited and indefinite; however, the key is to be able to encode information in such ways that it can be retrieved at a later time. The next section describes how the active processing of this information occurs.

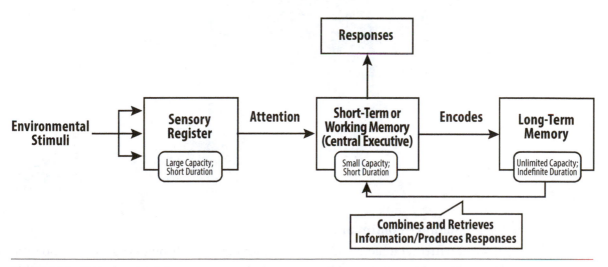

FIGURE 4.1.1: Memory

Source: Angela Vaughan and Brett Wilkinson

PROCESSING INFORMATION

Understanding how memory is structured is the first step. These models demonstrate that the key for learners is the ability to encode or process information, and to move it from working memory to long-term memory. The next step is to understand how information is processed and how to encode it effectively.

Read the following words:

- Bed
- Rest
- Tired
- Yawn
- Snore

Quickly, what is the next word that comes to mind? Was it dreams? Or maybe sleep? In doing a free recall demonstration, people will almost always recall words such as dreams or sleep. Why is that the case? It is probably easy to see that these words are associated with each other. This pattern of association also resembles how the brain is structured. Your brain is similar to an interconnected network where your brain links new knowledge to prior knowledge. In fact, the most powerful way to learn new information is to connect it to information you already know. This is an important distinction that will provide the basis for processing information and using effective learning strategies.

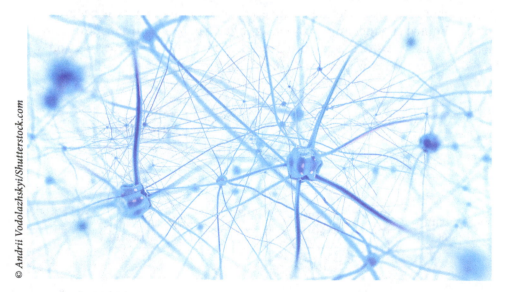

© Andrii Vodolazhskyi/Shutterstock.com

Memory Continuum

To further understand how information moves through your senses and into long-term memory, it would be helpful to think of your memory more simply as a continuum with short-term memory on the left and long-term memory on the right (Weinstein, Woodruff, & Await, 2004). As you pay attention to

FIGURE 4.1.2: Memory Continuum   *Source: Angela Vaughan and Brett Wilkinson*

stimuli or information, it moves or makes "jumps" in your memory. Consider information that you know automatically and without thought, such as your name. From birth until now, there have been countless times that this information, your name, has been processed or made jumps across the continuum: people have called you by your name, you learned to write your own name, you have thought of yourself by your name, etc. Considering the sheer number of times this information has been processed, the only way you would forget your name is, if you suffered brain damage.

Although a simple idea, visiting course material, or reading your textbook the number of times required to move or "jump" concepts from short-term memory into long-term memory would be overwhelming and unrealistic for most learners. Fortunately, there is a way to manipulate how you process information so that you can be more effective and efficient (and not read your textbook 50 times).

Consider the two lists of study strategies that a student might use to prepare for an exam:

List 1	List 2
• Read and highlight textbook • Create and review flashcards • Read and review notes • Rewrite notes	• Create your own examples • Paraphrase textbook notes • Teach someone else • Write and answer practice examination questions

What are the differences between these two lists? There are several differences to notice. First, the strategies in List 2 are likely more difficult and would take more time. More importantly, the strategies in List 2 rely on something that is critical to long-term processing, the learner's own knowledge. List 2 consists of elaboration strategies that involve something *the learner* creates. The strategies in List 1 are rehearsal strategies, and are based on other people's knowledge and words (e.g., professor's PowerPoints, the author's textbook).

Remember the previous list of words related to sleep? The elaboration strategies in List 2 take advantage of how your brain is structured by connecting new information to prior knowledge. Because this connection is more meaningful to the individual learner, the new information takes a bigger "jump" across the memory continuum. Therefore, information processed using strategies in List 2 are more likely to move more quickly and efficiently into long-term memory. Considering the differences in these strategies, are rehearsal strategies "bad"? The short answer is no. Rehearsal strategies are a fundamental part

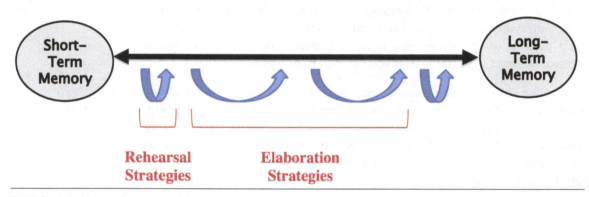

FIGURE 4.1.3: Memory Continuum with Learning Strategies

Source: Angela Vaughan and Brett Wilkinson

of learning; however, for rehearsal strategies to be effective, they require much more repetition to move the information into long-term memory. Therefore, an effective study plan incorporates both types of strategies.

Yet, many students primarily use rehearsal strategies (Cao & Nietfeld, 2007). In fact, Cao and Nietfeld's study found that even when students were presented with more difficult content, they still did not adjust their strategies and relied on less effective rehearsal strategies. This probably occurs for a couple of reasons. First, some students may be unaware of different ways to study new information. Others may have effectively used rehearsal strategies during middle or high school, and so they are comfortable with these types of strategies. However, once students or professionals are faced with an increase in the volume or level of difficulty of new information that must be learned, it becomes far more difficult to exclusively use rehearsal strategies and still be effective. Table 4.1.2 includes an extended list of both types of strategies.

How often do you self-test? In addition to identifying gaps in your knowledge, self-testing is a powerful learning strategy to encode information into long-term memory.

TABLE 4.1.2 REHEARSAL AND ELABORATION STRATEGIES

Rehearsal (ST)	Elaboration (LT)

• Read the textbook
• Read professor's lecture handouts/PowerPoints
• Highlight the textbook
• Take lecture notes verbatim
• Take textbook notes verbatim
• Review notes
• Create flashcards with vocabulary defined verbatim
• Review flashcards
• Type notes
• Look up vocabulary and use definitions from the textbook/lectures/Internet
• Attend class and listen to lecture
	• Create your own examples of concepts, ideas, visuals
	  • From textbook readings
	  • From lectures
	• Paraphrase textbook notes
	• Paraphrase lecture notes
	• Review notes after class with classmate and identify gaps
	• Connect concepts to prior or current:
	  • Knowledge
	  • Experience
	  • Courses
	• Ask questions
	• Teach someone else from class
	• Teach someone else not in class
	• Discuss in study groups
	• Write your own explanation of a topic
	• Create graphic organizers
	  • Concept/mind maps
	  • Tables
	  • Figures
	  • Timelines
	• Draw pictures
	• Write practice exam questions
	• Answer practice essay questions
	• Self-test and use recitation (retrieving information from memory)
	• Complete problems (math/statistics)
	  • Write out problem explanations
	• Answer unit objectives
	• Go to professor's office hours and discuss questions and ideas
	• Go to tutoring
	• Create a mnemonic or story
	• Create a memory palace
	• Define vocabulary using your own words

Writing to Learn

There are a couple of specific points to note from the list of strategies. One is the use of writing. As a student, you have spent many years learning how to write. When trying to process information more deeply, *writing to learn* can be very effective. Some are obvious uses of writing such as defining vocabulary in your own words, or paraphrasing your textbook notes. Others may not be as obvious. Have you ever written out the process of solving an algebra or statistics problem? Have you stopped to write a one-page summary immediately after a lecture? Have you written an explanation of a new concept such that a fifth grader would understand? These types of learning strategies force you to think deeply about what you know as well as to identify any gaps in your knowledge. Many times, writing tasks also give you an opportunity to process the information differently in your brain, thereby leading to deeper learning.

What are other ways (or other courses) in which you could incorporate writing to learn?

Flashcards

When you think of a flashcard, you likely envision a vocabulary word on one side and its definition on the other. In this format, flashcards are a rehearsal strategy that requires repetition. It is an easy way to study "on the run" and to use frequently throughout the day; however, an adjustment to their design can make them more meaningful. Consider the following examples:

EXAMPLE 1: PREDICTING AN ESSAY QUESTION

What were the key causes of the American Revolution?	1. The British taxed the colonies to help pay their debt from the French and Indian War.
	2. The Boston Tea Party, in response to continued taxation, dumped approximately $800,000 in modern currency into the harbor.
	3. The Intolerable Acts which led to several punishing bills on the colonists including closing the Boston port and denying trials in colonial courts.
	4. The Battle of Concord, as a result of King George trying to capture colonial leaders.

EXAMPLE 2: SOLVING MATH PROBLEMS

Solve the following problem: $2(x + 1) - 4 = 10$	1. Add 4 to both sides $2(x + 1) - 4 + 4 = 10 + 4$
	2. Divide by 2 on both sides $\dfrac{2(x + 1)}{2} = \dfrac{14}{2}$
	3. Subtract 1 one from both sides $x + 1 - 1 = 7 - 1$
	4. $x = 6$

Many elaboration strategies can be applied to flashcards. This provides the benefit of processing the information in a more meaningful way when making the cards, and allows you to revisit the information frequently.

Study Groups

Study groups are another effective way to incorporate elaboration strategies. In addition to teaching others in the group, you have the opportunity to ask questions and hear others' perspectives about topics. Some other benefits of a study group include:

- Increased motivation by working with others
- Increased commitment as the group members hold each other accountable
- Opportunity to learn other strategies
- Establishing a routine for studying

As helpful as study groups can be, it is rare that they happen spontaneously. Establishing a group requires intentional effort. Make an effort to know your classmates and invite those who share your motivation and commitment to do well. Once you have formed your group of three to five members (the ideal number), be sure to do the following:

- Establish a regular time and place to meet (i.e., a weekly routine within your schedule)
- Set an agenda *each time* the group meets and *assign responsibilities*
- Select a leader to help facilitate the meeting and keep everyone on track (this can change from meeting to meeting, or stay the same)
- Meet only for about 60–90 minutes (marathon sessions are ineffective)
- Hold each other accountable such that everyone participates and comes prepared

Another advantage to working with a study group is opportunities to tackle large amounts of information. The following table includes some ideas for strategies and activities to use in your study group.

TABLE 4.1.3 STUDY GROUP ACTIVITIES

Example	Description
1. Create your own examples	• Each group member picks a topic. • Individually create examples using both lecture and textbook notes. (Be creative!!) • In the large group, each member shares their examples with the group.
2. Paraphrase textbook and lecture notes	• Each group member picks a topic. • Individually rewrite your lecture and textbook notes into short paragraphs. • In the large group, share your paragraphs (see if you can paraphrase without reading off your paper). • Email your written paragraphs to each group member, so now all members have paraphrased copies of their lecture and textbook notes.
3. Review and connect	• Pair up with another study group member and pick a topic. • Review your notes together, looking for gaps in your notes. • Connect the concepts in your notes with things you have already learned, experiences you have had, or other courses you have taken. • In the large group, share any gaps found in your notes and the connections you created for your topics.
4. Prepare test questions	• All topics for the test are divided amongst the group. • Individually come up with 5 multiple choice questions and 2 short answer questions for your topic. • Email your questions to the group leader, who can compile all the questions into a test. • Bring your answers (and why the answer is correct) to the group meeting. • As a group, take the test together, and grade the test together. Use any incorrect answers as a way to discuss that topic and why that answer is incorrect.
5. Create a graphic organizer	• All topics are divided amongst the group. • Individually create a graphic organizer of your topic (Make it creative! The more colorful, the better!). • Share your organizer with the group. Group leaders: use each graphic organizer as a way to ask the group questions about the topic (e.g., there seems to be a connection between enabling goals and long-term goals, why is that?).

6. Teach your topic	• All topics are divided amongst the group.
	• Individually learn your topic in-depth; create some discussion questions about your topic.
	• Think like a teacher!!! This is your chance to teach it your way. Use your notes and textbook to highlight the important points.
	• In the group: Each member teaches their topic their way. Group members should participate by asking questions to the "teacher" like you would in a classroom.
7. YouTube examples	• Divide up topics.
	• Individually find a YouTube video that is related to your topic. (Be creative! It does not have to be exactly explaining your topic, just related to it).
	• In the large group, share your YouTube video and have group members guess which topic you had, and why you picked that video.
	• Share your reasons behind using that particular video.
	• To mix it up, you could draw topics out of a hat to keep them secret. You could also create your own YouTube video on your topic.
8. PowerPoint	• Divide up topics.
	• Individually use lecture notes and the textbook to create several PowerPoint slides (complete with pictures) on your topic.
	• Share your slides with your group members.
	• Be prepared to email your slides to everyone else.
9. Lead a discussion	• Divide up topics.
	• Individually create 3 to 4 discussion questions about your topic (the harder or more complex, the better).
	• In the group, each member leads a discussion on their topic. Discussions should be about 10 to 15 minutes per topic.

Notice that there has not been the mention of learning being "easy" in this discussion of memory and learning strategies. The focus has been on becoming more efficient and effective. So when you do invest the time and effort, you see results and feel the time was worthwhile. But make no mistake, deep learning *requires* time and effort. The following describes how to use this information about memory in your day-to-day preparation and studying.

PUTTING IT TOGETHER

Cluster 3 described several time management strategies that are related to processing information and the memory continuum. Taking this view of memory, the more consistently a learner visits the information, the more likely it will move across the continuum. This reinforces the need to study material multiple days and times over the course of a week (or multiple times over a day). By consistently revisiting the information, whether with

DISTRIBUTED PRACTICE:
Studying information over multiple periods of time to increase recall.

rehearsal or elaboration strategies, you will be more effective in processing new ideas into long-term memory. This is also called *distributed practice* and is consistently linked to higher recall and achievement (Cepeda et al., 2009; Cepeda, Pashler, Vul, Wixted, & Rohrer, 2006).

Cluster 3 also suggested studying 1 to 3 hours outside of class for every hour in class, and, as a college student, that you are always preparing for an exam. By viewing your studying as "units of study" (see Figure 4.1.4), you can combine both rehearsal and elaboration strategies, and prepare over several weeks. This type of approach does several things. First, the use of

Unit Exam		
Go to professor's office hours and ask questions and discuss course topics	Long Term
Share practice exam questions with study group – answer each other's practice questions and discuss	Long Term
Create and answer practice exam questions	Long Term
Go to tutoring	Long Term
Create graphic organizer that combines textbook and lecture notes	Long Term
Review flashcards each day	Short Term
Create flashcards with textbook definitions	Short Term
Type notes	Short Term
Paraphrase lecture notes	Long Term
Review notes with peer after class and identify gaps	Long Term
Take verbatim notes during the lecture	Short Term
Ask questions during class	Long Term
Attend class	Short Term
Review notes before class	Short Term

Read textbook and paraphrase notes
  – Write examples & connections
  – Write questions
	Long Term

Start of Unit		

FIGURE 4.1.4: Unit of Study

many different learning strategies allows you to commit the time necessary. Many of the elaboration strategies are complex and require time to complete. A specific plan of action over several weeks also allows you to process the information over time (i.e., distributed practice) rather than "cramming" for an exam in the last few days. Lastly, both the complexity of the tasks and a defined plan of action tends to increase motivation because tackling a challenge and knowing exactly what you need to do, gives you a sense of purpose.

With an understanding of memory and how information is processed, the next two modules describe additional learning strategies and how to apply this information to note-taking and reading.

MODULE 4.1 SUMMARY

- Everyone can improve and become a more effective learner.
- Memory models typically include three components: a sensory register, short-term or working memory and long-term memory.
- Storing refers to keeping information in memory, encoding refers to changing the information so that it can be stored, and retrieving refers to finding the information in memory when needed.
- Memory can be viewed as a continuum where information moves from short- to long-term memory, based on the use of rehearsal or elaboration strategies.
- Writing to learn, elaborative flashcards and study groups are effective learning strategies for processing information.
- Using a unit of study approach is an effective way to make use of different strategies and to prepare for exams over time.

KEY TERMS

- **Distributed Practice** – Studying information over multiple periods of time to increase recall.
- **Encoding** – The process of meaningfully changing information so that it can be stored in memory.
- **Elaboration Strategies** – Learning strategies that rely on the learner's prior knowledge to process new information.
- **Learning** – Acquiring new knowledge and skills.
- **Long-Term Memory** – The memory component where large amounts of information are stored indefinitely.
- **Memory** – Retrieving information that has been previously learned.
- **Rehearsal Strategies** – Learning strategies that rely on repetition and others' ideas, words and knowledge to process new information.
- **Retrieving** – The process of finding information in your memory when needed.
- **Sensory Register** – The memory component where information from the environment enters through the five senses.

- **Short-Term or Working Memory** – The memory component where information is briefly stored until it is either encoded or lost.
- **Storing** – The process of putting new information into memory.

REFERENCES

Ashcraft, M. H., & Radvansky, G. A. (2010). *Cognition* (5th ed.). Upper Saddle River, NJ: Prentice Hall/Pearson.

Atkinson, R. C., & Shiffrin, R. M. (1968). Human memory: A proposed system and its control processes. In K. Spence & J. Spence (Eds.), *The psychology of learning and motivation* (Vol. 2, pp. 89–195). New York, NY: Academic Press.

Cao, L., & Nietfeld, J. L. (2007). College students' metacognitive awareness of difficulties in learning the class content does not automatically lead to adjustment of study strategies. *Australian Journal of Educational & Developmental Psychology, 7,* 31–46.

Cepeda, N. J., Coburn, N., Rohrer, D., Wixted, J. T., Mozer, M. C., & Pashler, H. (2009). Optimizing distributed practice: Theoretical analysis and practical implications. *Experimental Psychology, 56,* 236–246. doi:10.1027/1618-3169.56.4.236

Cepeda, N. J., Pashler, H., Vul, E., Wixted, J. T., & Rohrer, D. (2006). Distributed practice in verbal recall tasks: A review and quantitative synthesis. *Psychological Bulletin, 132*, 354–380. doi:10.1037/0033-2909.132.3.354

Goodman, K., & Pascarella, E. T. (2006). First-year seminars increase persistence and retention. A summary of the evidence from how college affects students. *Association of America Colleges and Universities, 8*(3), 26-28.

James, W. (1890). *Principles of psychology.* New York, NY: Holt.

Pascarella, E. T., & Terenzini, P. T. (1998). Studying college students in the 21st century: Meeting new challenges. *Review of Higher Education, 21*, 151–165.

Pashler, H. (1992). Attentional limitations in doing two tasks at the same time. *Current Directions in Psychological Sciences, 1*, 44–48.

Sternberg, R. J., & Sternberg, K. (2012). *Cognitive psychology* (6th ed.). Belmont, CA: Wadsworth.

Swanson, N. M., Vaughan, A. L., & Wilkinson, B. D. (2015). First-year seminars: Supporting male college students' long-term academic success. *Journal of College Student Retention: Research, Theory & Practice*. doi: 10.1177/1521025115604811

Tuckman, B. W., & Kennedy, G. J. (2011). Teaching learning strategies to increase success of first-term college students. *The Journal of Experimental Education, 79*, 478–504.

Vaughan, A. L., Lalonde, T., & Jenkins-Guarnieri, M.A. (2014). Assessing student achievement in large-scale educational programs using hierarchical propensity scores. *Research in Higher Education, 55*(6), 564-580. doi: 10.1007/s11162-014-9329-8

Vaughan, A. L., Parra, J., & Lalonde, T. (2014). First-generation college student achievement and the first year seminar: A quasi-experimental design. *The Journal of The First-Year Experience & Students in Transition, 26*(2), 53–69.

Weinstein, C., Woodruff, A., & Await, C. (2004). Information processing module. In C. Weinstein, A. Woodruff, & C. Await, *Becoming a strategic learner: LASSI instructional module*. Clearwater, FL: H&H.

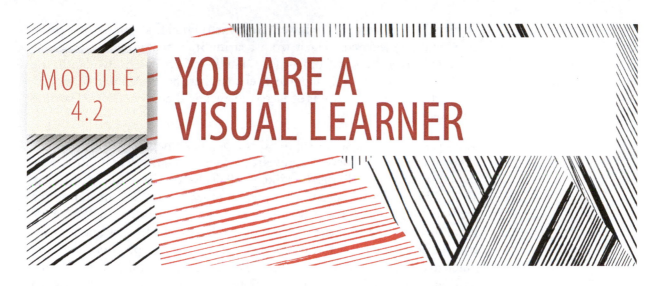

CLUSTER 4 OBJECTIVE COVERED IN THIS MODULE

☐ **OBJECTIVE:** Describe learning strategies that use visual imagery to process information.

OVERVIEW

This module focuses on one critical area of information processing: visual imagery. After describing the basis for using visual learning strategies, several techniques and examples will be shared. Visual learning is typically an area that most students have not tried or considered, yet, it is a powerful information processing tool for everyone.

THE MYTH OF LEARNING STYLES

REFLECTION: When someone says they are a visual learner, or perhaps when you have said this about yourself, what has that meant for you?

Most students have been introduced to the idea of learning styles at some point in their education. Many have also tried to identify their particular learning style, whether it is visual, auditory, or kinesthetic. The basic premise is threefold:

1. Different senses are used to process different types of information,
2. Learners have natural strengths in the use of a particular sense and learning style, and
3. Instruction that aligns with individual learning styles leads to better learning outcomes.

So visual learners are said to benefit from instruction that emphasizes visual cues, auditory learners benefit from hearing information aloud, and kinesthetic learners benefit from a more "hands-on" approach. By identifying the learning styles of individual learners, teachers have been told to modify instruction to meet the needs of each student, and thereby optimize learning outcomes.

The idea of learning styles captured the popular imagination in the early 1980s with the introduction of research on visual, auditory and kinesthetic modality strengths (Barbe & Milone, 1980; Barbe, Swassing, & Milone, 1979). This model was expanded upon by other researchers, including the introduction of reading as a distinct learning style measured by the VARK learning styles questionnaire (Fleming, 1992). As with any new and innovative set of learning ideas, teachers, administrators, and parents alike were quick to adopt these concepts. These ideas were simple, intuitively appealing, and easily marketable to the public. They were quickly and readily adopted worldwide and are still in use today.

However, recent evidence suggests that the importance of learning styles has been both overestimated and improperly researched. A comprehensive review of the learning styles research (Coffield, Moseley, Hall, & Ecclestone, 2004) found that among the fully 71 different models proposed and published in the literature, only 13 can be considered major models and only three of those models met the minimal standards of scientific rigor. These included the Cognitive Style Index (Allinson & Hayes, 1996), reversal theory (Apter, 2001), and the Inventory of Learning Styles (ILS; Vermunt, 1995). Needless to say, each of these are far more complex than the oversimplified idea of visual, auditory, and kinesthetic learning styles.

Additionally, there is a difference between learning styles and multiple intelligences. Gardner (1999) developed research on multiple intelligences as a counterpoint to the idea of learning styles. The difference is that the model of multiple intelligences does not indicate that one method or approach to learning new information is better than another. Learners may have stronger information processing capabilities in a particular cognitive area, but this does not mean that certain senses are better used than others. In this respect, the multiple intelligences model is aligned with personality differences and does not indicate that students can learn more effectively by using specific senses. The multiple intelligences include areas of visual (spatial), aural (auditory-musical), verbal (linguistic), logical (mathematical), physical (kinesthetic), social (interpersonal), and solitary (intrapersonal) processing.

Learning styles models suggest that individuals are universally better at using one specific sense in *every situation*. Therefore, it is proposed that the learning approach should be tailored to match a specific learning style in every situation to get the best results. The multiple intelligences model suggests that while individuals learn by using every type of intelligence, preferences arise in certain situations. Here, successful learning is more a matter of what works best in what situation. For example, a great musician may learn how to play or sing a song best by listening to the song rather than reading the sheet music, but he may also learn the history of music best by reviewing slides and reading texts rather than by hearing a lecture. This musician may have a strength in auditory-musical learning, but it does not apply to every learning situation.

The takeaway is that every learner is a visual, auditory, and kinesthetic learner. The relative benefits of each type of learning really depends on the situation. More recent advances in neuroscience also indicate that the use of all three sensory modalities can enhance memory retention and recall. In fact, when using multiple senses to process information, memory traces are formed in different areas of the brain that lead to deeper learning (Shams & Seitz, 2011). As such, combining different strategies using more than one sensory modality is the most effective learning approach (Sadoski & Paivio, 2001). However, of the different senses, it should be noted that the strongest level of retention is associated with visual learning for *all* learners (Cuevas, 2015). Regardless of any learning style, either tested for or self-described, information is retained and recalled more effectively when that information is provided in a visual-spatial format. Everyone is a visual learner.

> How often do you draw as a learning strategy?

VISUAL IMAGERY

An early study by Shepard (1967) showed the power of visual imagery. College students were shown 600 images, and later were able to recall and select previously-viewed images from other random images with 98% accuracy. Since then, research has been consistent about the effectiveness of storing information into long-term memory using visual images (Cuevas, 2015; Dewhurst & Conway, 1994; Forrest, 1981; Sadoski & Paivio, 2001). In addition to drawing images within your notes or when annotating your textbook, there are other specific techniques that you can use to incorporate visual imagery. The remainder of the module will describe two of these strategies: memory palaces and graphic organizers.

METHOD OF LOCI—MEMORY PALACE

> *"The general idea with most memory techniques is to change whatever boring thing is being inputted into your memory into something that is so colorful, so exciting, and so different from anything you've seen before that you can't possibly forget it"* (Foer, 2011, p, 91).

Moonwalking with Einstein by Joshua Foer (2011) is a book that describes the author's journey in training for and competing in the Memory Championships. In the book, he describes how people have accomplished amazing recall tasks, such as memorizing 405 random digits in five minutes, or 2,080 random digits and 27 shuffled decks of cards in an hour, or 80,000 plus digits of pi. What is truly amazing is that all of these tasks were accomplished with the competitors using visual imagery.

MEMORY PALACE:
A memory technique that uses visualization to connect images with places.

As described previously, your brain has a natural propensity to remember images (Cuevas, 2015; Shepard, 1967). The method of loci, or memory palace also takes advantage of your brain's inherent talent for remembering physical spaces. Think about someone's home you have visited. Even if you only visited it once, it is likely that you can still picture the location of the rooms and the general layout. More importantly, you probably remembered the layout without noticing or trying. The memory palace uses your brain's aptitude for both spaces and images. With this method, "the idea is to create a space in the mind's eye, a place that you know well and can easily visualize, and then populate that imagined place with images representing whatever you want to remember" (Foer, 2011, p. 96).

The following activity allows you to try a memory palace for yourself.

ACTIVITY 4.2.1 MEMORY PALACE

You're going to learn a shopping list; however, you will learn the items by using a memory palace. You do not need to try and memorize the list. Just follow the instructions and you will be able to recall the list when you're done. First, read the shopping list:

- Butter
- Wine
- Milk
- Muffins
- Mustard
- Waffles
- Pork Chops
- Carrots
- Cottage Cheese
- Pizza

Now, read the following statements. As you read, pause and take time to create the image in your mind. Try to visualize as many of the details as you can and to fully experience the senses (e.g., smell, feel, etc.) described. This memory palace will occur in your home. If you are now living in a dorm room, this palace will probably work better in your home before college. After you have read each of the statements, continue with the next set of instructions.

1. You are at your front door and the doorknob has been replaced with a stick of butter. You grab the soft butter, and it squishes and oozes between your fingers.

2. The door opens and just inside the door, you see a bottle of red wine and a carton of milk boxing. They are arguing about who tastes better. You hear a loud pop as the wine bottle falls over and the cork flies across the room. The milk carton is also on its side. You take a step and almost slip and fall on the red-and-white puddles of wine and milk at your feet.

3. You then carefully walk into your living room. The floor has been replaced with a room-sized top of a blueberry muffin. It is still warm from baking, but not hot, you can feel the warmth beneath your feet and you can smell the fresh baked muffin. Your feet begin to sink in. You decide to place your hands, still covered in butter, on it. The butter melts off of your hands and into the top of the muffin.

4. You look at your sofa, and sitting on the sofa is your favorite teacher, squeezing a bottle of yellow mustard onto his or her head. The mustard is dripping down the sides of his or her nose, and off the tip of his or her ears.

5. You then look at your TV. It has been replaced with a giant waffle wearing black frame glasses who is giving a very serious editorial about how The Walking Dead is the best show ever made.

6. You then go to the kitchen, and for pork chops, you see a pig taking a bubble bath in the sink. He's wearing a lime green shower cap, and singing *Somewhere Over the Rainbow* at the top of his lungs.

7. You then try to leave the kitchen, but a massive army of carrots are bouncing around on pogo sticks, eyes wide and laughing crazily, blocking your way. You push past.

8. You then go to your bedroom, and your bed has been replaced by a very large pool of cottage cheese. Abraham Lincoln is in swimming trunks. He runs across the room, jumps and does a cannonball into the pool of cottage cheese. Cottage cheese flies into the air and you feel a cold slimy piece land on your cheek. He asks you to join him.

9. You then walk into the bathroom and the toilet seat is replaced with a pepperoni pizza. The pepperonis look at you and scream, "No! No! Please No!"

Without pausing, take a tour of your home. As you visit each place in your home, write down the grocery item. Start the tour:

1. You are at your front door and you grab your doorknob.
2. The door opens and you step just inside the door.
3. You then carefully walk in your living room and look at the floor.
4. You then look across the room at your sofa.
5. You hear something, and turn and look at your TV.
6. You then go to the kitchen, and go to the sink.
7. You then turn and walk out to leave the kitchen.
8. You then go to your bedroom and see your bed.
9. Lastly, you walk into the bathroom and see the toilet.

Did you write down all 10 items correctly? At some point in taking the tour, did you stop reading the statements and visualize the tour strictly in your mind? To recall these items, did you have to "study" them, or were they readily available in your memory? What was it about these descriptions that were helpful in recalling the items?

Although the method of loci or memory palace is a useful tool, this activity also illustrates the raw power of mental imagery. These images were specifically easy to recall because they are:

- Silly or funny,
- Outrageous, unique or impossible, and
- Connected to something you already know (i.e., your house, your teacher, etc.).

Images can also be easier to recall if they are related to something that is racy or sexy. Imagine one of the characters (e.g., Abe Lincoln) instead as your favorite celebrity crush. Our brains naturally pay attention to, and encode these image characteristics with very little effort. Lastly, as described in the previous module, creating *your own* memory palace is an even more effective means of processing and encoding the items. As a result, the images are truly your own creation, and are thus more meaningful.

Is a memory palace a rehearsal or elaboration strategy? How do you know?

You can use a memory palace to assist your retention, but more importantly, you can use visual imagery as an ongoing information processing strategy. As mentioned previously, drawing pictures can be incorporated into your notes, when annotating your textbook, or when creating other study aids. The power of visual imagery is also effective when creating and using the following set of study aids: graphic organizers.

GRAPHIC ORGANIZERS

Graphic organizers are another method that uses visual imagery and organization to process information. Graphic organizers use different structures, visual imagery, and symbols to show ideas, relationships, and concepts. In this area, research provides evidence that students who use and create graphic organizers, tend to achieve at higher levels (Corkill, 1992; Katayama & Robinson, 2000; Robinson et al., 2006; Robinson & Kiewra, 1995). In Robinson et al.'s study (2006), undergraduate students who created graphic organizers scored higher on examinations and quizzes as compared to students who created outlines or summary notes, or those who studied graphic organizers completed by others. Additionally, graphic organizers tend to support student learning by clearly showing relationships that may only be implicit, and hence, missed in outlines or summary notes (Robinson & Kiewra, 1995). As a result, graphic organizers aid in "factual and relational learning, application, and integrated writing" (p. 466).

Graphic organizers can take many forms (e.g., concept maps, timelines, hierarchies, Venn diagrams, etc.) and can vary in complexity. Typically, *the process* of creating the graphic organizer forces the learner to analyze the information more deeply, and to select the appropriate information and create applicable structure and organization. This is not an easy task and requires time; however, it is this level of effort and time spent that supports deeper learning. The disadvantage of these methods is that they are not meant to be done at the last moment; however, once completed, a graphic organizer becomes a one-page study aid that can be revisited multiple times for review. There are several websites that include free software that makes completing these organizers easier. These include:

- https://www.lucidchart.com
- https://bubbl.us/
- https://udltechtoolkit.wikispaces.com/Graphic+organizers
- https://www.mindmup.com
- https://www.edrawsoft.com/graphic-organizer-software.php

The following are several examples of graphic organizers. In addition to the structure and organization, notice how many of these examples use colors, shapes, and drawings to reinforce the study aid as a visual tool.

GRAPHIC ORGANIZER:
A study aid that uses different structures, visual imagery and symbols to show ideas, relationships, and concepts.

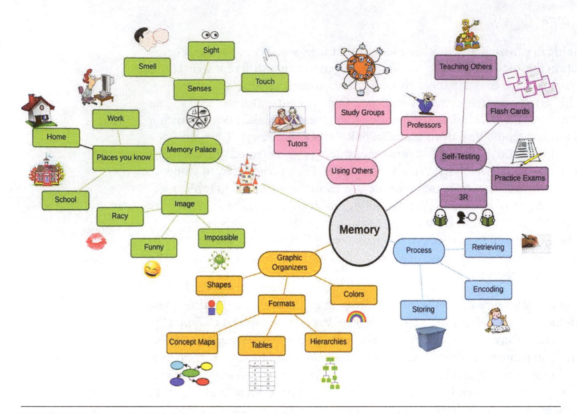

FIGURE 4.2.1: Concept Map With Colors and Drawings

Source: Angela Vaughan and Brett Wilkinson
Illustrations from Microsoft Word®

TABLE 4.2.1 TABLE THAT ILLUSTRATES EXPONENT RULES

Rule Name	Rule	Example
Product Rules	$a^n \cdot a^m = a^{n+m}$	$2^2 \cdot 2^3 = 2^{2+3} = 2^5 = 32$
	$a^n \cdot b^n = (a \cdot b)^m$	$2^2 \cdot 3^2 = (2 \cdot 3)^2 = 6^2 = 36$
Quotient Rules	$a^n / a^m = a^{n-m}$	$2^6/2^3 = 2^{6-3} = 2^3 = 8$
	$a^n / b^n = (a/b)^n$	$8^2/2^2 = (8/2)^2 = 4^2 = 16$
Power Rules	$(b^n)^m = b^{n \cdot m}$	$(3^2)^4 = 3^{2 \cdot 4} = 3^8 = 6561$
	$^m\sqrt{(b^n)} = b^{n/m}$	$^2\sqrt{(2^8)} = 2^{8/2} = 2^4 = 16$
	$b^{1/n} = {^n\sqrt{b}}$	$16^{1/4} = {^4\sqrt{16}} = 2$
Negative Exponents	$b^{-n} = 1/b^n$	$3^{-2} = 1/3^2 = 1/9$

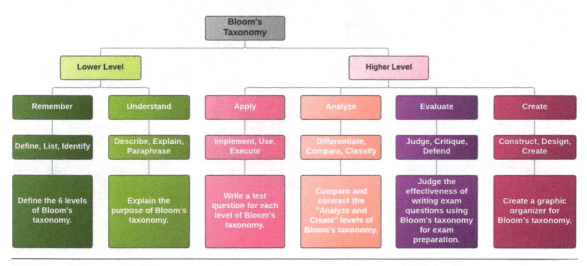

FIGURE 4.2.2: Hierarchy that Illustrates Bloom's Taxonomy

Source: Angela Vaughan and Brett Wilkinson

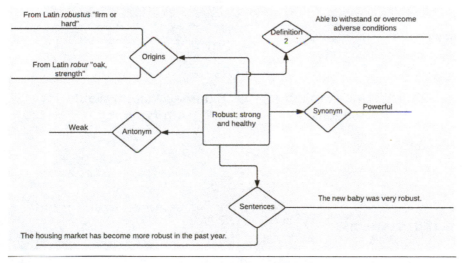

FIGURE 4.2.3: A Vocabulary Graphic Organizer

Source: Angela Vaughan and Brett Wilkinson

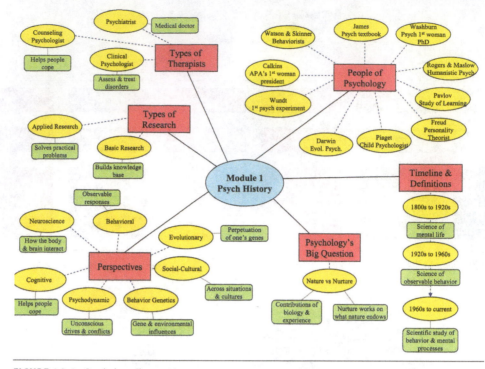

FIGURE 4.2.4: Psychology Chapter Map

Source: Angela Vaughan and Brett Wilkinson

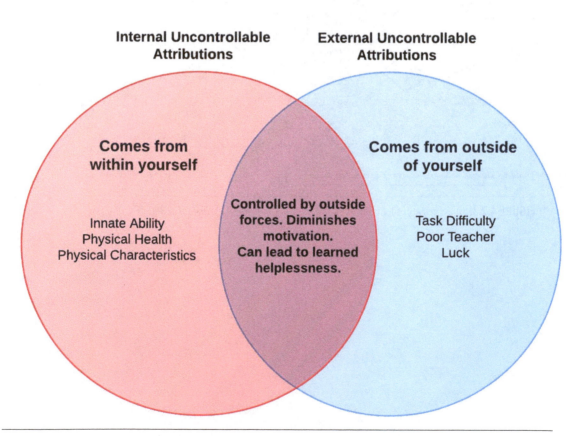

FIGURE 4.2.5: Venn Diagrams

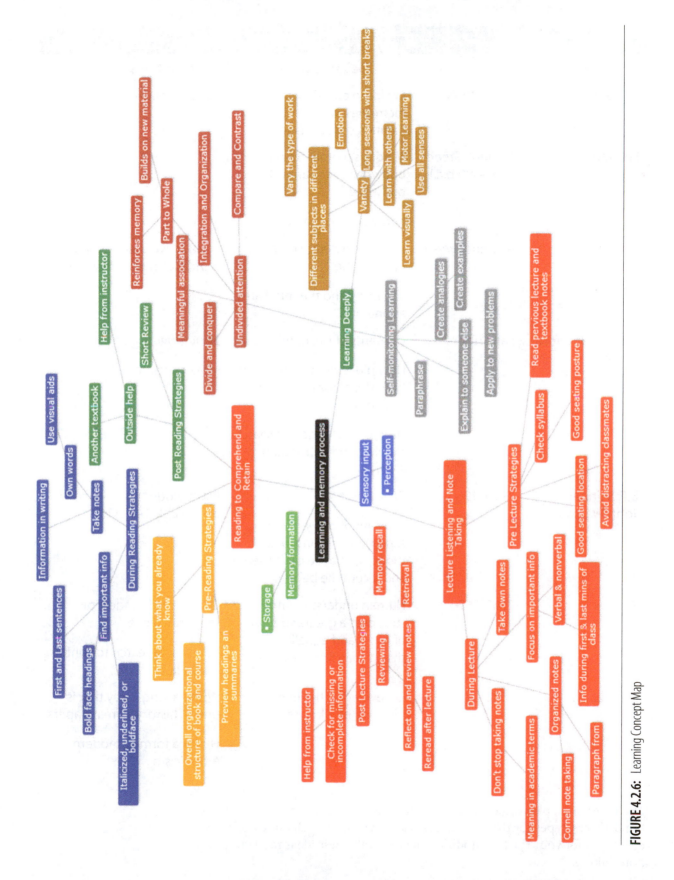

FIGURE 4.2.6: Learning Concept Map

FIGURE 4.2.7 PSYCHOLOGIST COMPARISON CHART (STUDENT EXAMPLE)

Psychologist	Year	Beliefs/Studies	Contributions
William James	Late 1800's	Explored emotions, memories, will power, habits & consciousness	Functionalism
Socrates/Plato	Ancient Greece (469–399 b.c.)	Mind is separate from the body/continues after the body dies Knowledge is innate	
Aristotle	Ancient Greece	Logic/knowledge is not pre-existing The body and the mind are as one	1st to derive theories and principles from observations
Edward Bradford Tit Chener	Late 1800's	Elements of the mind How did feelings/sensations from the senses relate to each other Used introspection to search for the mind's structural elements	Structuralism Introspection
B.F. Skinner John Watson	1920–1960	Behaviorist You cannot observe a sensation, a feeling, or a thought, but you can observe and record the behavior	Psychology "the science of observable behavior"
Francis Bacon	1561–1626	Human understanding supposes a greater degree of order and equality in things than it really finds	One of the founders of moden science Foresaw research to confirm our beliefs
John Locke	1632–1704	Believed that the mind at birth is a blank slate	Wrote a long essay that is one of history's great papers His idea formed modern empiricism

The types of graphic organizers and visual study aids are limitless. Try creating different types for different courses and evaluate which ones work most effectively for you. The last module will now apply these ideas to reading and note-taking.

MODULE 4.2 SUMMARY

- Using visual imagery as a learning strategy is a powerful way to store and retrieve information from long-term memory.
- A memory palace or method of loci is a learning strategy that uses visual and spatial descriptions to process information.
- Graphic organizers come in many different forms, and are learning strategies that use both visual information and learner-created structures to process information.

KEY TERMS

- **Memory Palace** – A memory technique that uses visualization to connect images with places.
- **Graphic Organizer** – A study aid that uses different structures, visual imagery, and symbols to show ideas, relationships, and concepts.

REFERENCES

Allinson, C. W., & Hayes, J. (1996). The cognitive style index: A measure of intuition-analysis for organizational research. *Journal of Management Studies, 33*(1), 119–135.

Apter, M. J. (2001). *Motivational styles in everyday life: A guide to reversal theory.* Washington, D.C.: American Psychological Association.

Barbe, W. B., & Milone, M. N. (1980). Modality. *Instructor, 89,* 44–47.

Barbe, W. B., Swassing, R. H., & Milone, M. N. (1979). *Teaching through the modality strengths: Concepts and practices.* Columbus, OH: Zaner-Bloser.

Coffield, F., Moseley, D., Hall, E., & Ecclestone, K. (2004). *Learning styles and pedagogy in post 16 learning: A systematic and critical review.* London: Learning and Skills Research Centre.

Corkill, A. J. (1992). Advance organizers: Facilitators of recall. *Educational Psychology Review, 4,* 33–66.

Cuevas, J. (2015). Is learning styles-based instruction effective? A comprehensive analysis of recent research on learning styles. *Theory and Research in Education, 13*(3), 308–333.

Dewhurst, S. A., & Conway, M. A. (1994). Pictures, images, and recollective experience. *Journal of Experimental Psychology: Learning, Memory, and Cognition, 20,* 1088–1098.

Fleming, N. D., & Mills, C. (1992) Not another inventory, rather a catalyst for reflection. *To Improve the Academy, 11,* 137–149.

Foer, J. (2011). *Moonwalking with Einstein.* New York, New York: Penguin Group.

Forrest, E. B. (1981). Visual imagery as an information processing strategy. *Journal of Learning Disabilities, 14*(10), 584–586.

Gardner, H. E. (1983). Multiple approaches to understanding. In C. M. Reigeluth (Ed.), *Instructional design theories and models: A new paradigm of instructional theory* (Vol. 2, pp. 69–89). Mahwah, NJ: Lawrence Erlbaum Associates.

Katayama, A. D., & Robinson, D. H. (2000). Getting students "partially" involved in note-taking using graphic organizers. *The Journal of Experimental Education, 68,* 119–133.

Robinson, D. H., Katayama, A. D., Beth, A., Odom, S., Hsieh, Y., & Vanderveen, A. (2006). Increasing text comprehension and graphic note-taking using a partial graphic organizer. *The Journal of Educational Research, 100*(2), 103–111.

Robinson, D. H., & Kiewra, K. A. (1995). Visual argument: Graphic organizers are superior to outlines in improving learning from text. *Journal of Educational Psychology, 87*(3), 455–467.

Sadoski, M., & Paivio, A. (2001). *Imagery and text: A dual coding theory of reading and writing.* Mahwah, NJ: Erlbaum.

Shams, W., & Seitz, K. (2011). Influences of multisensory experience on subsequent unisensory processing. *Frontiers in Perception Science, 2*(264), 1–9.

Shepard, R. N. (1967). Recognition memory for words, sentences, and pictures. *Journal of Verbal Learning and Verbal Behavior, 6,* 156–163.

Vermunt, J. D. (1995). Process-oriented instruction in learning and thinking strategies. *European Journal of Psychological Education, 10,* 325–349.

ACTIVE READING AND NOTE-TAKING

OVERVIEW

REFLECTION: Have you ever read a 20- or 50-page textbook chapter, and after finishing, realized you do not have any clue as to what you just read?

Many people have experienced completing their reading only to feel like it was a waste of time. Now, think about a time that you read something for fun. Even if you only read it once (and even a long time ago), can you remember the plot, the characters, etc.? Your answer is most likely yes. What is the difference between these two types of readings? The difference is related to memory and the information processing that was discussed in Module 4.1. This module will discuss how to apply those ideas in effective ways that allow you to gain more from the time you spend reading and listening to lectures.

ACTIVE READING

Like other learning how to learn strategies, active reading can be taught to students in order to improve their reading comprehension and academic achievement (Helms & Helms, 2010; Hill, Brozel, & Heiberger, 2014). This includes traditional courses with a heavy text such as biology (Hill et al., 2014) as well as more technical disciplines such as college-level mathematics

(Helms & Helms, 2010). Hill et al.'s (2014) study assessed the effectiveness of teaching active reading strategies to freshmen in a non-major biology course. The results showed that student reading comprehension more than doubled. This is quite significant, considering the level of difficulty in most freshmen biology courses.

But what does it mean to be an "active" reader? To help understand the difference between passive and active reading, read the following word:

STOP

Reading "stop" is not a difficult task; however, it helps illustrate a critical point. For those of you who have been an English language reader since you were little, reading the word "stop" is an automatic process. In fact, it would be impossible for you at this point to *not* read the word. This helps explain why you read something, and then cannot remember the details shortly after finishing. Without active reading strategies, your brain has to do very little work to read. So how do you change this result and make your time reading worthwhile? The short answer is to apply elaboration strategies (described in Module 4.1) to your reading.

Think back to your experience of reading for fun. Most of the time, especially if you are enjoying the book, you are using active reading strategies without noticing it. Consider how the following typically occurs when reading a book for pleasure:

- You visualize what the characters or settings look like.
- You predict what might happen next.
- You build an emotional attachment to the outcomes (e.g., I cannot believe he died!!).
- You have emotional responses throughout (e.g., fear, surprise, happiness, sadness, etc.) as you connect to what is happening in the plot.
- You continue to think about the book even when you are done reading.
- You make connections to your personal experiences, or what you see in the world.

All of these are elaboration strategies that make meaningful connections to you as the reader. But how do you do this with a chemistry textbook?! Although it may not be as fun, the same ideas apply. Before going forward, one other point needs to be clarified: active reading is neither easy nor fast, and requires some initial practice to gain expertise. However, connecting to your reading with an active approach will help you see a return on your time investment. When you finish reading and you feel you have learned something, your confidence will increase and you will build a solid foundation for long-term information processing.

ACTIVE READING:
A reading approach that uses elaboration strategies to process read information into long-term memory.

INITIAL PROCESSES

There are a couple of strategies that are necessary to set the stage for your active reading. The first strategy was described in Cluster 3 (Time Management). To maintain concentration, attention and motivation, you should schedule your readings over several time periods. As mentioned previously, active reading is more difficult, and will take more time. With that in mind, you should determine the appropriate amount of time in which you can maintain focused effort. This will vary, based on the difficulty of the textbook, and your level of prior knowledge in the course. For some textbooks, you may be able to easily sit down for an hour and effectively apply active reading strategies. For others, it may be difficult to complete 15 minutes. Begin by making an initial judgment, and then re-evaluate if the amount of time (or the number of pages) was appropriate and adjust if needed. In addition to promoting concentration and motivation, scheduling your readings will also help you take advantage of distributed practice (see Module 4.1). By reading and continuously reviewing previously-read material throughout the week, it is more likely that the information will be encoded and stored into long-term memory.

> *Where* do you typically read? Is it a distraction-free zone, or are you reading in bed trying to stay awake? Set yourself up for success and pick a place where you can maintain focus (e.g., desk or table at the library).

So, step one is to schedule your readings. Step two is to activate prior knowledge. This is directly related to helping your memory connect new information, to information already stored in memory (see Module 4.1). To demonstrate the necessity of this step, read the following passage:

> *With hocked gems financing him, our hero bravely defied all scornful laughter that tried to prevent his scheme. 'Your eyes deceive,' he had said. 'An egg, not a table, correctly typifies this unexplored planet.' Now three sturdy sisters sought proof. Forging along, sometimes thru calm vastness, yet more often over turbulent peaks and valleys, days became weeks as many doubters spread fearful rumors about the edge. At last from nowhere welcome winged creatures appeared, signifying the momentous success* (Dooling & Lachman, 1971, p. 217).

What do you think this passage is about? How comfortable would you be if 50% of your essay exam was based on your comprehension and analysis of this passage? Before going any further, go to the Module 4.3 Summary, and read what the passage is about.

Now, knowing the topic, re-read the passage. Does the information make more sense? How do you feel about writing an essay about this topic now? Most students agree (as well as the original researchers, who used this passage) that having even the smallest amount of prior knowledge is critical to comprehension.

There are several ways to activate prior knowledge when beginning to read. The following lists some ideas:

- Read any unit objectives within the textbook, or those provided by your professor.

- Read the chapter summary first.

Are there other ways you could activate prior knowledge before reading?

- Try to answer any end-of-chapter questions or reviews.

- Scan the titles, headings and margin information throughout the text.

- Review the syllabus to see how the reading fits into the course and schedule of topics.

- Review any previous lecture or textbook notes.

- Create any questions that could be answered by the text.

With this foundation, it is now time to read.

ACTIVE READING STRATEGIES

There is not one magical way to apply elaboration strategies to your reading. The following describes different possibilities. Give yourself the opportunity to try different strategies and see which ones are more effective for you. You may find that different strategies are more helpful based on the course or topics. You will also find that many of these require practice, and you will gain expertise and efficiency over time.

Annotating or Highlighting the Text

This strategy takes advantage of the fact that the college textbooks you bought are yours, and you can write all over them (if you are not able to write on your textbooks, you can do these same strategies on your own paper or document; electronic textbooks have the means for you to do this as well). But this strategy is very intentional. Have you ever highlighted your textbook only to find almost every sentence is highlighted? Consider these things when marking your textbook:

- Within the margins, write connections, questions, your personal response, and anything else that comes to mind. The important point here is to connect the information to something that is from your previous knowledge set.

- Instead of highlighting, write in the margins *WHY* you would highlight the text. For example, is this a new, important term? Does the information provide significant support? Do you have a question about the ideas, etc.?

Reading and Note-Taking Structures

Another strategy that can be used with or after the above strategies includes a more formal note-taking approach. The key here is to consistently apply the following approaches within your notes:

- Summarizing and paraphrasing

- Connections, examples, and questions

- Drawings, diagrams, and timelines

The notes themselves could be in an outline form, or you may decide to write out your notes in sentence or paragraph form. There are different recommended structures for your notes (although your own personal designs may be just as effective); however, the structure is not as important as including the elaboration strategies listed. Some of these structures include Cornell Notes, SUNY notes, modified approaches and summary/response approaches. There is also a structure to consider for math and statistics classes.

Many students have been introduced to the Cornell Note-Taking approach in high school. This consists of notes in the middle of the page, questions that are answered by the notes in the left-hand margin, and summaries at the bottom of the page (Figure 4.3.1).

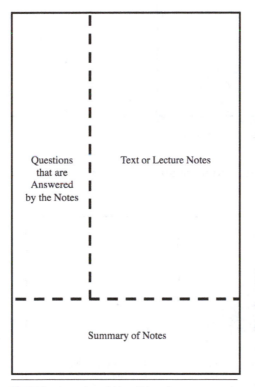

FIGURE 4.3.1: Cornell Note-Taking Structure

The SUNY method is similar, except that it is intended to use two pages. See Figure 4.3.2.

In both of these structures, the intent is to write questions that are answered by the notes. This provides a means to self-test yourself on the information. You can also go into your notes and highlight the key words or terms that reflect the answers to the questions.

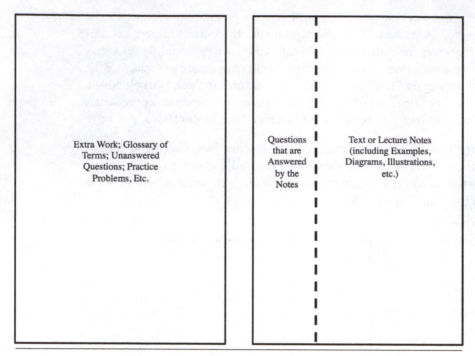

FIGURE 4.3.2: SUNY Note-Taking Structure

A potential modification to the above structures is shown in Figure 4.3.3.

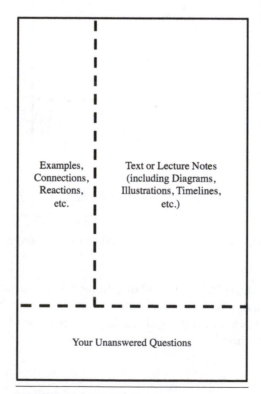

FIGURE 4.3.3: A Modified Structure

Educational Psychology for Learners: Connecting Theory, Research & Application

The primary difference with this structure is that your connections, examples and reactions are in the margin, and any unanswered questions are at the bottom of the page. Collecting your questions at the bottom can serve as a quick resource, when reviewing before class or when reviewing for an exam. Which questions have been resolved and which questions are still unanswered?

The summary/response approach is simply using one page to write and summarize the information from the text and using the adjacent page to write personal responses or reflections on the information. Your responses can include connections and illustrations to your own experiences, as well as any questions, doubts, or predictions you have at the time. This is your opportunity to meaningfully engage with the information.

The last structure can be helpful with math and statistics classes. As in your other courses, it is important to read *before* attending the lecture. This structure involves simply dividing the page, whereby one side includes practice problems from the text, and the other side includes the explanations, or the "why", behind the steps involved. An adjacent page could also be used for questions or vocabulary, etc.

Again, your particular note-taking structure is not important. As long as you have an organization that you understand, and you are incorporating elaboration strategies, your note-taking process will be effective.

Paraphrasing and Summarizing

Within each of the structures described, there was a place in your notes where you should be paraphrasing or summarizing information from the text. This will likely be the most time-consuming part of taking notes. It is also a skill that is usually underdeveloped among students who are incorporating active reading strategies for the first time. Think about when you sit down to read and take notes. Do you tend to glance back and forth between the text and your paper? Do you usually try to write down words and phrases verbatim? This type of note-taking does very little, above and beyond the automatic reading process described earlier.

For note-taking to be more effective, start with a small section or paragraph, and read it in its entirety. Once you are done, stop and think about what you just read. What stood out to you? What was unfamiliar? What seemed important? Now, try writing those ideas in your own words in your notes. Be sure to use full sentences or phrases. Once done, go back and read the section again, and confirm that your notes included all of the important points. It should be clear that this is a more time-consuming process than what you are used to. It will also be slow going because you will need to start with small sections. Once you have practiced and gained more skill, you will be able to expand the amount of information that you tackle each time. Paraphrasing and summarizing information into your own words is a critical elaboration strategy. Not only does it help encode the information into long-term memory, but it is an effective tool to identify gaps in your understanding.

A quick way to get your professor's attention is to come into lecture with a question from the readings. One, you accomplished the readings *before* lecture and two, you used active reading strategies, and identified gaps in your understanding!

Once you have completed your notes within a single session, repeat this process until your reading is complete. At the beginning of the next session, be sure to briefly revisit your previous reading and notes, as this is another opportunity to encode the information into memory. In the process, you may also discover additional ideas or generate new connections. Take advantage of these new ideas and connections, and add them to your notes.

At this point in your reading, you should have completed the following process or steps (Figure 4.3.4):

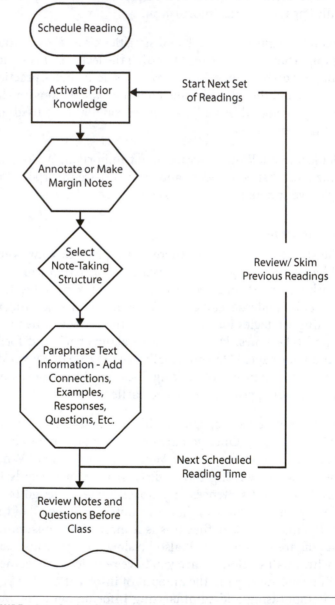

FIGURE 4.3.4: Reading Process   *Source: Angela Vaughan and Brett Wilkinson*

OTHER ACTIVE READING STRATEGIES

The following are some additional ways to engage with your texts. These can be effectively used as a supplement to your reading process.

TABLE 4.3.1 MORE ACTIVE READING STRATEGIES

Name of Strategy	Description
"What it Says" and "What it Does" (Ramage & Bean, 1995, p. 32–34)	First, write a summary of the content of the text and then write the purpose or the function accomplished within the text or essay.
"Believing and Doubting Game" (Elbow, 1973, 1986)	First, try to identify and relate with the author as you read. Then, play devil's advocate by questioning, looking for flaws, and raising objections.
"Dialogical Thinking" (Paul, 1987)	Similar to the strategy above, its intent is "to argue for and against each and every point of view" (p. 140).
"Focused Reading Notes" (Bean, 2001)	First, activate prior knowledge and skim the readings. Then try to predict four or five important themes or concepts within the reading. Divide your paper into the four or five columns (with each of these themes) and begin taking detailed notes by entering information within the appropriate columns.
Multiple Choice or Essay Examination Questions	After reading specific sections, try to create examination questions that test the material. Later, use these as a review.

Another strategy is called the Active Reading Document (Dubas & Toledo, 2015). This five-task strategy helps the reader move from a comprehension of the text to an in-depth analysis of the information. The following briefly outlines the strategy. For a more detailed description, read the article by Dubas and Toledo (2015).

Task 1: Represent the broad topics and key concepts with a hierarchical organization.

Task 2: Paraphrase the information with your own words, drawings, diagrams, etc.

Task 3: Identify and explain three connections that exist within the current reading.

Task 4: Identify and explain two connections that exist to other chapters or units within the same text or course.

Task 5: Identify and explain two additional connections. The first should connect to other courses or disciplines, and the other should connect to the reader's own personal experiences (p. 29).

The variety of elaboration strategies to help with your active reading is limitless. Try some of the strategies described here and try creating some of your own. In the end, the investment of time will be well worth it. The following describes how these same ideas apply to taking notes during lectures.

LECTURES AND NOTE-TAKING

REFLECTION: Have you ever skipped class or been tempted to skip class?

Although sometimes there is a temptation to skip class, you are missing out on one of the easiest strategies for success: attending class. Research has shown consistent relationships between class attendance, achievement, and GPA (Credé, Roch, & Kieszczynka, 2010; Jenne, 1973; Moore et al., 2003). A meta-analytic study (with 28,000+ students, covering 82 years in 68 studies) showed this positive relationship was an even stronger predictor of class grades and college GPA than high school GPA, college entrance exams (e.g., SAT scores) and study strategies (Credé et al., 2010). In addition to the effects on achievement, there are other benefits to attending class:

- Discover what the professor feels is important information.
- Get questions answered from textbook readings.
- Understand how different concepts are interconnected.
- Get another explanation that is possibly different from the textbook.
- Create another memory trace of the information in your brain (as well as the effects of distributed practice).

However, once you are in class, there are ways to maximize your time.

PRE-, DURING, AND POST-LECTURE

Much of the information about note-taking in the previous section also applies during lecture; however, there are some other points to consider when trying to process lecture information as compared to textbook information. Similar to reading, you want to activate prior knowledge. In fact, activating prior knowledge for a lecture has obvious effects. But how do you activate prior knowledge for lectures? The following are effective ways to activate prior knowledge:

- Read your textbook (of course!)
- Review the syllabus to see how this lecture fits into the schedule of topics and the course
- Review previous lecture notes
- Review any professor PowerPoints provided

Professors ask you to read prior to lecture for real reasons. Think about any of your classes now, or even in high school. In any of these, was the vocabulary and information so unfamiliar that it felt like the professor was talking a different language? What was the result? This typically makes it more difficult to take accurate notes, and to stay on pace with the professor, especially if he or she is going quickly, or speaks with a heavy, unfamiliar accent. However, by carefully reading beforehand, you can gain familiarity with the vocabulary and some of the concepts, even if you do not quite understand the materials yet. As a result, you spend less time trying to identify or detect unfamiliar words and ideas, and more time trying to build comprehension. Think again about the unfamiliar passage you read before. Listening to this story in class and taking notes would feel very different, depending on whether or not you knew the topic beforehand. So step one is to activate prior knowledge.

Step two, as mentioned before, is to attend class. In class, pay close attention to your distractors and try to minimize them. Where should you sit so that you have focused attention? Many recommend sitting front row center, which may be helpful, but you are the best judge of what will work for you. While listening to lecture, take notes. Any of the structures described before, can work in lecture as well, including your own-designed structures. However, professors sometimes make it difficult to effectively use these structures. If your professor is going too fast, then try to get as much of the information into your notes as possible, even verbatim. And if you are having difficulty understanding the concepts, do not stop writing. Hopefully, your professor encourages students to ask questions, but if that is not the case, continue to write knowing you can revisit the information later (e.g., with peers, tutors, study group, one-on-one with professor, etc.).

> If your professor provides PowerPoints ahead of time, do you still need to attend class? Based on the ideas of information processing, what would be the advantage to attending? How could you use the PowerPoints?

Once the lecture is complete, there are several strategies that will help you to process the information more fully. These include:

- Reviewing with a peer immediately (or as soon as possible) after class to identify gaps, answer questions, etc.
- If writing lecture notes verbatim, treat these notes as a text and now rewrite notes as you would during reading (i.e., paraphrasing, examples, drawings, questions, etc.).
- Combine lecture and textbook notes into a cohesive whole.
- Write potential multiple choice and essay exam questions from the lecture and use them to review later.
- Create a graphic organizer that combines lecture and textbook notes.

Once these activities are complete, review your work prior to the next lecture, and begin the process again.

Encoding information from both your textbooks and lectures requires deliberate and intentional processes. However, by incorporating elaboration strategies throughout, you will maximize the return on your investment of time and effort.

MODULE 4.3 SUMMARY

- Active reading is a learning "how to learn" skill that can be taught and developed.
- Scheduling your reading and activating prior knowledge is helpful to set the stage for active reading strategies (the passage is about Christopher Columbus).

- Active reading incorporates elaboration strategies and takes advantage of distributed practice.
- Note-taking structures are an effective way to organize your notes and incorporate multiple elaboration strategies.
- Attending class has multiple benefits including increased course grades and GPA.
- Processing information for lectures is a similar process as to reading: activate prior knowledge, incorporate elaboration strategies, and take advantage of distributed practice.

KEY TERMS

- **Active Reading** – A reading approach that uses elaboration strategies to process read information into long-term memory.

REFERENCES

Bean, J. C. (2001). *Engaging ideas. The professor's guide to integrating writing, critical thinking, and active learning in the classroom* (1st ed.). San Francisco, CA: Jossey-Bass.

Credé, M., Roch, S. G., & Kieszczynka, U. M. (2010). Class attendance in college: A meta-analytic review of the relationship of class attendance with grades and student characteristics. *Review of Educational Research, 80*(2), 272–295.

Dooling, D. J., & Lachman, R. (1971). Effects of comprehension on retention of prose. *Journal of Experimental Psychology, 88*(2), 216–222.

Dubas, J. M., & Toledo, S. A. (2015). Active reading documents (ARDS): A tool to facilitate meaningful learning through reading. *College Teaching*, 63(1), 27–33.

Elbow, P. (1973). *Writing without teachers*. New York: Oxford University Press.

Elbow, P. (1986). *Embracing contraries: Explorations in learning and teaching*. New York: Oxford University Press.

Helms, J. W., & Helms, K. T. (2010). Note launchers. Promoting active reading of mathematics textbooks. *Journal of College Reading and Learning, 41*(1), 109–119.

Hill, K. M., Brözel, V. S., & Heiberger, G. A. (2014). Examining the delivery modes of metacognitive awareness and active reading lessons in a college nonmajors introductory biology course. *Journal of Microbiology & Biology Education, 15*(1), 5–12.

Jenne, F. H. (1973). Attendance and student proficiency change in a health science class. *Journal of School Health, 43,* 135–126.

Moore, R., Jensen, M., Hatch, J., Duranczyk, I., Staats, S., & Koch, L. (2003). Showing up: The importance of class attendance for academic success in introductory science courses. *American Biology Teacher, 65,* 325–329.

Paul, R. W. (1987). Dialogical thinking: Critical thought essential to the acquisition of rational knowledge and passions. In J. B. Baron & R. J. Sternberg (Eds.), *Teaching thinking skills: Theory and practice.* New York: Freeman.

Ramage, J. D., & Bean, J. C. (1995). *Writing arguments: A rhetoric with readings* (3rd ed.). Needham Heights, MA: Allyn & Bacon.

CASE STUDY

Desiree had always done very well in high school. To prepare for her high school exams, she would read her textbooks carefully and take notes. She would complete all of her assigned homework and she would use flashcards to help her with any vocabulary words. Right before exams, she would re-read her textbook and notes. These strategies worked well, and she was satisfied with her grades.

Desiree is now in college, and after her first round of exams, she is beginning to worry. She tried using the same approach as before, and has continued to use the same learning strategies; however, she earned less than 70% on each of her exams. She thought maybe she needed to read and review her text more, but there was so much material, this strategy just felt overwhelming and not very effective. She was starting to think, maybe college was too hard for her.

QUESTIONS

1. What are some reasons Desiree's learning strategies may no longer be effective at the college level?

2. What are potential approaches and learning strategies Desiree could use to help her encode, store and retrieve the information when needed?

3. Who are the people Desiree could easily reach out to for help?

1. Desiree is primarily using rehearsal strategies (e.g., reading, re-reading and flashcards). These strategies are less effective due to the volume of information given in the short amount of time at the college level, and as a result, Desiree is having difficulty learning.

2. Desiree should try to incorporate more elaboration strategies such as visual imagery (e.g., drawings and graphic organizers), working in a study group, creating her own examples and connections, writing practice exam questions, etc. She should also be using these same strategies when she is taking notes during reading and lecture.

3. Desiree could form a study group for each of her classes and have them meet on a weekly basis. She could also form partnerships with peers in each of her classes, who could review notes with her after each class. She could use campus tutors to help her discuss and apply any course information. She can also meet with her professors and ask questions she has formed from both the readings and lectures.

ADDITIONAL READINGS

Baddeley, A. (2003). Working memory: looking back and looking forward. *Nature Reviews Neuroscience, 4*(10), 829–839.

Cowan, N. (2008). What are the differences between long-term, short-term, and working memory? *Progress in Brain Research, 169,* 323–338.

Cukras, G. G. (2006). The investigation of study strategies that maximize learning forunderprepared students. *College Teaching, 54*(1), 194–197.

Elliot, A. J., McGregor, H. A., & Gable, S. (1999). Achievement goals, study strategies, and exam performance: A mediational analysis. *Journal of Educational Psychology, 91*(3), 549–563.

Ericsson, K. A. (2003). Exceptional memorizers: Made, not born. *Trends in Cognitive Sciences, 7*(6), 233–235.

Hershner, S. D., & Chervin, R. D. (2014). Causes and consequences of sleepiness among college students. *Nature and Science of Sleep, 6,* 73–84.

Karpicke, J. D., Butler, A. C., & Roediger III, H. L. (2009). Metacognitive strategies in student learning: Do students practice retrieval when they study on their own? *Memory, 17*(4), 471–479.

Karpicke, J. D., & Roediger, H. L. (2008). The critical importance of retrieval for learning. *Science, 319*(5865), 966–968.

Oberauer, K. (2002). Access to information in working memory: Exploring the focus of attention. *Journal of Experimental Psychology: Learning, Memory, and Cognition, 28*(3), 411–421.

Plant, E. A., Ericsson, K. A., Hill, L., & Asberg, K. (2005). Why study time does not predict grade point average across college students: Implications of deliberate practice for academic performance. *Contemporary Educational Psychology, 30*(1), 96–116.

Wissman, K. T., Rawson, K. A., & Pyc, M. A. (2012). How and when do students use flashcards? *Memory, 20*(6), 568–579.

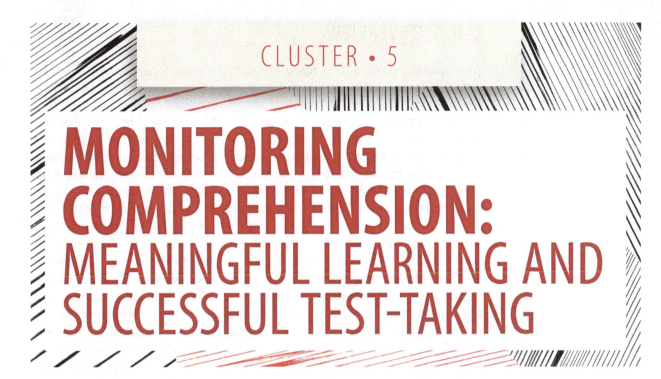

MONITORING COMPREHENSION:
MEANINGFUL LEARNING AND SUCCESSFUL TEST-TAKING

CASE STUDY

Joe was preparing for his first set of college exams. During the week before the exams, he re-read his textbook and his notes several times. He felt confident that he would do well, especially because he had always done pretty well on exams in the past. However, once he started to take his first exam, several things happened. As he was reading the items, he realized that they seemed familiar; however, he could not remember which of the answers were correct. So many of them seemed very similar, and he could not distinguish between them. He started becoming anxious. He also started noticing that other students were finishing, turning in their papers, zipping their backpacks, and leaving the room. He could feel his anxiety increasing and started thinking about how he might fail this exam, and potentially fail the course. Knowing that he needed to finish, he tried to focus on the remaining items; however, he felt his mind go blank.

QUESTIONS

1. What strategies could Joe have used during his preparation that would have helped him judge his readiness?

2. Are there ways in which Joe could have managed his anxiety during the exam that would have helped him to remember as much as possible?

CLUSTER OVERVIEW

As a student, learning is typically measured by some form of assessment. In school, this may be an exam, or perhaps a paper. Once outside of school, learning as a professional is still assessed in different ways. This assessment may be in the form of completing a job successfully, or being able to incorporate new software into your daily routine. As a student, the result of poor learning is usually a bad grade. As a professional, the consequences could be losing a promotion, or worse, losing your job. With so much at stake, people who *hope* they will do well are testing fate. Fortunately, there are ways to assess your level of understanding, so that you can adequately prepare prior to being evaluated, and feel confident about your future results. As other strategies described in this book, monitoring your comprehension is an intentional process. Although it is closely related to self-regulation (see Cluster 7), there are some distinctions that warrant a more detailed discussion. The first module will describe comprehension monitoring and helpful strategies including self-testing, active reading and listening, and the use of learning taxonomies. As the first module helps you in the preparation of exam situations, the second module provides you with strategies to maximize your performance during exams. These strategies include minimizing anxiety, predicting future exam items, and using appropriate test-taking strategies.

CLUSTER OBJECTIVES

- Outline the purpose and features of comprehension monitoring, and its relationship to self-testing, active reading and listening.
- Describe self-testing strategies that minimize illusions of knowing.
- Describe the role of learning taxonomies in the practice of comprehension monitoring and provide illustrative examples using Bloom's taxonomy.
- Describe the relationship between stress, anxiety, and performance.
- Identify strategies that will help minimize levels of anxiety.
- Describe strategies that will help predict exam items.
- Describe general and specific test-taking strategies related to successful exam performance.

COMPREHENSION MONITORING AND LEARNING TAXONOMIES

CLUSTER 5 OBJECTIVES COVERED IN THIS MODULE

☐ **OBJECTIVE:** Outline the purpose and features of comprehension monitoring, and its relationship to self-testing, active reading and listening.

☐ **OBJECTIVE:** Describe self-testing strategies that minimize illusions of knowing.

☐ **OBJECTIVE:** Describe the role of learning taxonomies in the practice of comprehension monitoring, and provide illustrative examples using Bloom's taxonomy.

WHAT IS COMPREHENSION MONITORING?

REFLECTION: How do you know what you know, and more importantly, what you don't know? Have you ever felt confident prior to taking an examination, only to be surprised by what you didn't know?

Few things are more important in the learning process than comprehension, or the ability to fully understand learned materials. In order to know whether or not something is well understood, one must actively and regularly monitor the learning process in order to detect and address gaps in knowledge. Therefore, *comprehension monitoring* is the ability to observe and assess the quality of one's understanding of learned materials. It is a skill that requires active decision-making, attention to detail, and intentionality in the learning process. It also promotes deep learning and critical thinking.

COMPREHENSION MONITORING:

The ability to observe and assess the quality of one's understanding of learned materials.

This idea is closely related to the concept of metacognition (see Cluster 7) insofar as both comprehension monitoring and metacognition entail a certain degree of self-awareness and self-observation. The difference is that metacognition consists of thinking about the process of thinking, whereas comprehension monitoring involves the *direct assessment* of knowledge acquisition. In this respect, the primary purpose of comprehension monitoring is to determine how complexly a given subject matter is understood (Pitts, 1983). In other words, how do you know when you know it?

All learners tend to acquire certain habits. When those habits lead to high levels of understanding, the process of comprehension monitoring ensures that the most effective strategies are being implemented. When those habits interfere with learning, comprehension monitoring becomes the tool for assessing the problematic strategy and determining what new course of action needs to be taken. When you pay close attention to how well you understand what you are learning, making changes to your study habits and learning goals becomes much easier. As a result, new learning strategies can be implemented that improve not only understanding, but retention and retrieval as well. That is to say, good comprehension monitoring skills can be a powerful learning tool in preparing for exams, and for overall career success.

There are several important aspects of comprehension monitoring, each of which requires an active approach to learning and studying. This module outlines strategies related to self-testing, active reading and listening, and the use of learning taxonomies to significantly improve learning outcomes.

ILLUSION OF KNOWING

Before discussing strategies, it is important to understand some of the challenges to comprehension monitoring. Unfortunately, learners of all ages have a tendency to be overconfident when assessing their level of knowledge in an area (Ormrod, 2004; Hacker, Bol, Horgan, & Rakow, 2000). This phenomenon has been called an illusion of knowing (Ormord, 2004) or illusion of competence (Koriat & Bjork, 2005). Both can lead to students making decisions to stop studying prematurely (Bjork, Dunlosky, & Kornell, 2012) or to incorrectly predict future performance on an exam (Hacker et al., 2000). Unfortunately, in Hacker et al.'s (2000) study of student exam prediction and performance, the researchers found that the most confident students were those who scored the lowest on their exams, "with overconfidence becoming greatly exaggerated the lower they scored" (p. 168).

To understand illusions of knowing, it is helpful to recognize how hindsight and foresight biases interfere with one's comprehension monitoring (Fischhoff, 1975; Koriat & Bjork, 2005). These biases are similar in that they tend to occur when studying and preparing for exams. Consider the following example:

> Min is studying for her psychology examination. As part of her exam preparation, she is re-reading her notes, textbook, and the unit objectives. As she is reading, she feels relieved because she recognizes the

What ineffective study habits have you acquired and how do you plan to address them?

ILLUSION OF KNOWING:
Overconfidence about the level of knowledge and understanding in an area.

vocabulary and the concepts. All of the information is familiar to her and she believes that she understands and knows all of the required material. She is also reviewing some sample multiple choice questions, and believes that she will be able to answer similar items on her exam. However, during her exam, she struggles throughout the exam and realizes that she knows very little of the information.

Min's example illustrates how hindsight and foresight biases can easily blind someone's ability to make an accurate judgment of their comprehension. Hindsight bias comes into play when Min is reading the information and believes, "yeah, I know it." It is "the tendency [students] have, once information is available, to think that [they] knew it all along" (Bjork et al., 2013, p. 423).

Foresight bias happens when Min views the example items and believes she can retrieve the information in the future and answer similar items. She primarily feels this way, because both the questions and answers are presented together while she studies.

Inherently, these problems occur because of the different contexts of studying and taking exams. While studying, information and answers are readily available, but during an exam, they *are not*. Fortunately, there are ways to mitigate these problems and to accurately assess your level of knowledge and avoid illusions of knowing. The first set of strategies involves self-testing.

HINDSIGHT BIAS:
The tendency for people to believe they already knew information, once the information is made available.

FORESIGHT BIAS:
The tendency for people to be overconfident in their ability to recall information in the future.

SELF-TESTING

Cluster 4 identified self-testing as an effective strategy to promote encoding and storage of information into long-term memory. In fact, research consistently provides evidence that self-testing (including taking practice tests) can be more effective than other types of preparation (Karpicke & Roediger, 2008; Roediger & Karpicke, 2006; Runquist, 1983). This includes self-testing in one format (e.g., free recall) and being formally assessed in another (e.g., multiple-choice; McDaniel, Howard, & Einstein, 2009; Vaughn & Rawson, 2011). However, self-testing is also critical to minimize hindsight and foresight bias, and to identify gaps in your knowledge.

Self-testing, as a general strategy, means recreating the testing context while studying. In other words, the learner creates multiple testing situations where the answers are not readily available or visible. Table 5.1.1 lists some examples of self-testing. Notice many of these are the elaboration strategies described in Cluster 4. Many will seem familiar and others only require a slight modification to assist in monitoring comprehension.

TABLE 5.1.1 SELF-TESTING STRATEGIES

Strategy	Description
Flashcards	Quiz yourself on vocabulary words, potential essay questions, practice problems, etc.
Unit Objectives	Use the unit objectives as a written exam. Without using your text or notes, write complete answers to each of the objectives.
3R: Read-Recite-Review	After reading a section in the textbook, set the book aside and then state *out loud* as much information as you can recall. Then read it again.
Graphic Organizers	Create a graphic organizer. Then recreate the organizer, but leave critical information blank throughout. Use the organizer to quiz yourself on the information.
Create Exam Items	Create practice multiple-choice and essay exam items, and then answer them. Cluster 4 also described using study groups to create practice exams.
Textbook Resources	Use any textbook or online practices to quiz yourself on the content.
Teach Someone Else	When teaching someone else, you should be able to give clear explanations, as well as examples that illustrate your points.

These strategies can be used during specific exam preparation, but they can also be used throughout the learning process. Consider incorporating comprehension monitoring strategies in every study session. Not only will the strategies promote deeper processing, but they will also help you to identify further areas of study during your next scheduled session. Later in the module, a taxonomy useful to self-testing will be described in more detail.

ACTIVE READING AND LISTENING SKILLS

Being an active learner means finding ways to elevate your interest in the learning process. The most salient areas in which this can be activated are also the most basic: reading and listening. As described in Cluster 4, shifting from a passive to an active approach when reading texts and listening to lectures is one of the most fundamental methods for improving learning outcomes. Active reading and listening are also a prerequisite for comprehension monitoring. If you intend to monitor your understanding, then it is vital that you be actively engaged in the process of consuming raw information. The differences between active and passive states of learning are outlined below, and basic tips for becoming an active reader and listener are provided.

ACTIVE READING

Understanding the difference between passive reading and active reading is an essential component of comprehension monitoring. Passive reading happens when a student does not connect with the materials due to feeling rushed (e.g., quickly reading chapters for the first time right before an exam), disinterested (e.g., reading because it is required but without any interest in the material), or otherwise preoccupied (e.g., texting or watching television while reading). As described previously, much of the information from the text is quickly forgotten, even if all of the words have technically been read.

Can you identify three causes of passive reading in your own experience?

In addition to the active reading strategies described in Cluster 4, comprehension monitoring is further enhanced when learners pause to reflect on certain ideas, cross-check information, or question their understanding. Passive reading occurs when the learner reads the passage, section, or chapter from beginning to end without hesitation and therefore, feels that the reading is complete. Although the reading has technically been done, most students will not be able to retain or later recall important ideas from the text. Information that is not consciously processed in a deep and meaningful way cannot be readily assimilated by the mind. Only bits and pieces of the text will be remembered when reading passively, meaning that a period of study time has been essentially wasted using an ineffective approach.

Active reading takes more time and energy than passive reading, because it requires decision-making and attention to detail. In other words, it requires comprehension monitoring. Active readers formulate questions, evaluate pre-established goals, integrate prior knowledge, make predictions, and construct meaning using a selective reading process (Duke & Pearson, 2008). Although this might seem time-consuming to some students, shifting to an active reading process might actually be a time saver when you consider how much time can be spent passively reading texts without retaining any of the information. Precious energy is wasted when chapters have to be read multiple times because the information was not retained during an initial, passive reading attempt. Alternatively, the process of active reading is not difficult, significantly improves memory retention, and makes it far easier to retrieve and recall information for exams. The following are some additional strategies to monitor comprehension while reading.

- Use textbook headers to generate questions. After reading, pause to see if you can answer the questions (preferably in writing or reciting out loud).
- Similarly, use headers to pause and predict what the section will be about. After reading, compare your prediction with the information that was actually included.
- Create reading goals. For example, use any unit objectives given by your professor, and seek the information that answers these objectives.
- To incorporate prior knowledge, try to connect previous information included in your lecture and textbook notes to the new information you are reading.
- After reading a section, stop and generate any questions that could be answered the next time you attend a lecture.

ACTIVE LISTENING:

Listening attentively to another person with the intention of understanding the entire message beyond the words being spoken.

Think of a time when someone was genuinely listening to you. How was this experience different from other experiences in which you felt that someone was not entirely listening?

ACTIVE LISTENING

There is a significant difference between passive listening and active listening in classroom environments. Passive listening is simply hearing the words spoken during a lecture. It is passive because hearing is an automatic process (similar to reading) that requires little engagement or conscious thought. Active listening, on the other hand, is an effortful process of finding meaning and drawing connections between the ideas presented in a lecture. It not only requires concentration and engagement with the learning materials, but also a desire to grasp the broader meaning of what is being taught.

Consider the experience of listening to background music, compared to analyzing the structure and lyrics of a song. Background music is not consciously processed and as a result, the nuances of a song can be easily overlooked. At times, you may not even know a particular song has been playing in the background if your attention is fully focused elsewhere. However, the musical experience is completely different when your intention is to listen closely to a new song. You can hear the distinct instruments, feel the rhythm of the bassline, and become enraptured by the story being told. You might even draw connections between the lyrics and your life experiences, actively imagining or remembering events that are personally significant. The power of music exposes the real value of active listening: it makes experiences meaningful.

By applying the skill of active listening in the classroom, students have an opportunity to hear and connect with the nuanced stories of human knowledge. Whether through the use of instruments or lyrics, a song tells the story of how a musician perceives and experiences the world. Similarly, the instructor of a college classroom tells the aggregated story of countless academic minds who have labored through history to question, understand, create, and explain the various workings of the world. There can be a lyrical quality to knowledge when an idea is genuinely comprehended. However, understanding the larger tapestry of human insights in a field of study requires a desire to engage with the content and see the bigger picture.

Active listening is a crucial part of the learning process. It requires going beyond the words of a lecture to find the underlying message in what is spoken. It also involves paying attention to how those ideas connect with other concepts in a relevant and meaningful way. Finally, it entails closely monitoring your understanding in order to find knowledge gaps and to ask questions that fill those gaps. However, as mentioned in Cluster 4, sometimes it is challenging to pause and make connections due to the speed at which your professor is talking. Consider some note-taking strategies that will highlight areas that you specifically want to revisit. Maybe it is simply placing a question mark in the margins, or perhaps you use some symbol to show potential connection. Maybe you use different colored highlights to cue specific meanings. Even when moving quickly, create methods that will allow you to identify areas where there are potential gaps or areas for deeper consideration. Once the lecture is over, the other strategies described in Cluster 4 can be very helpful in monitoring your comprehension (i.e., sharing notes with a peer to identify gaps and questions, paraphrasing your lecture notes and adding connections, examples, etc.).

Of course, none of this is possible when a student is bored or disinterested; and yet the responsibility for classroom engagement lies squarely in the hands of college students. Fortunately, entering lectures with specific goals for learning, trying to gain as much information as possible, and using specific note-taking strategies that keep you actively engaged, can give you purpose and help conquer boredom.

LEARNING TAXONOMIES

Is it possible to gauge your *level* of understanding? For example, given the term "electoral college," what does it mean to be able to recall its definition, versus being able to provide justification for its use in the United States? Learning taxonomies are a valuable tool to monitor your comprehension, such that you acquire deep levels of understanding, as well as meet the expectations of your professors. A taxonomy is a classification system used to clarify and simplify a complex set of processes. In the realm of education, a number of such classification systems have been developed to help teachers and learners recognize the various types, levels, or stages of learning and understanding. As a result, these learning taxonomies are useful for monitoring comprehension and choosing effective study strategies. They can be incorporated into the active reading or studying process by posing questions used to gauge level of understanding, thereby serving as clear markers for the genuine and lasting comprehension of learning materials.

LEARNING TAXONOMY: A classification system used to clarify and define the different levels of human knowledge and understanding.

The most widely acclaimed learning classification system is Bloom's taxonomy, developed by an educational psychology committee that was chaired by Benjamin Bloom in the early 1950s. It has long served as the primary educational tool for assessing learning outcomes and building new learning approaches. Due to later concerns about its taxonomic structure, a revised version was created to strengthen its basic conceptual foundation.

BLOOM'S TAXONOMY

The original taxonomy by Bloom et al. (1956) was crafted over the course of five years, in order to build a common language of learning among educators. It has been used by teachers, researchers, administrators, and learners as the principal learning framework for the last 60 years. Bloom's taxonomy is composed of three major domains: cognitive, affective, and psychomotor. In terms of comprehension monitoring, only the cognitive domain is relevant and will be attended to exclusively. To read more about the affective and psychomotor domains, please reference the *Additional Readings* section at the end of this cluster.

Although used for many years, researchers and educators voiced concerns about the structure of Bloom's original taxonomy; therefore, a new committee was organized to address these issues (Krathwohl, 2002). A complete explanation for why the revisions were considered necessary is beyond the scope of this particular text.

The revised Bloom's taxonomy maintains the spirit of the original while incorporating the results of research conducted over many years since the original was developed (Pickard, 2007). The following terms reflect a shift in language used to describe each category, and provide a more clear framework for applying them in the learning process. Sample self-testing questions that could be used to monitor comprehension in each category are provided for illustrative purposes.

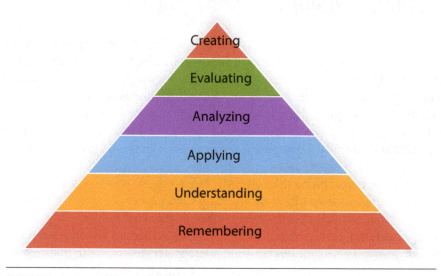

FIGURE 5.1.1: Revised Bloom's Taxonomy   *Source: Angela Vaughan and Brett Wilkinson*

- *Remembering*: The ability to memorize and recall learned materials such as terms, facts, basic concepts, and general theories. This category involves knowledge of specifics, and is the foundation for all subsequent learning processes.
  - When did the French Revolution begin?
  - What is the definition of comprehension monitoring?
  - What are the six categories of the original Bloom's taxonomy?
- *Understanding*: The ability to use remembered learning materials in order to compare, interpret, describe, and explain ideas or relationships between ideas. This category involves a deeper grasp of how factual information is contextual, or how it is related to other ideas in a more complex way.
  - Explain the circumstances that led to the French Revolution.
  - What is the relationship between comprehension monitoring and active reading?
  - How does the original Bloom's taxonomy differ from the revised version?

- *Applying*: The ability to utilize remembered and understood knowledge in order to solve problems or implement learning materials in concrete situations. This category involves the application of prior knowledge in thoughtful and meaningful ways.

  - What lessons from the French Revolution can be applied to the world today?
  - What question might you ask to determine if you are using active reading strategies?
  - How would you use Bloom's taxonomy to improve your study habits?

- *Analyzing*: The ability to examine and distinguish between the separate parts of a learning material in order to better understand its structure. This category involves breaking down concepts that are part of a whole, and using inferences to explain how those parts are interrelated.

  - Explain how the combination of political, economic, and socio-cultural forces led to the French Revolution.
  - Identify and explain how the six categories of Bloom's taxonomy are used to enhance learning outcomes.
  - Compare the original Bloom's taxonomy to the revised version and explain the relative benefits of the latter.

- *Evaluating*: The ability to make informed judgments about information, develop critiques or opinions, and provide recommendations for advancements in knowledge. This category involves using all of the previous categories to construct a thoughtful, complex, and personal evaluation of learned materials.

  - Argue for or against Edmund Burke's suggestion that the French Revolution was a direct consequence of ideals set forth by philosophers of the French Enlightenment.
  - Assess the structure of the revised Bloom's taxonomy and discuss whether or not it is a helpful contribution to the field of educational psychology. Provide justification for your stated position.

- *Creating*: The ability to combine learning elements together into a coherent structure or whole, or to reorganize learning elements in a new and original way. This category involves the creation of new ideas, patterns, or solutions based on knowledge accrued across all previous categories, and is regarded as the most complex and abstract mental function.

  - Formulate a new explanation for the causes of the French Revolution.
  - Create a new technique for the implementation of active reading strategies.
  - Propose a modified learning taxonomy with new approaches to learning acquisition.

FINAL THOUGHTS ON COMPREHENSION MONITORING

Can you identify a subject area in which you might like to become a highly proficient and learned professional?

Learning taxonomies are meant to be used as tool for evaluating how comprehensively certain materials have been learned. By identifying personal level of understanding, it becomes far easier to address knowledge gaps in a systematic way. Otherwise, you are left to assume just how well the material is really understood. Growing your comprehension requires active monitoring as well as the ongoing use of metacognitive strategies (see Cluster 7). Once missing knowledge is recognized, learning strategies can be thoughtfully selected that address the gap. You can then move towards more complex levels of thought and higher levels of educational attainment.

The larger purpose of learning taxonomies and comprehension monitoring strategies alike, is to enhance depth of understanding and improve critical thinking. As discussed throughout this book, solid transferrable learning skills are the supreme measure of self-regulated learning. Learning taxonomies provide a classification system by which, one can determine just how adept a learner is, when it comes to harnessing transferrable skills. Additionally, comprehension monitoring is a fundamental component of self-regulated learning; an underlying skill that will serve you well throughout life.

Becoming a more intentional learner takes practice and a willingness to test out new learning methods. Try applying some of the ideas from this module in your next study session to measure your comprehension as you prepare for upcoming exams. When using active reading strategies during your next study session, or active listening strategies during an upcoming lecture, remember to formulate thoughtful goals and to seek the bigger picture. You will likely be surprised by how much more interesting the materials become when you do! The next module focuses on more practical aspects of exam preparation, including strategies to overcome poor test-taking skills and test anxiety.

MODULE 5.1 SUMMARY

- Comprehension monitoring involves the observation and assessment of how well, one understands learned materials.
- Hindsight and foresight biases contribute to students' illusion of knowing.
- Self-testing is an effective method to minimize biases and overconfidence.
- Active reading is an intentional comprehension monitoring process that can be enacted using multiple strategies.
- Active listening is an intentional comprehension monitoring process that involves seeking to connect ideas to larger concepts in a meaningful way.

- The revised Bloom's learning taxonomy includes six categories (remembering, understanding, applying, analyzing, evaluating, and creating).

KEY TERMS

- **Active Listening** – Listening attentively to another person with the intention of understanding the entire message beyond the words being spoken.
- **Comprehension Monitoring** – The ability to observe and assess the quality of one's understanding of learned materials.
- **Foresight Bias** – The tendency for people to be overconfident in their ability to recall information in the future.
- **Hindsight Bias** – The tendency for people to believe they already knew information, once the information is made available.
- **Illusion of Knowing** – Overconfidence about the level of knowledge and understanding in an area.

REFERENCES

Bjork, R. A., Dunlosky, J., & Kornell, N. (2013). Self-regulated learning: Beliefs, techniques, and illusions. *Annual Review of Psychology, 64*, 417–444.

Bloom, B., Englehart, M., Furst, E., Hill, W., & Krathwohl, D. (1956). *Taxonomy of educational objectives: The classification of educational goals.* New York: McKay.

Duke, N. K., & Pearson, P. D. (2008). Effective practices for developing reading comprehension. *The Journal of Education, 189*(1/2), 107–122.

Fischhoff, B. (1975). Hindsight ≠ foresight: The effect of outcome knowledge on judgment under uncertainty. *Journal of Experimental Psychology: Human Perception and Performance, 1*(3), 288–299.

Hacker, D. J., Bol, L., Horgan, D. D., & Rakow, E. A. (2000). Test prediction and performance in a classroom context. *Journal of Educational Psychology, 92*(1), 160 –170.

Karpicke, J. D., & Roediger, H. L., III. (2008). The critical importance of retrieval for learning. *Science, 319*, 966–968.

Koriat, A., & Bjork, R. A. (2005). Illusions of competence in monitoring one's knowledge during study. *Journal of Experimental Psychology: Learning, Memory, and Cognition, 31*(2), 187–194.

Krathwohl, D. R. (2002). A revision of Bloom's taxonomy: An overview. *Theory into Practice, 41*(4), 212–218.

McDaniel, M. A., Howard, D. C., & Einstein, G. O. (2009). The read-recite-review study strategy: Effective and portable. *Psychological Science, 20*, 516–522.

Myers, M. (1981). Comprehension monitoring, memory, and study strategies of good and poor readers. *Journal of Literacy Research, 13*(1), 5–22.

Ormrod, J. E. (2004). *Human learning* (4th ed.). Columbus, Ohio: Prentice Hall.

Pickard, M. J. (2007). The new Bloom's taxonomy: An overview for family and consumer sciences. *Journal of Family and Consumer Sciences Education, 25*(1), 45–55.

Pitts, M. (1983). Comprehension monitoring: Definition and practice. *Journal of Reading, 26*(6), 516–523.

Robinson, F. P. (1946). *Effective study.* New York: Harper & Row.

Roediger, H. L., III, & Karpicke, J. D. (2006). The power of testing memory: Basic research and implications for educational practice. *Perspectives on Psychological Science, 1*, 181–210.

Runquist, W. N. (1983). Some effects of remembering on forgetting. *Memory & Cognition, 11*, 641–650.

Vaughn, K. E., & Rawson, K. A. (2011). Diagnosing criterion level effects on memory: What aspects of memory are enhanced by repeated retrieval? *Psychological Science, 22*, 1127–1131.

MAXIMIZING EXAM PERFORMANCE

CLUSTER 5 OBJECTIVES COVERED IN THIS MODULE

☐ **OBJECTIVE:** Describe the relationship between stress, anxiety and performance.

☐ **OBJECTIVE:** Identify strategies that will help minimize levels of anxiety.

☐ **OBJECTIVE:** Describe strategies that will help predict exam items.

☐ **OBJECTIVE:** Describe general and specific test-taking strategies related to successful exam performance.

OVERVIEW

The previous module outlined methods for promoting deep learning and critical thinking through the use of comprehension monitoring. Although careful preparation and monitoring are the best strategies to earn the exam grades you want, other factors can sometimes interfere. These factors include anxiety, misguided studying (i.e., studying the wrong content), and poor test-taking skills. Therefore, this module will provide additional strategies to optimize your exam performance and to ensure that you can fully enact the knowledge and understanding that you worked so hard to gain.

ANXIETY

REFLECTION: Are there times when you feel that text anxiety interferes with your ability to perform your best?

Anxiety can prevent learners from performing at their best, not only during exams, but also throughout the learning process. This module will first describe how anxiety relates to information processing and performance, and then offer some strategies to minimize its effects. Although it is likely that you have personal experiences in which anxiety seemed to decrease your performance, research has also consistently shown the same anxiety-related effects for learners at all levels (Schwarzer, 1990). Studies revealed that higher levels of anxiety are related to significantly lower GPAs (Chapell et al., 2005), and lower exam scores (Hsieh, Sullivan, Sass, & Guerra, 2012; Schwarzer, 1990). However, there is a distinct difference between anxiety and stress. Anxiety is the result of high levels of stress, but not all stress (sometimes expressed as arousal) is negative. It should seem clear that moderate levels of stress can help propel you to action, whereas the complete absence of stress means you are either asleep, or dead! Hebb (1955) described the relationship between performance and arousal, in terms of optimal and suboptimal ranges (see the adapted version in Figure 5.2.1).

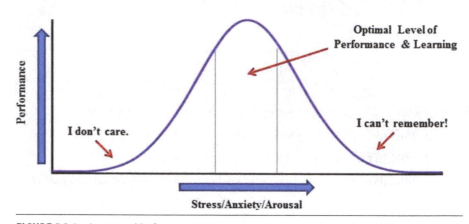

FIGURE 5.2.1: Anxiety and Performance   *Adapted from Herb (1955, p. 250)*

In addition to feelings of panic, or even paralysis, high levels of anxiety can interfere with the cognitive functions of working memory (Chen & Chang, 2009). Recall in Cluster 4 that working memory acts as the central executive, and not only encodes and stores information, but also retrieves information from long-term memory to produce appropriate responses. With high levels of anxiety, these functions are overloaded. You may have experienced this, when you take an exam and your mind feels like it has gone "blank." The pivotal question is this: how can you regulate a level of stress that promotes optimal performance and learning?

PERCEPTIONS OF STRESS

Recent research indicates that some of the negative outcomes of stress are partially based on *one's perception* of the effects (Jamieson, Nock, & Mendes, 2012; Keller et al., 2012). In other words, if you believe stress is bad for you, then you are more likely to experience its negative effects and suffer from decreased cognitive performance. In fact, a study conducted by Keller et al. (2012) provides evidence that a negative perception of stress corresponds with a 43% increased risk of premature death! Fortunately, there is also evidence that the opposite can be true. If you believe that stress provides benefits, then you are likely to have more positive experiences and outcomes. What can this look like? To change your perception, consider that certain levels of stress are an indication that you care and want to do well. Also, remind yourself that moderate stress levels tend to improve alertness, concentration, and memory (Sapolsky, 2004). Gaining awareness of your perception of stress is a powerful strategy. Gaining awareness of your triggers is also important.

RECOGNIZING TRIGGERS

Most events, on their own, in a person's daily life, are not stressful. Consider how some people love to speak in public and do very well with this task. Now, think of others who would rather do anything else, other than speaking publicly because it makes them feel ill. Is public speaking, by its very nature, a stressful event? It depends on the individual's perception of the event. Similarly, your perception of stress and its general effects can be an insight into your thoughts about, or interpretations of a particular event. Your interpretations are important because they lead to both emotional and physiological feelings that can interfere with your concentration and performance. Do the thoughts and feelings in Table 5.2.1 seem familiar?

INTERNAL TRIGGERS:
Negative thoughts leading to increased feelings of anxiety that could potentially interfere with performance.

TABLE 5.2.1 INTERNAL TRIGGERS

I find myself thinking...	I find myself feeling...	I am physically feeling...
• The other students must be smarter than me. • I'll fail this task, and then I'll fail the course. • I can't and won't graduate from college. • What's the point? • There is not enough time to finish this exam. • It doesn't matter how much I studied, I won't do well. • Why does this teacher give more exams than papers? • Because of these racing thoughts in my head, I can't concentrate.	• Concerned • Alarmed • Depressed • Saddened • Mad • Annoyed • Frustrated • Anxious	• Racing heart • Rapid breathing • Perspiration • Knots in the stomach • Change in appetite • Shaking/trembling • Muscle aches • Numbness/tingling • Headaches • Nausea • Dizziness • Too hot or too cold • Like crying • Clammy hands • Teeth grinding
My negative thoughts:	**My negative feelings:**	**My negative physical feelings:**

If so, what can you do? Once a negative thought enters your mind, *stop* the negative self-talk and analyze what you are thinking. Is the thought a true statement? Consider the following situations:

Laura was getting ready to take her Calculus mid-term exam. She had been studying hard but started feeling really nervous about two weeks before the exam. By the morning of the exam, all Laura could think about, was how she had to do well and if she failed, she would fail the class entirely. These thoughts continued to escalate and became increasingly irrational, eventually persuading Laura to fear that she might actually fail all of her classes and lose her scholarship. She was so consumed by anxiety that she "froze" during the exam and could not recall the necessary information.

Now consider Flora:

Flora was also getting ready to take her Calculus mid-term exam. She had been studying and started to feel nervous because the material was much more difficult than she had anticipated; however, she also thought about how hard she was working, how carefully she had planned her preparation, and how effectively she used the resources available to her (e.g., tutoring and her professor). As a result, she started to get excited about the opportunity to "prove" what she had learned. She knew she belonged in college and was ready to take on the challenges. Anyone could do easy work; she wanted to show that she could do what was challenging!

What are some positive messages and self-talk that you can tell yourself about, when negative thoughts start to happen?

The difference in self-talk in each example is evident. For Laura, negative thoughts led to real cognitive and physiological consequences. For Flora, the challenge was welcomed. As a result, Flora was able to retrieve the information she needed and effectively shared her knowledge and understanding.

Everything discussed so far, has been related to internal triggers. What about external triggers? What are some of the environmental conditions that can become a distraction and lead to additional stress and anxiety? Consider Table 5.2.2.

EXTERNAL TRIGGERS:
Outside sights and sounds that could increase levels of anxiety and potentially interfere with performance.

TABLE 5.2.2 EXTERNAL TRIGGERS	
Visual Triggers: The sight of…	**Auditory Triggers: The sound of…**
• Students turning in their tests	• Pencils dropping on the table
• The room becoming empty	• Students zipping their backpacks
• People turning the pages of their exams	• Desks moving
• The hands of the clock moving	• Clocks ticking
	• The door opening and closing as people leave
	• People outside the classroom
My visual triggers:	**My auditory triggers:**

Possible Solutions:
• Choose your seat wisely:
  • What seat might be exposed to the least amount of distractions?
  • Perhaps sitting in the front might prevent you from scanning the room for distractions.
  • Sitting away from a window might be wise for those who feel they are easily distracted.
• Avoid the temptation to look up often. Stay focused on the exam in front of you.
	Possible Solutions:
	• Drown out the sound by sitting near a noisy fan or vent.
	• Use ear plugs.
	• Ask the instructor if you can listen to music while taking your exam.

Strategies that will work for you:	**Strategies that will work for you:**

OTHER STRATEGIES

Gaining awareness of your perception and triggers should provide some relief; however, there are other specific strategies that will allow you to take control and minimize some of the effects of stress and anxiety. The following test-taking strategies are important in general, but can also help specifically target and reduce anxiety.

- Get a good night's sleep and eat a proper meal prior to the exam. Give yourself the opportunity to be in peak performance, mentally and physically.

- Physical activity can help burn off adrenaline. If possible, build in time to do a physical activity for at least 10 minutes before your exam (however, do not do anything too strenuous that will lead to fatigue). This physical activity can help the body process the chemical release of adrenaline you might be experiencing.

- Avoid extra amounts of caffeine and sugar, on and around the day of the exam, as these substances will naturally raise your arousal, which can look and feel like anxiety.

- Share your exam anxiety issues with your instructor (but not an hour before an exam!). The instructor may be willing to explore options such as taking the exam in the instructor's office, or being allowed a break during the exam. Just sharing your issue with your instructor may provide some relief.

- No last minute cramming! Create a schedule for allotted exam studying times and stick to it. Effective preparation will also help you build confidence, and increase your positive self-talk, if you start to feel nervous.

- Avoid excessive socializing and the consumption of alcohol or drugs during the critical days before an exam.

- Organize all of your materials for the exam the night before (e.g., pencils, blue books, note cards, etc.). You do not want to add to your stress levels because you forgot to bring exam materials.

- Get to the exam on time, but not too early. Arriving too early may cause your anxiety to balloon.

- Avoid speaking with fellow students who are not prepared, or who express negativity. Be cautious of talking with other students about the exam material (e.g., they may have a different interpretation of the material information) just before going into the exam, especially if this situation has made you nervous or confused in the past.

- If you have a disability, work with the Disability Support Services office on your campus. There are likely accommodations that will allow you to take your exam in an environment that is free from distractions.

- Because you will likely have a jolt of adrenaline at the onset of the exam, start by answering the questions you feel confident about. You will benefit in two ways from this strategy. Given some time, your brain will eventually recover from the adrenaline rush and you will be able to slow down, and tackle the more complicated questions. You will also create confidence and a positive momentum for moving through the rest of the exam.

- During the exam, give yourself permission to worry about the consequences of any outcomes later. This does not mean that you do not care about the outcomes. It just means that you will focus on your exam now, and handle anything else later.

- If, after incorporating these strategies, you continue to experience high levels of anxiety that severely interfere with your performance, seek out someone (e.g., advisors at the campus counseling center) who can help and support you. These professionals can help you with strategies to calm your mind, as well as assist you with facing personal stressors that may be contributing to your anxiety.

Moderate amounts of stress are beneficial, and reflect that you care about what you are doing. However, if you have struggled in the past, be as intentional about your approach to stress management as you are in any other area of learning. Over time and with practice, you will acquire coping skills and self-awareness to manage your stress, reduce your anxiety, and increase your effectiveness under pressure. These skills will allow you to be at your most effective self during exams.

PREDICTING EXAM QUESTIONS

REFLECTION: Have you ever taken an exam and realized that you did not study the "right" information?

Deep learning and getting the most out of your education means much more than answering questions on an exam; however, exam performances are typically the primary tool used to measure your knowledge and understanding. Therefore, how do you know what the professor will include on an exam? First and foremost, attending class will help you gain some understanding of your professor's focus. Also, any materials that your professors share, such as unit objectives and study guides, will be valuable. Use these, and when self-testing, treat them as an exam. This means *writing* your responses to unit objectives or study guide questions, rather than just reading them and saying to yourself, "Yeah, I know that!" (see Module 5.1). As described earlier, this is critical to avoiding the "illusion of knowing" and identifying any gaps in your knowledge.

In addition to these resources, you can use your first exam as an essential source for predicting future exam questions. Most professors do not let you keep your exam and may only let you briefly review it; however, professors also tend to be predictable when designing their exams. As a result, your first exam can provide helpful information. The following outlines the steps for taking advantage of this information:

Step 1—Immediately after the exam, write down everything you can remember.

- Exam questions, concepts, topics, etc.
- Areas you feel you did well
- Areas where you may have struggled, including questions that you were not expecting

Step 2—Find the information.

- Take the information from step 1 and find it in your class resources (e.g., lecture notes, PowerPoints, textbook, homework, etc.). If you cannot find the information, it would also be helpful to visit with your professor to try and gain some understanding of his or her expectations.
  - Textbook
    - Was the information pulled from the text, bolded vocabulary, summaries, chapter reviews, etc.?
  - Lecture
    - Was the information in your lecture notes?
    - Do you remember hearing the information, but did not include it in your notes?
    - Did the professor clearly emphasize this particular topic?
  - PowerPoints
    - Was the information included in the lecture PowerPoints?
    - Were these PowerPoints available to you before or after class?
  - Homework
    - Were exam problems similar to assigned problems?
    - Were there other suggested problems that would have been helpful?
  - Study Guides
    - Were most of the topics included on the study guide, or was there information on the exam that was not included?

Step 3—Identify any patterns.

- Does your professor pull more items from a particular source, or does he or she use all of them equally?
- Did you do better with information from a particular source?
- Did you do worse with information from a particular source?
  - Was this a result of less studying with a particular source, or did you struggle with understanding information from that source?

- Did you feel confident about some information, but then got it wrong on the exam?
    - Do you know why this occurred? (You may need to visit with your professor to identify areas of misunderstanding.)
- Are there any other patterns?

Although ongoing, consistent preparation is your single best strategy, predicting future exam questions can help you prioritize and build confidence.

TAKING THE EXAM

You have completed your preparation and incorporated the strategies listed earlier (e.g., not too much caffeine, avoiding negative students, etc.) and you are now ready to take the exam. The following will discuss some general strategies, as well as more specific strategies for particular types of exams (i.e., multiple choice, open book, etc.). There are also strategies that are helpful when you are unsure of your response and have to use "testwise" skills.

GENERAL STRATEGIES

- When you receive your exam paper, write your name on it!
- Write down any formulas or other memory cues on the backside of your exam paper or available scratch paper, immediately upon receiving the exam.
- Then, preview the exam. Make sure you have all of the pages and the numbers are sequential.
- When previewing, see how many items there are, how much they are worth, and the different types that are included.
- Take a moment to plan your time. If the essay question is worth 50% of your exam, you will want to make sure you give yourself enough time to complete it. If your exam is for a duration of 60 minutes and you have 60 multiple choice items, know that you are budgeting about a minute per item.
- Read all of the directions. You want to make sure you understand your professor's expectations (e.g., deducting points for wrong answers; expectations for rounding math answers, etc.).
- Answer the easy items first. This builds confidence, helps to minimize initial anxiety and allows you to earn all points possible. With this, be sure you leave time for items that are worth a significant amount of points, regardless of ease or difficulty.
- Mark the items that you skip so that you do not miss any of these items when reviewing your exam (and be careful to skip that bubble and continue sequentially if answering on a scantron sheet—this can throw off the answers to the rest of your exam!).

- When you are unsure of an answer, skip the item and pay attention to other items on the exam for potential relevant information. Sometimes, the information you need is given (or inferred) in another item. Reading other items may also trigger some information in your memory.

- Change answers only when you remember something new, unless you made a careless mistake, or if another item on the exam provides needed information. Second-guessing yourself can often lead to changing correct answers to incorrect answers, and increase test anxiety.

- Use your time. Carefully review your exam when you are done, and check for any mistakes. When taking a multiple choice exam, compare your answers circled on the exam to answers filled in on the scantron to avoid costly mistakes.

MULTIPLE CHOICE ITEMS

Many of these are general approaches to multiple choice items, and some are useful when you have to make an "educated" guess.

- Carefully read the directions. Some exams may want you to choose all of the correct answers.

- As you read the question, underline key terms.

- Watch the meaning of sentences containing double negatives. Cross out both negatives and then answer the question.

- Do not read anything into or out of the question. Make sure you restrict your response only to the topic at hand. Do not infer reasons—go with what is stated in the question.

- For long questions, break up the question into smaller parts. Sometimes, long questions are hard to keep up with. Read slowly, sentence by sentence, and make sure you understand each part, rather than focusing on the question as a whole. It may help to cover part of the stem or some of the options with your hand, so you can focus better.

- It is often better to cover up the options while you read the question. Once you have read the question, think of the correct answer first, then uncover the options and find your response(s) among them.

- Read each possible option individually and decide on the correctness of each. Students often become stressed when they see terms such as "all of the above" or "none of the above," and try to read all of the responses together.

- Read all of the responses before making a selection.

- Eliminate and cross off any answers you know are not correct.

- When you do not know the correct response, compare each option with the stem and analyze how each is different. One response may have something that others do not have.

- If unsure, select the response that seems to contain more information, or is more inclusive.

- If you are guessing between two responses, avoid options containing words such as "none," "all," "always," and "never." Choices using "some" or "often" are more likely to be correct.

- If two options are identical, they are both wrong, unless there is a choice that includes both options.

- Examine opposites carefully: one is definitely incorrect, and one is likely to be correct.

- Explain answers in the margins, especially when you feel like there are "two" best answers. Some professors may give credit or partial credit after seeing your thought process surrounding an answer.

- Choose "all of the above" when two or more choices are definitely correct. However, only one response has to be wrong for this choice to be incorrect.

- Try to focus on each question in turn. Do not worry about one question while trying to answer another. You might even want to cover up all of the other questions besides the one you are working on.

- When absolutely guessing, select the middle choice or the longest response.

ACTIVITY 5.2.1

Using only your testwise skills, answer the following multiple choice questions:

1. In the readings, Smith described a number of problems with the SNM theory. The most important of these was:
   a. Its explanation was very clear
   b. It easily predicted other issues
   c. It provided answers to some troubling questions
   d. It is inconsistent with BAC's theory

2. When comparing TIJ and PAF, Miller's experiments found that:
   a. TIJ is easier
   b. PAF is easier
   c. PAF is more difficult
   d. Both (a) and (b)
   e. Both (b) and (c)

Source: Adapted from http://www.lacitycollege.edu/services/learningskills/mctest.html

How easy was it to answer these questions? What were the clues that you used to select the correct response? In question 1, notice that the question asked for a "problem." The only response that appears to include a problem is response (d). Without knowing anything else about the topic, you should be able to read carefully and select the right answer. Question 2 is a matter of reading the choices carefully and eliminating them. Notice that choices (a) and (c) mean the same thing, so neither of these can be correct. Choice (d) includes conflicting information (i.e., they both cannot be easier). Choice (e) includes opposite information, so it cannot be correct. Once you eliminate each of these choices, the only remaining response is (b).

TRUE/FALSE ITEMS

- Look for qualifiers. "All," "only," "never," and "always" are usually false. "Generally," "often," "usually," and "sometimes" are almost always true.

- Every part of a true statement must be true. If any one part of the sentence is false, the whole sentence is false despite many other true statements.

- Negatives are confusing. If the question contains negatives, like "no," "not," "cannot," circle the negative and read the sentence that remains. Decide whether that sentence is true or false. If it is true, the opposite or negative is usually false.

ESSAY EXAMS

With essay exams, it is helpful to answer practice essay questions beforehand, to gain skills with organizing your responses, responding with clarity, and completing an essay within a time limit.

- Read all of the essay questions.
- If you have a choice of answering select essay questions (e.g., answer two out of the three questions), decide which ones you are going to answer.
- Read the questions carefully and do everything that it asks you to do—some essay questions contain more than one part.
- Budget your time and begin to plan.
- Outline or diagram the main points you want to cover.
- Write out examples, sources and quotes you want to use to support your essay. Include this and your outline writing on the paper you turn into your professor—if you run short of time to complete the essay, it may improve your score because your professor can see the knowledge you intended to share.
- Start with a thesis statement or idea that explains what you will be covering in your essay. Thinking of a title can also help provide a focus for your essay.
- Write legibly. Neatness, organization, good grammar and accurate spelling is important.
- Save time at the end so you can re-read and revise your essay.

- Keep your eye on the time. Make sure you are not spending too much time on one answer at the expense of others.
- If you run out of time, jot down the last few ideas in point form. Your professor will be able to see where you were going with your answer, especially if you used an outline before you began.

OPEN BOOK EXAMS

Contrary to what students may believe, open book exams can be some of the most difficult exams. Just because it seems that all of the information will be available, many students do not prepare for open book exams as thoroughly as for other in-class exams. As a result, many students are surprised by their difficulty and do not earn desired outcomes. More specific preparation can help you be as successful in these exams, as with others.

- As part of the preparation, know what information is found in each chapter.
- If allowed:
  - Highlight important points, use post-it notes, bookmarks, and make notes in your book. Open book exams are often very time-constricted to make up for the ease of information access, so knowing where information is located is critical.
  - Write down any formulas and definitions on a separate piece of paper, along with the page numbers, where more information can be found.
  - Use your notes and know where information can be found in your notes (create a table of contents for easy access).
- Bring all the resources that your professor or teacher allows.
- As in other exams, answer the easy questions that you know first, then go back and answer the questions where you need to reference your book.
- Use quotations from the book to support your view, but do not over-quote, be sure to give your own insight and commentary.

MATH AND STATISTICS EXAMS

When preparing for math and statistics exams, keep the following in mind:

- Repetition is important in math. You learn how to solve problems by doing them—so complete practice problems but do not do it blindly. Make sure you learn how to recognize when and why you should use a specific method to solve a problem.
- Work on practice problems for each topic ranging in levels of difficulty.
- When practicing, try to solve the problem on your own first, then look at the answer or seek help if you are having trouble.

- Mix up the order of the questions from various topics when you are reviewing, so you will learn when to use a specific method or formula.
- Make up a sheet with all the formulas you need to know, and memorize all the formulas on the sheet.

When taking the exam:

- Write down all the key formulas on the margin of your paper as soon as you receive your exam. This will ease some of the cognitive load and will allow you to reference them later. This will also help make sure you do not make "silly" mistakes when you see and use the formulas.
- Read the directions carefully and do not forget to answer all parts of the question.
- Make estimates for your answers (i.e., if you are asked to answer 48 x 12 = ? , you could expect a number around 500, but if you end up with an answer around 5000, you will know you did something wrong).
- Show all of your work (especially when partial credit is awarded) and write as legibly as possible.
- Even if you know the final answer is wrong, do not erase your entire work because you may get partial credit for using the correct procedure.
- Check over your exam after you are done. If you have time, redo the problem on a separate piece of paper and see if you come up with the same answer the second time around. Look for careless mistakes. Are your decimals in the right place, did you read the directions correctly, did you copy the numbers correctly, is your arithmetic correct, etc.?
- If you are able to use a calculator, use one that lists out the data entered, so you can review for errors when computing.

AFTER THE EXAM

Once you have completed an exam, take advantage of opportunities to evaluate your preparation and performance. Every exam is an opportunity to learn and improve. Cluster 7 specifically describes strategies to assess your preparation and learning strategies. Based on your results, should you make changes to your preparation? These changes could include the amount of time spent studying and the learning strategies used in the process. Be open to making changes and adding new strategies that could significantly improve your performance. Additionally, visit with your professor and seek *specific* and *immediate* feedback on how to improve your outcomes on future exams.

Even if you have struggled with exams in the past, know that your abilities will continue to improve over time and with practice. Ongoing and intentional preparation for your exams combined with the regular and practiced use of specific strategies during exams, will allow you to achieve the results you want!

MODULE 5.2 SUMMARY

- High levels of stress can lead to anxiety, and reduced performance and cognitive ability.
- There are several strategies that can help learners minimize stress and anxiety, including awareness of stress perception and anxiety triggers.
- Attending lectures, answering unit objectives, and using study guides are effective ways to predict exam items. The first exam is also a helpful source for predicting future exam items.
- General and specific test-taking strategies can help maximize your performance on exams.

KEY TERMS

- **Anxiety** – High levels of concern or worry that can negatively affect mental and physiological performance.
- **External Triggers** – Outside sights and sounds that could increase levels of anxiety and potentially interfere with performance.
- **Internal Triggers** – Negative thoughts leading to increased feelings of anxiety that could potentially interfere with performance.
- **Stress** – Perceptions of concern due to life events.

REFERENCES

Chapell, M. S., Blanding, Z. B., Silverstein, M. E., Takahashi, M., Newman, B., Gubi, A., &McCann, N. (2005). Test anxiety and academic performance in undergraduate and graduate students. *Journal of Educational Psychology, 97*(2), 268–274. doi:10.1037/0022-0663.97.2.268

Hebb, D. O. (1955). Drives and the C.N.S. (Conceptual nervous system). *The Psychological Review, 62*(4), 243–254.

Hsieh, P., Sullivan, J. R., Sass, D. A., & Guerra, N. S. (2012). Undergraduate engineering students' beliefs, coping strategies, and academic performance: An evaluation of theoretical models. *Journal of Experimental Education, 80*(2), 196–218. doi:10.1080/00220973.2011.596853

Sapolsky, R. (2004). *Why zebras don't get ulcers*. New York, NY: W. H. Freeman.

Schwarzer, R. (1990). Current trends in anxiety research. In P. J. D. Drenth, J. A. Sergeant, & R. J. Takens (Eds.), *European perspectives in psychology* (Vol. 2, pp. 225–244). Chichester, England: Wiley.

CASE STUDY

Joe was preparing for his first set of college exams. During the week before the exams, he re-read his textbook and his notes several times. He felt confident that he would do well, especially because he had always done pretty well on exams in the past. However, once he started to take his first exam, several things happened. As he was reading the items, he realized that they seemed familiar; however, he could not remember which of the answers were correct. So many of them seemed very similar, and he could not distinguish between them. He started becoming anxious. He also started noticing that other students were finishing, turning in their papers, zipping their backpacks, and leaving the room. He could feel his anxiety increasing, and started thinking about how he might fail this exam, and potentially fail the course. Knowing that he needed to finish, he tried to focus on the remaining items; however, he felt his mind go blank.

QUESTIONS

1. What strategies could Joe have used during his preparation that would have helped him judge his readiness?
2. Are there ways in which Joe could have managed his anxiety during the exam that would have helped him to remember as much as possible?

POTENTIAL RESPONSES

1. Joe could have used different self-testing strategies such as flashcards, answering, in writing, any unit objectives, and meeting with his study group to create and complete a practice exam. Before this week of exam preparation, he could have also used active reading strategies each time he completed his reading, such as the 3Rs (read-recite-review), creating questions for lecture, and connecting previous lecture and textbook information to new readings.

2. Once Joe realized he was not as prepared as he should have been, he could have given himself permission to worry about the consequences later. He could reassure himself that it is only one exam, and that he will adjust his learning strategies and come back better prepared on subsequent exams. As far as external triggers are concerned, he could increase his focus on his exam and not look around the room. He could also remind himself that the time-frame in which other students finish the exam, does not reflect on his abilities, and that he can use all the available time. If sounds are a particular problem, it may be helpful for him in the future, to bring ear plugs to exams.

ADDITIONAL READINGS

Biggs, J. B., & Collis, K. F. (2014). Evaluating the quality of learning: Th SOLO taxonomy (Structure of the Observed Learning Outcome). New York: Academic Press.

Everson, H. T., & Tobias, S. (1998). The ability to estimate knowledge and performance in college: A metacognitive analysis. *Instructional Science, 26*(1-2), 65–79.

Harrow, A. (1972) *A Taxonomy of psychomotor domain: A guide for developing behavioral objectives*. New York: David McKay.

Krathwohl, D. R., Bloom, B. S., & Masia, B. B. (1964). *Taxonomy of educational objectives: The classification of educational goals, Handbook II: Affective domain*. New York: David McKay.

Lothes, J. II., Mochrie, K., Wilson, M., & Hakan, R. (2019). The effect of dbt-informed mindfulness skills (what and how skills) and mindfulness-based stress reduction practices on test anxiety in college students: A mixed design study. *Current Psychology*, 1–14. doi: 10.1007/s12144-019-00207-y

Pressley, M. (2002). Metacognition and self-regulated comprehension. In A. Farstrup & S. J. Samuel (Eds.), *What research has to say about reading instruction* (pp. 291–309). Newark, DE: International Literacy Association.

Rane, D. B. (2011). Good listening skills make efficient business sense. *The IUP Journal of Soft Skills, 5*(4), 43–51.

Spielberger, C. D., Anton, W. D., & Bedell, J. (2015). The nature and treatment of test anxiety. *Emotions and Anxiety: New Concepts, Methods, and Applications*, 317–344.

Van Etten, S., Freebern, G., & Pressley, M. (1997). College students' beliefs about exam preparation. *Contemporary Educational Psychology, 22*(2), 192–212.

THE FUNDAMENTAL CAUSES OF BEHAVIOR:
YOUR MOTIVATION

CASE STUDY

Jessica is a second-semester freshmen. She is majoring in accounting because her mother is an accountant. She never misses her classes and turns in all of her work; however, she always waits until the last minute to complete her assignments. Additionally, she only does exactly what is required to get the grade. She does not enjoy her classes but still manages to go through the motions and get decent grades. When asked about her major, Jessica says: "I guess accounting is alright. I mean, the classes are pretty boring but I still get the work done and my grades are pretty good. And even when I do not understand what the instructors are talking about or why it is important, I still pass the exams, so that is good too. I don't know. A friend of mine said that I shouldn't worry about remembering this stuff right now anyway because we will review it all in my sophomore classes."

QUESTIONS

1. What type of motivation do you think is primarily influencing Jessica's behavior?

2. How is this related to her goal orientation?

3. Do you think that her motivation and goal orientation will ultimately affect her persistence and achievement over the long-term? Why or why not?

4. What recommendations would you give Jessica that could potentially help her going forward?

205

CLUSTER OVERVIEW

"Broad theories that combine multiple processes should generally give priority to motivation as fundamental, because the full causal chain that leads to behavior and beyond will generally start with motivation." (Baumeister, 2015, Primacy of motivation, para. 1).

Most people would agree that motivation is necessary to accomplish life's goals. Yet, many times motivation is viewed as a character trait that is static and as such, not within your control. Sometimes students have heard teachers say, "Well, he is just not motivated," or maybe you have made these same comments about yourself. Unlike your hair or eye color, you are not born with a motivation gene. Motivation is fully under your control. The key to manipulating your own motivation is to understand the types of motivation, to recognize their influences on your own behaviors, and then to use strategies that will promote and maintain your motivation.

This cluster will begin by helping you understand different types of motivation. Although there are many motivation theories with decades of supporting research, this cluster will focus on only a few theories that have a clear and direct relationship to learning and academic success. These include: intrinsic and extrinsic motivation, achievement motivation (goal orientations), self-efficacy, and attributions. There will also be a discussion that highlights the evolving conversation on growth mindset and its relationship to these motivational principles. The last module in this cluster will specifically discuss how to cultivate self-awareness and the strategies you can use to increase your own motivation.

CLUSTER OBJECTIVES

- Describe the relationship between intrinsic and extrinsic motivation and their effect on behaviors.
- Describe the different kinds of achievement motivation (goal orientations) and their influences on motivation.
- Discuss the role of self-efficacy in learning.
- Describe attributions and their relationship with growth mindset and achievement motivation.
- Describe the relationship between motivation and other areas (e.g., goals, time management, etc.) that influence students' educational experiences.
- Identify strategies to promote and maintain higher levels of motivation.

SOME MOTIVATION THEORIES

CLUSTER 6 OBJECTIVES COVERED IN THIS MODULE

- ☐ **OBJECTIVE:** Describe the relationship between intrinsic and extrinsic motivation and their effect on behaviors.
- ☐ **OBJECTIVE:** Describe the different kinds of achievement motivation (goal orientations) and their influences on motivation.

MOTIVATION THEORIES

Philosophers and psychologists have been contemplating the motives of human beings for centuries. Put simply, why do people do the things that they do? Theories around motivation have ranged from more basic ideas such as drive (e.g., when you are hungry, you find food) to more complex ideas such as social cognitive theory, which integrate cognitive factors (such as beliefs and expectations) with observational learning and reinforcements (Bandura, 1991). This module will focus on specific motivation theories that are of direct concern to learners, intrinsic and extrinsic motivation, and achievement motivation (or goal orientations).

INTRINSIC AND EXTRINSIC MOTIVATION

REFLECTION: Think about the classes you are taking. Are there some classes you truly enjoy? In these classes, do you put in extra effort, read more than assigned, visit with the professor, etc.? Do you have classes where it may be the opposite? You only do what is assigned, perhaps miss classes, procrastinate, etc.? How does your performance compare in these two types of classes?

OVERVIEW

When people pursue tasks and activities that are inherently enjoyable, it is said they are intrinsically motivated. Deci (1975) further stated that a person intrinsically motivated would engage in activities to "feel competent…[and to] seek out challenge" (p. 61).

Incentives or rewards are not needed or required. deCharms (1968) described intrinsic motivation in terms of locus of causality. When people feel like their behaviors are the result of their own choices and decisions, they have an inner locus of causality and are "free" (p. 273). He further compared these behaviors and choices in terms of play. Play is something you choose to do because you want to. For example, think of the things you choose to do because you enjoy the activity. It may be playing a sport or reading a book for leisure or engaging in a hobby. No one has to tell you to do these activities; you choose to do them for yourself. You are intrinsically motivated to complete these tasks.

The opposite of intrinsic motivation is extrinsic motivation. People who are extrinsically motivated will engage in activities because they expect a reward or incentive or they are trying to avoid negative consequences. deCharms (1968) would say they have an external locus of causality and are being "forced" (p. 273). As intrinsic motivation is compared to play, extrinsic motivation is compared to work. Many times, work is something you have to do. Subsequently, a person may not value these activities as much and may feel controlled.

One way to identify extrinsic motivation is whether a person continues the tasks or activities once the reward or incentive is removed. If the answer is no, then the person is likely extrinsically motivated. Some easy examples of extrinsic motivation are people who go to work for the sole purpose of earning a paycheck. If the employer decides to stop paying the employee, it is likely he or she would stop showing up for work. Many times students are extrinsically motivated and complete academic tasks exclusively for the grade. Going further, many students attend college because they are seeking a high-paying job or career.

In contrast to these types of motivation is amotivation. Simply, this means that a person has no motivation for a task. Many times, this type of motivation is linked to feelings of helplessness, lack of control, and a perceived inability to affect the outcome of a situation (Deci & Ryan, 2002). As a result, a person who is amotivated may quit the task or activity entirely as he or she may see no point in continuing.

The Relationship between Intrinsic and Extrinsic Motivation

Deci (1975) argued that human beings are born intrinsically motivated and have an innate passion to learn and explore the world. As such, elementary-aged children engage in academic tasks for their inherent enjoyment and fulfilling their need to gain competence. It is interesting to wonder at what

---

INTRINSIC MOTIVATION:
Type of motivation based on inherent enjoyment and satisfaction.

LOCUS OF CAUSALITY:
Individuals' perception of where their choices and behaviors originate, from within themselves or dictated by others.

EXTRINSIC MOTIVATION:
Type of motivation based on gaining rewards or avoiding negative consequences.

Which type of motivation is more powerful, intrinsic or extrinsic? Does this hold true in every circumstance?

AMOTIVATION:
A complete lack of motivation.

Are intrinsic and extrinsic motivation mutually exclusive? Can your motivation for a task be equally influenced by both?

point and by what means many students lose this intrinsic motivation for learning. Several early researchers have directly tied this change in motivation to the introduction of rewards, incentives, and grades in a child's academic experience (Bruner, 1962; Holt, 1964; Montessori, 1967).

This line of research has continued in other domains. Do extrinsic rewards diminish a person's intrinsic motivation for a task or activity? Much of the research, historically, would argue that this is true (Deci, 1971; Deci, Koestner, & Ryan, 1999). However, a recent meta-analytic study that examined 40 years of research argued that this relationship is more complex and that both intrinsic motivation and incentives could predict higher levels of performance (Cerasoli, Nicklin, & Ford, 2014). Considering that people tend to seek careers that are personally meaningful and yet would still like to be paid and recognized for their work, there is a need for theories that encompass the intricacy of the relationship between intrinsic and extrinsic motivation. Similarly, there are students who inherently enjoy a particular class and its associated academic tasks, yet are also decidedly motivated to earn a high GPA. Where does one motivation end and the other begin?

Recognizing this complexity inherent to human motives, Reiss (2012) has identified the limitations of a dualistic view of motivation and proposed a more multifaceted theory on motivation. In fact, Reiss proposed there are 16 universal reinforcements that better reflect the diversity of human motives. Some of these include acceptance, power, and tranquility. It is likely that more research will continue to try and explain motivation's diversity.

Hierarchical Model of Intrinsic and Extrinsic Motivation

In addition to the three types of motivation, Deci and Ryan (2002) also proposed that people experience motivation at the global, contextual, and situational levels. Global level refers to general personality types where individuals may or may not have several areas grounded in intrinsic or extrinsic motivation. For example, a young woman may have several interests in her life where she is intrinsically motivated such as a particular sport, several hobbies, and an area of study. Contextual refers to the specific domains. In the young woman's example, she could be intrinsically motivated to play softball; however, she is extrinsically motivated towards her math classes. Situational refers to specific circumstances within a context. Although this young woman is extrinsically motivated in her math class, verbal encouragement from her professor during a particular class may cause her to enjoy her success and learning and prompt her to put in additional effort.

Vallerand's (1997) proposed model integrates these three levels and describes the interrelationship between them. More significant is the potential for motivation to change at each level due to repeated exposure to positive experiences. Using the same example as above, if the young woman continues to have favorable experiences in her math class, it is possible that her motivation at the contextual level could shift from extrinsic to intrinsic motivation. As will be discussed further in the next section, understanding how and why

GLOBAL LEVEL:
Level of motivation that reveals a person's tendency towards activities influenced by either intrinsic or extrinsic types of motivation.

CONTEXTUAL LEVEL:
Level of motivation that is specific to a domain or area in a person's life.

SITUATIONAL LEVEL:
Level of motivation within a domain that is specific to a particular instance or circumstance within that domain.

motivation can change is critical to your ability to promote and maintain your own motivation.

LINKS TO SELF-DETERMINATION THEORY

Perceived feelings of self-determination have been closely linked to higher levels of intrinsic motivation in various domains for many decades (Deci & Ryan, 2002; Vallerand, 1997). Due to these consistent and ongoing findings, a discussion of self-determination theory is important in fully understanding intrinsic and extrinsic motivation. According to self-determination theory, individuals must perceive three constructs—autonomy, competence, and relatedness—to feel self-determined as well as to maintain psychological well-being. Although autonomy is typically related to choice, it also reflects the ability of individuals to adapt their behaviors when only one option is available. Competence does not necessarily refer to a person's set of abilities; rather it reflects the individual's perceptions of self-confidence and "effectance in action" (Deci & Ryan, 2002, p. 7). Lastly, relatedness refers to an individual's relationship with others and a sense of belongingness. Deci and Ryan (2002) have defined these constructs as basic psychological needs that must be met for an individual to function optimally. Over the years, self-determination has evolved to reflect the contributions of related foundational theories. One of the major theories that integrates the concepts of autonomy, competence, and relatedness include Organismic Integration Theory (Deci & Ryan, 2002). This theory is described due to its specific relationship to intrinsic and extrinsic motivation as well as individuals' potential to transform their own motivation.

Organismic Integration Theory

This theory outlines a motivation continuum ranging from amotivation to intrinsic motivation. Deci and Ryan (2002) stated that previous research has focused on a more dichotomous view of motivation. Either people are motivated to do something due to some extrinsic reward or they are not, in which case they are amotivated. To counter this idea, Deci and Ryan introduced a taxonomy of motivation that is more of a continuum with amotivation on the extreme left, extrinsic motivation in the middle, and intrinsic motivation on the extreme right. This continuum represents the degree to which extrinsic rewards are necessary for an individual to be motivated. It is assumed that on the extreme right, individuals are intrinsically motivated and do not require an extrinsic reward; however, as an individual moves further to the left on the continuum, more extrinsic rewards are required. Deci and Ryan further represented this idea by dividing extrinsic motivation into four parts: external regulation, introjection, identification, and integration. Because integration reflects individuals valuing an activity, it is the closest to intrinsic motivation; therefore, it is the most self-determined of the extrinsic types of motivation. On the opposite end of the extrinsic continuum, closest to amotivation, is external regulation. Individuals with external regulation tend to require more external rewards and usually do not value the activity; therefore, it is the most extrinsic type of motivation.

SELF-DETERMINATION:
A motivational construct that requires individuals to perceive feelings of autonomy, competence, and relatedness.

AUTONOMY:
The perceived ability of individuals to either choose a course of action from several options available or to adapt their behaviors when there is only one option.

COMPETENCE:
An individual's perception of self-confidence and ability to affect outcomes.

RELATEDNESS:
An individual's sense of belongingness with others.

INTEGRATION:
Type of extrinsic motivation closest to intrinsic motivation where an individual values the activity.

EXTERNAL REGULATION:
Type of extrinsic motivation closest to amotivation and requiring the most external rewards to complete tasks.

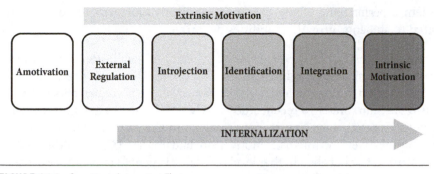

FIGURE 6.1.1: Organismic Integration Theory   *Source: Angela Vaughan and Brett Wilkinson*

Based on Organismic Integration Theory, motivation can transform. A person can have no interest in an activity and begin it solely based on external regulation. However, by fostering autonomy and self-determination, an environment can facilitate a transformation. In this type of environment, individuals can begin to see the value in an activity and their motivation may shift towards intrinsic motivation. This transformation is called internalization (Deci & Ryan, 2002). The authors contend that anyone can begin at any point along the continuum and either move towards intrinsic or extrinsic motivation based on the value the person places on the activity. As students face daily activities that are not necessarily inherently enjoyable, it is possible for them to *transform their own extrinsic motivation* by connecting these activities to broader goals and interests. For example, a student who must take a math class to become a nurse may only be extrinsically motivated (and in some extreme cases, amotivated) to complete the required tasks. However, if the student clearly recognizes that the skills developed in the math class will directly contribute to their abilities as a nurse, his or her motivation can transform towards integration, a more intrinsic form of motivation. The individual's newfound intrinsic motivation in the class can lead to more persistence, less procrastination, more complex learning strategies, and higher achievement (Deci & Ryan, 2002). The relationships between intrinsic motivation and higher achievement outcomes are discussed next.

INTERNALIZATION:
The process of motivation transforming towards intrinsic motivation due to increased perceived value of an activity.

What courses are you taking right now that you could connect to your goals and create more value and intrinsic motivation for yourself?

INTRINSIC MOTIVATION AND POSITIVE OUTCOMES

Intrinsic motivation has been consistently linked to positive outcomes in many domains (Deci & Ryan, 2002). Within education and learning, these findings have been repeated at all levels (Brophy, 1998; Pintrich, Marx, & Boyle, 1993; Schunk, 1991; Zusho, Pintrich, & Coppalo, 2003). Earlier research by Vallerand and Bissonnette (1992) examined students at a junior college where higher levels of intrinsic motivation were related to persistence in the course whereas higher levels of extrinsic motivation were more related to dropping the course. Intrinsic motivation has also been related to academic self-efficacy or confidence in abilities in a particular domain (Siu, Bakker & Jiang, 2014) and long-term growth in academic achievement (Murayama, Pekrun, Lichtenfeld, & vom Hofe, 2013). Interestingly, Murayama et al.'s study found intrinsic motivation to be related to mathematics achievement above and beyond students' intelligence. Intelligence could predict current academic performance; however, intrinsic motivation was more strongly related to students' growth in abilities over time.

Another earlier study by Ferrer-Caja and Weiss (2002) supported the relationship of task persistence and intrinsic motivation. Furthermore, these students tended to select more challenging tasks and put forth greater effort. These findings are mirrored in a recent study by Uyulgan and Akkuzu (2014) where the authors determined that student teachers in their educational programs with higher levels of intrinsic motivation had higher GPAs. Additionally, these student teachers had higher levels of commitment to their future profession, which the authors suggested would most likely lead to the student teachers following through and entering the teaching profession after graduation.

It is clear from the research that intrinsic motivation can be a critical factor in promoting important outcomes for students, higher persistence, achievement, effort, and learning.

ACHIEVEMENT MOTIVATION

REFLECTION: If you stop to think about some of your past achievements, can you recall what motivated you to succeed? Is there a consistent theme or pattern in your motivation towards success? How about your viewpoint on failure? Do you recognize anything notable regarding your motivational level in one area of interest compared to another?

> *"Life is a process of becoming, a combination of states we have to go through. Where people fail is that they wish to elect a state and remain in it. This is a kind of death." —Anais Nin*

Achievement is the process of becoming something more than who you are now. When you seek to attain some goal or outcome, you are essentially saying "I want or need something more in my life." When your actions result in the outcome you were seeking then you can claim to have achieved that end. However, accomplishing a goal also requires sustained effort and motivation. In this respect, achievement is not merely an outcome, but a complex motivational process leading to a particular set of desired outcomes (Hart & Albarracín, 2009).

ACHIEVEMENT MOTIVATION: The need or desire to meet realistic goals, attain success, or experience a sense of accomplishment.

The study of achievement motivation has largely centered on the question of process. Over the last 65 years, psychologists have approached this important topic from a number of perspectives and established a diverse array of theories and models. In this module, some of the most prominent ideas from the literature on achievement motivation will be described before illustrating their practical value for students in terms of self-regulated learning as an ongoing motivational process.

BRIEF HISTORY OF ACHIEVEMENT MOTIVATION RESEARCH

The earliest accounts of achievement motivation were founded on the idea of basic human needs. Personality psychologists such as McDougall (1932) and

Murray (1938) created expansive lists of basic psychological needs (e.g., curiosity, nurturance, self-assertion) to categorize and better define what motivates human action. Maslow (1954) developed a hierarchy of needs ranging from the physiological (e.g., food, shelter) to the self-actualizing (e.g., creativity, spontaneity). However, while these conceptual frameworks provided a valuable taxonomy of motivational factors, they did not address why there are individual differences in motivation (Deci & Ryan, 2000). In other words, why are you motivated in some situations and not others? Why is motivation inconsistent?

Addressing this issue required a shift in the underlying question itself. Instead of asking "what are the various human needs," scholars sought to explain how individuals differ in their motivation to meet those needs. In response to this shift, a group of theorists proposed that three fundamental needs—achievement, power, and affiliation—are acquired through life experience and can be used to explain individual differences in motivation (McClelland, Atkinson, Clark, & Lowell, 1953). In this framework, achievement-oriented people are less interested in external rewards and more interested in a personal sense of success. Atkinson (1957) also suggested that achieving success requires the avoidance of failure, and so a tendency towards achievement motivation can lead to a fear of failure when success is not consistently attained.

Based on extensive studies of achievement, McClelland (1965) determined that achievement motivation is tied to standards of excellence or ideal outcomes. Research indicates that the process of goal-setting involves a comparison of your present circumstances to either an ideal standard or an ought standard (Higgins, 1987). Both ideal and ought standards are often set by others. For example, a teacher sets standards when grading course papers even as a boss might expect your upcoming presentation to secure a new business contract. Yet, your level of motivation does not depend on these external standards alone. If it did, then you would always achieve success in accordance with the expectations set by other people.

IDEAL STANDARD: Values or attributes that either yourself or another person hope, wish, or aspire for you to possess.

OUGHT STANDARD: Values or attributes that either yourself or another person expect, demand, or believe you should possess.

According to both McClelland (1985) and Atkinson (1981), your motivation to achieve is largely determined by the way you imagine the route to success. It is influenced by your imagined expectations or achievement imagery. In this manner, your achievement motivation is based on not only your general drive for success, but how likely you think it will be to succeed and on how enticing you find the incentives tied to a successful outcome (Oettingen, 2000). Achievement imagery thus plays a vital role in motivation. You envision the likelihood of attaining the outcome, weigh the incentives, and choose your course of action accordingly.

ACHIEVEMENT IMAGERY: The use of mental visualizations or fantasies when considering how a future achievement outcome might be experienced.

MODERN ACHIEVEMENT MOTIVATION

Among modern accounts of achievement motivation, emphasis is placed on the notion of goal orientations rather than basic psychological needs (Elliot, 2005). Such ideas, while informed by needs-based theories, seek to provide a still more substantive account of situational goal formation by explaining why

GOAL ORIENTATION: The degree to which one develops or demonstrates ability in achievement situations.

individuals show different levels of achievement motivation. Whereas needs-based theories seek to explain achievement motivation in terms of personality dispositions, goal orientation theories focus on how specific types of achievement motivation influence both short-term and long-term learning outcomes.

Initial exploratory research on such individual differences by Eison (1981) and Nicholls (1984) led to robust discussions on how different approaches to achievement result in unique learning outcomes. This eventually led to the development by Dweck (1986) of a distinction between learning and performance goal orientations, as well as the work of Ames (1992) on mastery-focused and ability-focused achievement orientations. Based on these findings, researchers came to a consensus on the set of terms for achievement types used today: mastery and performance.

Mastery and Performance Orientations

MASTERY ORIENTATION:
The goal of learning and accomplishing tasks based on personal standards of excellence, with an emphasis on improvement and skill acquisition.

PERFORMANCE ORIENTATION:
The goal of learning and accomplishing tasks based on the desire to outperform others, display superior capability, or validate one's sense of ability.

An orientation represents the position, angle, or view you take on any given issue. In terms of achievement more specifically, mastery and performance orientations signify the major positions you take on a goal or task. Mastery orientation involves a "big picture" point of view or the understanding that time and dedication are often required to accomplish something masterfully. Many times, this is also described as having learning goals. Performance orientation (or performance goals) focuses on more immediate results, often guided by comparisons to others or some external standard of excellence. While a mastery orientation supports the role of effort and competence in learning, a performance orientation emphasizes ability and outcomes.

Mastery orientation is an internalized process that regards short-term failures as a natural consequence of seeking long-term gains (Elliot, 1999). Because the focus is on learning and enhancing skills, motivation can be sustained over time despite numerous challenges and without concern for the judgment of others. Performance orientation, on the other hand, is an externalized process that regards failure as a marker of inability or incompetence (Elliot, 1999). Because the focus is on performance relative to an external standard of excellence, it is difficult to sustain motivation in the face of obstacles or when confronted by the negative judgment of others.

Examples are provided below to clarify how each achievement motive might appear in a hypothetical classroom setting.

Performance Orientation

Mark consistently participates in class by raising his hand to answer questions and lead group discussions. He approaches the task at hand actively and with resolve. However, what others might not recognize is that Mark is less motivated by learning the course material than by demonstrating to others that he is an intelligent and capable student. While this may not be apparent to casual observers, Mark feels driven to prove his competence and ability. He approaches tasks with vigor and determination, but is sensitive to—and constantly aware of—how people judge his ability and performance.

For example, after answering a question incorrectly his first thought is about how others in the class might perceive him. This is not necessarily a consuming thought, but it signifies where his mind goes automatically when his performance is suboptimal. He displays a high level of public self-consciousness combined with a desire to be perceived in a good light. This form of achievement motivation has led Mark to perform well throughout his educational experience, yet he is far less interested in learning the materials than in being regarded positively by others.

Do you think Mark is intrinsically or extrinsically motivated? How do you know?

Mastery Orientation

Rachel participates as actively in class as Mark. She asks questions and takes risks in order to learn the materials. While her active engagement in the class appears remarkably similar to Mark's, Rachel is actually more interested in learning the content and building her understanding than being regarded as competent by others. The behavior she displays is similar to that guiding performance, but her relationship to the learning process is completely different. She approaches the class with curiosity and resilience, as well as with a desire to improve her ability in that area of study.

For example, when Rachel answers a question incorrectly, her first thought is about the new information provided and how it contrasts with her knowledge base. Her focus is on gaining clarity of understanding, which may lead her to ask follow-up questions in order to resolve her sense of uncertainty. Rachel is most focused on reorganizing and synthesizing course content, rather than being concerned with how others judge her. With lower public self-consciousness than Mark, Rachel is willing to take the risks necessary to improve her learning and enhance her ability to grasp the subject matter.

Do you think Rachel is intrinsically or extrinsically motivated? How do you know?

PUTTING IT ALL TOGETHER: ACHIEVEMENT MOTIVATION FOR THE SELF-REGULATED LEARNER

Motivation is purposeful, insofar as it energizes you to accomplish a goal. Achievement is intentional, meaning that the actions taken to attain specific end-goals require both forethought and sustained effort. The purposeful and intentional nature of achievement motivation is most clearly embodied by a mastery-approach style, which research indicates is the most beneficial style for long-term learning outcomes (Elliot, 1999). While performance-approach can also lead to beneficial outcomes, the effects are typically short-term, perfunctory, and directly related to external standards of excellence. Although performance-approach motives have been shown to support academic and work-related performance outcomes in competitive environments, such results come at the risk of forming life-long maladaptive habits including the use of superficial learning strategies, the development of negative attitudes towards learning, and tendencies to withdraw from challenging situations (Barron & Harachiewicz, 2003).

Ormrod (1999) assembled a comprehensive list of the typical characteristics of students with mastery or learning goals and students with performance goals:

People with Learning Goals	**People with Performance Goals**
Believe that competence develops over time through practice and effort	Believe that competence is a stable characteristic (people either have talent or they don't) and think that competent people shouldn't have to try very hard
Choose tasks that maximize opportunities for learning	Choose tasks that maximize opportunities for demonstrating competence and avoid tasks that might make them look incompetent
React to easy tasks with feelings of boredom or disappointment	React to success on easy tasks with feelings of pride or relief
Are more likely to be intrinsically motivated to learn course material	Are more likely to be extrinsically motivated—that is, motivated by expectations of external reinforcement and punishment
Invest considerable effort in tasks	Invest the minimal effort needed to succeed
Use learning strategies that promote true comprehension of course material (e.g., meaningful learning, elaboration, and comprehension monitoring)	Use learning strategies that promote only rote learning of course material (e.g., repetition copying, and word-for-word memorization)
Seek feedback that accurately describes their ability and helps them improve	Seek feedback that flatters them
Evaluate their own performance in terms of progress they make	Evaluate their own performance in terms of how they compare with others
View errors as a normal and useful part of the learning process and use their errors to help improve performance	View errors as a sign of failure and incompetence
Interpret failure as a sign that they need to exert more effort	Interpret failure as a sign of low ability and therefore predictive of continuing failure in the future
Are satisfied with their performance if they try hard and make progress, even if their efforts result in failure	Are satisfied with their performance only if they succeed
Persist in the face of failure	Give up easily when they fail and avoid tasks that have previously led to failure
View a teacher as a resource and guide to help them learn	View a teacher as a judge and as a rewarder or punisher
As students, are more likely to be enthusiastic about, and become actively involved in, school activities	As students, are more likely to distance themselves from the school environment

ORMROD, JEANNE ELLIS, HUMAN LEARNING, 3rd Ed., © 1999. Reprinted by permission of Pearson Education, Inc., New York, New York.

MODULE 6.1 SUMMARY

- Two types of motivation include intrinsic and extrinsic motivation.
- Amotivation is a lack of motivation.
- Extrinsic rewards given to intrinsically motivated tasks may diminish a person's motivation for the task.
- Three levels of motivation include global, contextual, and situational levels.
- Self-determination includes perceiving autonomy, competence, and relatedness and is strongly related to intrinsic motivation.
- Organismic Integration Theory suggests that a person can begin to value and internalize an activity such that his or her motivation transforms.
- Achievement is a basic psychological need.
- Two types of achievement orientation include mastery and performance.
- Mastery is an internalized process guided by the desire for personal development while performance is an externalized process designed to meet standards set by others.

KEY TERMS

- **Achievement Imagery** – The use of mental visualizations or fantasies when considering how a future achievement outcome might be experienced.
- **Achievement Motivation** – The need or desire to meet realistic goals, attain success, or experience a sense of accomplishment.
- **Amotivation** – A complete lack of motivation.
- **Autonomy** – The perceived ability of individuals to either choose a course of action from several options available or to adapt their behaviors when there is only one option.
- **Competence** – An individual's perception of self-confidence and ability to affect outcomes.
- **Contextual Level of Motivation** – Level of motivation that is specific to a domain or area in a person's life.
- **External Regulation** – Type of extrinsic motivation closest to amotivation and requiring the most external rewards to complete tasks.
- **Extrinsic Motivation** – Type of motivation based on gaining rewards or avoiding negative consequences.
- **Global Level of Motivation** – Level of motivation that reveals a person's tendency towards activities influenced by either intrinsic or extrinsic types of motivation.

- **Goal Orientation** – The degree to which one develops or demonstrates ability in achievement situations.
- **Ideal Standards** – Values or attributes that either yourself or another person hope, wish, or aspire for you to possess.
- **Integration** – Type of extrinsic motivation closest to intrinsic motivation where an individual values the activity.
- **Internalization** – The process of motivation transforming towards intrinsic motivation due to increased perceived value of an activity.
- **Intrinsic Motivation** – Type of motivation based on inherent enjoyment and satisfaction.
- **Locus of Causality** – Individuals' perception of where their choices and behaviors originate, from within themselves or dictated by others.
- **Mastery Orientation** – The goal of learning and accomplishing tasks based on personal standards of excellence with an emphasis on improvement and skill acquisition.
- **Ought Standards** – Values or attributes that either yourself or another person expect, demand, or believe you should possess.
- **Performance Orientation** – The goal of learning and accomplishing tasks based on the desire to outperform others, display superior capability, or validate one's sense of ability.
- **Relatedness** – An individual's sense of belongingness with others.
- **Self-Determination** – A motivational construct that requires individuals to perceive feelings of autonomy, competence, and relatedness.
- **Situational Level Motivation** – Level of motivation within a domain that is specific to a particular instance or circumstance within that domain.

REFERENCES

Ames, C. A. (1992). Classrooms: Goals, structures, and student motivation. *Journal of Educational Psychology, 84,* 261–271.

Atkinson, J. W. (1981). Studying personality in the context of an advanced motivational psychology. *American Psychologist, 36*(2), 117–128.

Bandura, A. (1991). Social cognitive theory of self-regulation. *Organizational Behavior and Human Decision Processes, 50,* 248–287.

Baranik, L. E., Stanley, L. J., Bynum, B., & Lance, C. E. (2010). Examining the construct validity of mastery-avoidance achievement goals: A meta-analysis. *Human Performance, 23*(3), 265–282.

Baranik, L. E., Lau, A. R., Stanley, R. J., Barron, K. E., & Lance, C. E. (2013). Achievement goals in organizations: Is there support for mastery-avoidance? *Journal of Managerial Issues, 25*(1), 46–61.

Barron, K. E., & Harackiewicz, J. M. (2003). Revisiting the benefits of performance-approach goals in the college classroom: Exploring the role of goals in advanced college courses. *International Journal of Educational Research*, *39*(4), 357–374.

Baumeister, R. F. (2015). Toward a general theory of motivation: Problems, challenges, opportunities, and the big picture. *Motivation & Emotion*. Online publication. doi: 10.1007/s11031-015-9521-y

Brophy, J. (1998). *Motivating students to learn*. Boston: McGraw Hill.

Bruner, J. (1962). *On knowing: Essays for the left hand*. Cambridge: Harvard University Press.

Cerasoli, C. P., Nicklin, J. M., & Ford, M. T. (2014). Intrinsic motivation and extrinsic incentives jointly predict performance: A 40-year meta-analysis. *Psychological Bulletin*, *140*(40), 980–1008.

deCharms, R. (1968). *Personal causation*. New York: Academic Press.

Deci, E. L. (1971). Effects of externally mediated rewards on intrinsic motivation. *Journal of Personality and Social Psychology*, *18*(1), 105–115.

Deci, E. L. (1975). *Intrinsic motivation*. New York: Plenum Press.

Deci, E. L., Koestner, R., & Ryan, R. M. (1999). A meta-analytic review of experiments examining the effects of extrinsic rewards on intrinsic motivation. *Psychological Bulletin*, *125*(6), 627–668.

Deci, E. L. & Ryan, R. M. (2000). The "what" and "why" of goal pursuits: Human needs and the self-determination of behavior. *Psychological Inquiry*, *11*(4), 227–268.

Deci, E. L., & Ryan, R. M. (Eds.). (2002). *Handbook of self-determination research*. Rochester: University of Rochester Press.

Dweck, C. (1986). Motivational processes affecting learning. *American Psychologist*, *41*, 1040–1048.

Eison, J. A. (1981). A new instrument for assessing students' orientations towards grades and learning. *Psychological Reports*, *48*, 919–924.

Elliot, A. J. (1999). Approach and avoidance motivation and achievement goals. *Educational Psychologist*, *34*, 169–189.

Elliot, A. J. (2005). A conceptual history of the achievement goal construct. In A. J. Elliot & C. S. Dweck (Eds.), *Handbook of competence and motivation* (pp. 52–72). New York: The Guilford Press.

Ferrer-Caja, E., & Weiss, M. R. (2002). Cross-validation of a model of intrinsic motivation with students enrolled in high school elective courses. *The Journal of Experimental Education, 71*(1), 41–65.

Hart, W., & Albarracín, D. (2009). The effects of chronic achievement motivation and achievement primes on the activation of achievement and fun goals. *Journal of Personality and Social Psychology, 97*(6), 1129–1141.

Higgins, E. T. (1987). Self-discrepancy: A theory relating self to affect. *Psychological Review, 94*(3), 319–340.

Holt, J. (1964). *How children fail. New York*: Dell.

Maslow, A. H. (1954). *Motivation and personality.* New York: Harper & Row.

McClelland, D. C. (1965). Toward a theory of motive acquisition. *American Psychologist, 20*(5), 321–333.

McClelland, D. C. (1985). *Human motivation.* Glenview, IL: Scott & Foresman.

McClelland, D. C., Atkinson, J. W., Clark, R. A., & Lowell, E. L. (1953). *The achievement motive.* New York: Appleton-Century-Crofts.

McDougall, J. (1932). *The energies of men: A study of the fundamentals of dynamic psychology.* Methuen: London.

Montessori, M. (1967). *The discovery of the child.* New York: Ballantine.

Murayama, K., Pekrun, R., Lichtenfeld, S., & vom Hofe, R. (2013). Predicting long-term growth in students' mathematics achievement: The unique contributions of motivation and cognitive strategies. *Child Development, 84*(4), 1475–1490.

Murray, H. A. (1938). *Exploration in personality.* New York: Oxford University Press.

Nicholls, J. G. (1984). Achievement motivation: Conceptions of ability, subjective experience, task choice, and performance. *Psychological Review, 91,* 328–346.

Oettingen, G. (2000). Expectancy effects on behavior depend on self-regulatory thought. *Social Cognition, 18,* 101–129.

Ormrod, J. E. (1999). *Human Learning* (3rd ed.). Columbus, Ohio: Prentice Hall.

Pintrich, P. R., Marx, R. W., & Boyle, R. A. (1993). Beyond cold conceptual change: The role of motivational beliefs and classroom contextual factors in the process of conceptual change. *Review of Educational Research, 63*(2), 167–199.

Reiss, S. (2012). Intrinsic and extrinsic motivation. *Teaching of Psychology, 39*(2), 152–156.

Schunk, D. H. (1991). Self-efficacy and academic motivation. *Educational Psychologist, 26*, 207–231.

Siu, O. L., Bakker, A. B., & Jiang, X. J. (2014). Psychological capital among university students: Relationships with study engagement and intrinsic motivation. *Journal of Happiness Studies, 15*(4), 979–994.

Uyulgan, M. A., & Akkuzu, N. (2014). An overview of student teachers' academic intrinsic motivation. *Educational Sciences: Theory and Practice, 14*(1), 24–32.

Vallerand, R. J., & Bissonnette, R. (1992). Intrinsic, extrinsic, and amotivational styles as predictors of behavior: A prospective study. *Journal of Personality, 60*, 599–620.

Zusho, A., Pintrich, P. R., & Coppalo, B. (2003). Skill and will: The role of motivation and cognition in the learning of college chemistry. *International Journal of Science Education, 25*(9), 1081–1094.

BELIEFS THAT DRIVE MOTIVATION

CLUSTER 6 OBJECTIVES COVERED IN THIS MODULE

- ☐ **OBJECTIVE:** Discuss the role of self-efficacy in learning.
- ☐ **OBJECTIVE:** Describe attributions and their relationship with growth mindset and achievement motivation..

BELIEFS

This module will focus on beliefs. These include your beliefs about your ability, about your reasons for success or failure, and your beliefs about growth and learning. Although there are many separate theories and principles about beliefs, the following will discuss three specific theories that can have a direct influence on your motivation and your ability to maintain motivation over the long term: self-efficacy, attributions, and mindsets. This module will conclude with a matrix that illustrates the overlapping nature of the theories in this cluster and how they contribute to your motivation.

SELF-EFFICACY

REFLECTION: Take a moment to think about an activity you enjoy and feel capable of accomplishing. Now imagine that you're doing this task right now and are about to finish. What feelings come up for you? Do you experience a boost in self-confidence as you imagine the outcome? Now imagine that you're working on a task that you don't quite understand or have difficulty accomplishing. Does your self-confidence waver when imagining this task? If you were given a choice between the two tasks, you'd likely prefer to engage in the one that you enjoy and complete with ease. Everyone likes the sense of competence that arises from doing well. But why do these feelings differ? How might these feelings betray one's ability to persist in the face of new challenges?

When faced with a challenge, most people have some sense of whether or not they are capable of accomplishing it. People complete many everyday tasks without much thought, such as brewing a pot of coffee in the morning despite being half-asleep with blurred vision. Other tasks require more concentration despite eliciting similar levels of confidence, such as driving to work in rush hour traffic or completing basic math problems. When you stop to consider how much of your daily life is comprised of tasks that are accomplished without hardly any critical thought, you might be inclined to give yourself a well-deserved, self-congratulatory pat on the back for a job well done!

However, many of the important tasks that confront individuals are neither so straightforward nor so simple. This is particularly true for college students because the very purpose of higher education is to introduce new learning opportunities and innovative ideas to those who have not yet acquired certain points of knowledge. The challenges vary from subject to subject and from class to class, often requiring students to perform well in unfamiliar content areas or on previously unfamiliar tasks. In such a unique learning environment, it is inevitable that students will believe in their ability to accomplish some tasks more readily than others and for their motivation to waver in kind. This relationship between personal beliefs in the ability to accomplish a task and the motivation to persist when confronted with challenges is best understood in terms of self-efficacy. To better grasp how self-efficacy beliefs influence achievement, motivation, and goal persistence, Social Cognitive Theory will be described next.

SOCIAL COGNITIVE THEORY

In the 1970's, Social Cognitive Theory was developed by the psychologist Albert Bandura to explain social learning and behavioral change. It asserts that learning occurs through the process of social interaction and observing the behavior of others. This is called modeling, a primary learning mechanism for reinforcing and inhibiting behaviors. Building upon earlier behaviorist theories, this idea presupposes that people can be conditioned to learn new behaviors through reinforcement. Up until this point, psychologists had widely viewed human behavior as an automatic response to environmental conditions. However, Bandura (1977) did not and so introduced the notion of reciprocal determinism: that a person's behavior both influences and is influenced by personal characteristics (i.e., cognitive, affective, motivational, and biological factors) as well as the social environment. Human behavior is thus regarded through a lens of personal agency—or the basic human capacity to make self-determined choices—as being subjective, interpersonal, and extraordinarily complex (Bandura, 2006).

Placing emphasis on personal agency was a significant conceptual shift in learning theory. In contrast to earlier behaviorist theories, Social Cognitive Theory regarded a multitude of factors—behavioral, cognitive, personal, and environmental—as influential determinants of human motivation (Bandura, Adams, & Beyer, 1977). Whereas behaviorists had long asserted that learning is an automatic process of imitation that is supported by rewards and deterred by punishment, Bandura (1982) took the alternative view that human beings are intentional agents who seek to control outcomes. As such, learning and behavioral change must be understood in terms of how actions, thoughts, beliefs, and situational environment collectively influence one's learning and personal change processes. Broadening the view of learning processes beyond the limits of behaviorism, Social Cognitive Theory successfully granted due respect to the dynamic and multifaceted features of actual human experience in the world.

According to Bandura (1997), there are four major processes that influence learning, motivation, and goal attainment: self-observation, self-evaluation, self-reaction, and self-efficacy. Each of these is relatively straightforward concepts that, taken together, provide a clear picture of how the theory frames learning. Whenever you attempt to learn a new skill, all four factors are used to enhance the likelihood that successful learning will occur. For example, you have finally decided to take your first ballroom dance class. As you take the first steps, several learning mechanisms suddenly kick into gear. You observe your thoughts, feelings, and actions as you move across the dance floor, making spontaneous adjustments as you go. You evaluate your current performance in terms of how well you thought you would do prior to arriving at the dance studio. You also react to your progress (or lack thereof) and judge yourself in light of your own self-evaluations and self-observations.

Depending on how these factors play out—regardless of whether you glide gracefully across the dance floor or stumble frustratingly over your own feet—your self-efficacy for the task of dancing may either suffer or flourish. Self-efficacy is a personal belief in your ability to accomplish specific tasks. It is contingent not only on task performance, but your evaluative judgments and subsequent reactions to that performance. So doing poorly at any given task, dancing or otherwise, can lead to a retreat from the learning process or a determination to redouble your efforts in mastering the task. It is largely a matter of how your beliefs are formed in response to your outcome expectations. If your self-efficacy beliefs are relatively high and you continue in the class, all three learning processes are continuously engaged. You closely observe your feet in motion, evaluate your progress in terms of a self-determined outcome, react to the progress made (or not), and find that your self-efficacy for the task either increases or decreases.

All of these learning processes also require specific cognitive elements that are distinctly human and serve as the foundation for Social Cognitive Theory. According to Pajares (2009), individuals use symbols to visualize their experiences, forethought to plan their actions, self-reflection to evaluate and explore their thoughts and behaviors, self-regulatory mechanisms to control

SENSE OF AGENCY:
The subjective awareness that one is initiating, executing, and controlling one's own actions in the world.

SOCIAL COGNITIVE THEORY:
Psychological theory that explains personality development in terms of thoughts, feelings, actions, and motivations derived from interaction with the social environment.

MODELING:
The process by which persons serve as an imitative example or to otherwise influence the behaviors of others.

their responses, and vicarious learning to translate observations into learned behaviors. In terms of your experience at the ballroom dance studio, you can visualize the step you are learning, plan for the next step, evaluate your progress, control your emotional response to a misstep, and watch the instructor to learn what to do next. It is an incredibly complex set of capabilities that you use every day, with or without effort depending on the task at hand. However, when the missteps outnumber the correct ones, (metaphorically speaking) your persistence may waver or even crumble. A closer examination of self-efficacy will help explain why.

SELF-EFFICACY BELIEFS

Self-efficacy beliefs are a task-specific version of self-esteem. Whereas self-esteem relates to a global sense of self-worth, self-efficacy "refers to beliefs in one's capabilities to organize and execute a course of action required to manage prospective situations" (Bandura, 1995, p. 2). Self-efficacy beliefs can have a significant effect on motivation, with higher self-efficacy relating to increased task-persistence and lower self-efficacy corresponding with reduced engagement or effort (Parajes, 2009). So the likelihood that you will engage in an activity depends largely on your belief that you can succeed. However, there is a self-fulfilling prophecy hidden therein: if you do not believe in your ability to perform a task then you are unlikely to persist, even when continued effort would lead to both increased ability and enhanced self-efficacy as a result (Gecas, 2004).

Even as self-efficacy is a cumulative response-outcome expectancy of processes such as self-observations, self-evaluations, and self-reactions, its influence on behavior largely depends upon how these factors are interpreted (Pajares & Schunk, 2001). It is interpretation that guides personal judgments of task-based efficacy. Doing well or poorly at a task does not necessarily determine persistence or self-efficacy beliefs; however, the positive or negative interpretation of those relative outcomes does. Such judgments are a central feature of Social Cognitive Theory, outlined by Bandura (1997) in terms of four major catalysts for growing or sustaining self-efficacy: mastery experiences, social modeling, verbal persuasion, and emotional arousal. It is by means of these mechanisms that you interpret whether or not you have the ability to complete a task.

Mastery Experiences

The judgment of past performance exerts the single greatest influence on self-efficacy beliefs (Bandura, 1997). Successful performances in the past tend to increase self-efficacy and task persistence while failures tend to reduce self-efficacy and subsequent effort. High levels of self-efficacy also correspond with a mastery achievement orientation, meaning that more difficult or challenging tasks are perceived as an opportunity to gain mastery rather than as a risk to avoid due to fear of failure (Williams & Williams, 2010). For example, noticing that you have made positive progress over the past four dance classes will increase your sense of efficacy and determination to continue learning.

Social Modeling

Social modeling involves observing others perform a task and then considering whether you would be able to perform the task with a greater or lesser degree of success (Bandura, 1997). Such vicarious experiences depend largely on how you compare yourself to the individual being observed. Observing someone similar to you succeed at a given task can increase self-efficacy beliefs regarding that task. If that similar individual fails, you will be less likely to engage in the task. For example, watching similar students in the dance class struggle as you do and also stumble over their feet will likely increase your willingness to persist in learning.

Verbal Persuasion

Supportive or discouraging remarks about personal performance or ability can have a significant effect on self-efficacy beliefs (Bandura, 1997). Positive, encouraging comments from credible individuals tend to increase self-efficacy and task persistence. Negative, discouraging comments have the inverse effect. The source of persuasion is an important factor to consider because greater significance is placed on support or discouragement provided by individuals perceived as credible (Pajares & Schunk, 2001). For example, positive feedback from your dance instructor will likely increase your efficacy and desire to continue in the class.

Emotional Arousal

Physiological feedback is a consistent source of information guiding self-efficacy beliefs. A prime example arises from giving a presentation to a large audience. In such a case, emotional arousal in the form of anxiety symptoms such as sweating, agitation, or racing thoughts provide negative feedback that can deter task persistence and lower self-efficacy. At the same time, positive emotional feedback stemming from feelings of joy, pleasure, or peacefulness can increase self-efficacy and effort (Bandura, 1997). The more capable and confident you feel in completing a task, the greater the positive emotional feedback. For example, the feeling of accomplishment upon finally mastering a new dance step will lead to positive emotional feedback and a desire to continue learning.

An important distinction to consider about physiological feedback is your interpretation. In the example of presenting to a large audience, you could interpret these feelings as not being prepared or you could interpret these feelings as excitement and eagerness to present. One interpretation will decrease self-efficacy, the other will promote it.

> What are some activities you have continued to participate in because you were successful? What are some activities that you have quit because you did not do well?

SOCIAL MODELING: The impact of observing others perform tasks, or handle situations, on subsequent task persistence, motivation, or self-efficacy beliefs.

VERBAL PERSUASION: The impact of either verbal support or discouragement on subsequent task persistence, motivation, and self-efficacy beliefs.

> Have you ever received feedback from a parent, coach or teacher that made you question your ability on a task? What were the short- and long-term consequences of that feedback?

EMOTIONAL AROUSAL: The impact of physiological feedback on subsequent task persistence, motivation, and self-efficacy beliefs.

PUTTING IT ALL TOGETHER: THE IMPACT OF SELF-EFFICACY ON PERSONAL AGENCY

So how might self-efficacy beliefs impact your experience of personal agency? This is an important question. Remember, personal agency is your basic capacity to make choices, while self-efficacy is the belief that you can enact specific behaviors to achieve certain outcomes (Bandura, 1992). In other words, the beliefs you hold about your abilities have a direct bearing on the choices you make. When your efficacy in a given area is low, your sense of agency diminishes and choices are restricted. When your efficacy is high, your sense of agency rises and the array of choices expand. A strong sense of agency is important for success and wellbeing because effective action depends upon the belief that you can overcome obstacles and achieve desired outcomes. According to Bandura (2006), "Unless people believe that they can produce desired effects by their actions, they have little incentive to act or to persevere in the face of difficulties" (p. 170).

An important consideration is whether specific self-efficacy beliefs are accurate or not. Because your optimism, aspirations, and persistence are heavily determined by self-efficacy, the accuracy of those beliefs should be of great concern. Inaccurate beliefs about your ability to accomplish a task can profoundly affect the decisions you make and, consequently, the course of your life (Bandura, 2006). Low self-efficacy can be accurate if it is grounded in a realistic assessment of skill and possibility. For example, some people will never be able to dunk a basketball regardless of how much training or effort they expend. Being realistic about certain limitations ensures that you do not put undue effort into a task that will not pay off. However, when the belief is inaccurate, you are likely to give up even though additional effort could change the result. For example, students who believe they are inherently "bad" at math ignore the fact that spending extra time and energy practicing would change this perception. Persistence and effort are often the key.

Another consideration is how certain self-efficacy beliefs influence thought and mood. A consequence of low self-efficacy is the tendency to believe some tasks are more difficult than they actually are. This misperception can lead to a "tunnel vision" effect, increasing stress levels and restricting your ability to think creatively about a problem and possible solutions (Bandura, 1997). The idea of an obstacle becomes so large as to seem insurmountable. As a result, self-doubt fuels both a sense of helplessness in the face of the task and a reduction in sense of personal agency. It harms your sense of competence as well as your range of behavioral choices.

A similar outcome arises from high self-efficacy when the difficulty of a future task is underestimated. Believing a task is easier than it actually is can lead you to ignore necessary preparations (Schunk, 1991). For example, with high self-efficacy in a given class you might decide not to study for the midterm examination, only to find that you seriously underestimated its difficulty. However, a positive result of high self-efficacy in this case would be the willingness to attribute your poor midterm examination grade to a lack of effort. For the student with low self-efficacy who receives a bad midterm grade, the poor performance is generally attributed to a lack of ability. This distinction between effort and ability has important implications for the self-regulated learner and will be discussed further in the next section on causal attributions.

TABLE 6.2.1 HIGH SELF-EFFICACY: INFLUENCES, TASKS, MOTIVATION, AND ATTRIBUTIONS	
Influences	• Past successes • Comparison to peers who are successful • Positive verbal feedback from credible people • Positive feelings or helpful interpretations of physiological symptoms
Academic Tasks	• More likely to give greater effort • More likely to choose challenging activities • More likely to persevere after failure or difficulties • More likely to use complex, elaborative learning strategies • Less likely to procrastinate
Motivation	• Higher intrinsic motivation • Mastery orientations and learning goals
Attributions	• More likely to identify success and failure as the result of controllable causes such as effort

ATTRIBUTIONS

REFLECTON: Think about the last time you succeeded at a task. What were the reasons for your success? Did you put in a lot of hard work or was the task just easy? Now think about the last time you failed at a task. What were your reasons for failing? Was the task too hard? Did you think it was beyond your abilities?

OVERVIEW

In the 1950s, Heider (1958) believed that to interpret other people's intentions and actions, you needed to first understand the factors related to their specific actions. Heider suggested that, "the result of an action is felt to depend on two sets of conditions, namely factors within the person and within the environment" (p. 82). These results (potential successes or failures) are then associated with causes related to these factors. Specifically, he identified three causes: ability and effort (related to internal conditions or within the person), as well as task difficulty (related to external conditions or the environment).

Weiner's Theory

Our interest in motivation is tied more directly to how someone interprets his or her own actions and the resulting outcomes. This leads to Weiner's theories of attributions, (1974, 1985, 2010; Weiner et al., 1971), which expanded on ideas of causality. Attributions are individuals' explanations for their success or failure. Weiner et al. (1971) suggested that these explanations integrate three causal dimensions:

- **Locus of causality**—This is the location of the cause whether it is internal or external to the person. For example, a student may believe he failed a test because he did not study, an internal cause or may believe he failed because the test was very difficult, an external cause.

- **Stability**—This refers to whether the cause remains the same over the long term and in different circumstances. For example, the student above can decide to study, an unstable cause that can change, and believe the test will retain its level of difficulty, an unchanging stable cause.

- **Controllability**—This refers to whether a person believes the cause is under his or her control. In the same example, the student can control the amount of effort and study time, but cannot control the design of the test.

ATTRIBUTION THEORY:

Theory that states there is a relationship between motivation and three causal dimensions: locus of causality, stability and controllability.

Does someone's attributions always reflect reality?

In his research, Weiner (2010) has concluded that most of the attributions made in learning contexts fall into the following four causes of achievement: ability (internal, stable, and uncontrollable); effort (internal, unstable, and controllable); difficulty of task (external, stable, and uncontrollable); and luck (external, unstable, and uncontrollable). Depending on the attribution, there can be subsequent cognitive and behavioral consequences as well as significant motivational effects.

TABLE 6.2.2 ATTRIBUTIONS

	Stable	Unstable
Internal	Innate Ability	Acquired Ability/Effort
External	Task	Luck

Controllable	Uncontrollable

Expectancy Principle

Weiner's expectancy principle ties the previous causal dimensions to expectations about the future and future results. For example, a student who fails a test and believes the reason for her failure is her lack of intellect or ability is making a stable, uncontrollable, and internal attribution. Put bluntly, this student may believe she is "just stupid." Because she believes this trait is unchanging and uncontrollable, it could lead to high expectancy for failure in the future. This has significant implications for motivation. A student who sees no chance for success will most likely procrastinate, not study, or not try at all. Over time, this can lead to learned helplessness where a person believes they have no control over the outcomes in their life (Seligman, 1975). In other words, 'Why try if I'm only going to fail?' This situation can be further intensified if external attributions are also made such as believing that the teacher was unfair. In each case, the student will feel as if she has no control, and more importantly, this feeling will not change over time (Weiner, 2010).

The other extreme occurs when a student fails a test and recognizes that she did not study or only used rote or rehearsal strategies to prepare. This person is making unstable, controllable, and internal attributions. It is likely in the future that this student will decide to make changes to her level of effort and possibly the strategies used to study. In this instance, the student believes there is an opportunity for success. Weiner would argue that the driving factor in a person's expectancy for success or failure is dependent on whether it is stable or changeable over time (Weiner, 2010).

ATTRIBUTIONS AND ATTRIBUTION RETRAINING AND ACADEMIC ACHIEVEMENT

The research supports significant relationships between student attributions and achievement and affective outcomes (Hamm, Perry, Clifton, Chipperfield, & Boese, 2014; Perry, Stupnisky, Daniels, & Haynes, 2008; Perry, Stupnisky, Hall, Chipperfield, & Weiner, 2010; Swinton, Kurtz-Costes, Rowley, & Okeke-Adeyanju, 2011). Achievements, including course grades and GPAs, motivation, and positive affect have been consistently related to attributions that emphasize internal, controllable attributions. Although some studies identify the given attributions and the resultant outcomes (Perry et al., 2008; Swinton et al., 2011), other studies examine the effect of attribution retraining on many of these same outcomes (Hamm et al., 2014; Perry et al., 2010).

Perry et al.'s (2008) study examined the attributions of first-year students entering college and their related achievement. In particular, the researchers found that students made complex attributions that identified multiple causes (e.g., low ability and unfair teacher) for their successes and failures.

From these, four groups of students were identified. The worst performing of these groups were the relinquished-control students. These were students who identified both internal (i.e., innate ability) and external (i.e., teacher, difficulty of task) uncontrollable causes for their failures. The result for these students was lower course grades and lower GPAs at the end of the year. Students who were more likely to persist and have higher achievement were identified as self-protective students. These students were more likely to identify internal *controllable* attributions (i.e., effort) as well as external uncontrollable attributions. Perry at el. argued that these students recognized the need to adapt their efforts to achieve success; however, they were also able to "save face" in light of the more difficult college-level tasks by identifying some of the uncontrollable, external factors.

Another study by Perry et al. (2010) also examined transitioning first-year students. The quasi-experimental design included attributional retraining where controllable attributions (e.g., effort) were emphasized and uncontrollable attributions (e.g., poor professor) were de-emphasized. The result for study participants included higher course grades and first-year GPAs and more positive affect in the second semester. Similarly, a study by Hamm et al. (2014) assessed the effects of attributional retraining for first-year students who were high risk. The results for these students also included higher intrinsic motivation, GPAs and fewer course withdrawals. The fact that students' attributions can be influenced by retraining is an important consideration, especially when examining your own attributions and their associated effects on your motivation and achievement. These will be discussed more in Module 6.3.

Attributions and these results are highly aligned with the following theories around mindsets and implicit theories of intelligence, which are discussed next.

GROWTH MINDSET DEFINED

> *"...they believe that a person's true potential is unknown (and unknowable); that it's impossible to foresee what can be accomplished with years of passion, toil, and training"* (Dweck, 2006).

FIXED MINDSET:
A belief that abilities and intelligence cannot be changed.

GROWTH MINDSET:
A belief that abilities and intelligence can be developed over time.

Mindset refers to how a person views their ability and intelligence. A person with a fixed mindset believes his or her intelligence and abilities cannot change over time (Dweck, 2006). A person with a growth mindset recognizes that with work and effort, any ability can be further developed. Mindsets align with Dweck's earlier work that described how individuals have an implicit theory of intelligence. People either have an entity view (ability is fixed) or an incremental view (ability is changeable) of intelligence (Dweck & Leggett, 1988).

Mindset Influences

Although your mindset is wholly your own, the people around you can have a significant influence on whether you have a fixed or growth mindset (Dweck, 2006, 2010). Messages, feedbacks, and even praise can have a positive or negative influence on your mindset. Consider the following statements:

> Teacher 1 to student: Wow, that's fantastic! You did really great on that test, you are really smart!

> Teacher 2 to student: Wow, that's fantastic! I know you studied really hard and it looks like it paid off!

What kind of attribution is Teacher 1 making for the student? Is this helpful for long-term motivation?

Both of these statements seem positive and on the surface may appear to help a student maintain motivation; however, the first statement is actually promoting a fixed mindset by emphasizing an innate trait: intelligence or "being smart." When people have a fixed mindset, they tend to believe that the outcomes in their life are not within their control. For tasks that are "easy," they will continue to have success; however, as soon as they face difficulties or failure, they may decide that they just are not "smart enough." For individuals with a growth mindset, they believe the outcomes in their life are under their control, and even in the face of failure, they regard these opportunities as areas for development and learning. Teacher 2's statement focused on effort and hence supports a growth mindset. As such, any internal or external messages or feedback that emphasizes stable, uncontrollable, and internal attributions, such as innate ability, tends to lead to fixed mindsets (Mueller, & Dweck, 1998). Messages that emphasize unstable, controllable, and internal attributions, such as effort, tend to lead to growth mindsets (Blackwell, Trzesniewski, & Dweck, 2007; Dweck, 2006, 2010). How do these mindsets affect your motivation? The following discusses both the research that supports the positive outcomes of a growth mindset as well as the relationship between mindsets and achievement motivation.

Mindset Outcomes

Specifically within the education domain, growth mindsets or incremental views of intelligence have consistently been related to positive achievement and motivation outcomes including persistence, grades, test performance, and enjoyment (Blackwell et al., 2007; Dweck, 2010; Good, Aronson, & Inzlicht, 2003; Mueller & Dweck, 1998). An experimental study by Blackwell et al. (2007) examined the effect of a direct intervention that sought to influence students' theories of intelligence. Students who were given information and lessons around growth mindsets not only had higher course grades, but their achievement continued to exceed for two more years (the length of the study). This growth in achievement also reflected an abrupt change, at the time of the intervention, in the students' achievement trajectory. Achievement was declining, and then, after the intervention, it began to increase. Additionally, these students' level of motivation was significantly higher from the control group as measured by their teachers (who were blind to who participated in the intervention).

Another experimental study by Good et al. (2003) examined whether promoting growth mindsets was related to higher standardized test scores for females and minority and low-income students. These students were examined due to consistent gaps in achievement on standardized tests. The study suggested that students who are exposed to stereotypical ideas about intelligence and ability may be more likely to have fixed mindsets in which they view their ability as inherent due to their identification within a group. After being mentored and encouraged to view their intelligence as malleable and changeable (i.e., a growth mindset), the participants in the experimental group outperformed their peers on these standardized tests.

Many of these studies identify the link between mindsets, associated outcomes, and goal orientation (Dweck & Leggett, 1988). If students view their intelligence and ability as incremental, then they are more likely to have learning goals or a mastery orientation, which, in turn, can lead to higher levels of intrinsic motivation. Students with a mastery orientation also tend to understand that learning is a process requiring effort and appropriate use of strategies. As a result, these students are more likely to persist through difficulties and failure by adjusting their efforts and strategies. Similarly, they are also more likely to attribute successes and failures to unstable, controllable, and internal attributions.

How do you think external attributions are related to mindsets and someone's achievement and motivation?

The opposite is true for students with fixed mindsets or entity views of intelligence (Dweck & Leggett, 1988). These students are more likely to have performance goals and will feel the need to "prove" their ability repeatedly (Dweck, 2006). Unfortunately, this can also mean that students will either give up in the face of challenges or not even try in an attempt to "save face" and avoid looking "stupid."

MOTIVATION MATRIX

From these discussions, it should be clear that motivation theories tend to overlap to help explain beliefs and behaviors. The following illustrates how each theory contributes to a person's motivation.

TABLE 6.2.3 CHARACTERISTICS OF HIGHER AND LOWER LEVELS OF MOTIVATION WITHIN EACH THEORY OF MOTIVATION

	Maximizing Motivation	Diminishing Motivation
Tasks and Activities	Intrinsic motivation leads to seeking activities that are inherently enjoyable and further competence	Extrinsic motivation leads to seeking activities that results in rewards or avoids failure
Locus of Causality and Self-Determination	Has an internal locus of causality and believes choices and behaviors are related to personal goals and values	Has an external locus of causality and believes choices are dictated by others
Achievement Motivation	Mastery orientation or learning goals leads to seeking opportunities to develop skills and advance learning	Performance goals leads to seeking tasks that will result in rewards or looking "smart"
Self-Efficacy	High self-efficacy leads to seeking tasks that are challenging, to utilizing more elaborative learning strategies and to planning more effectively	Low self-efficacy can lead to diminished effort, seeking easy tasks or quitting altogether
Attributions	Attributions for success and failure are typically unstable, internal, controllable factors, such as effort	Attributions for success and failure are typically external and/or stable, internal, uncontrollable factors, such as ability
Views of Intelligence	Views intelligence as incremental and capable of development and change with effort	Views intelligence as fixed

MODULE 6.2 SUMMARY

- Social Cognitive Theory holds that learning occurs in a social context and involves a combination of cognitive, affective, motivational, and biological factors.

- Self-efficacy beliefs are learned through mastery experiences, social modeling, verbal persuasion, and emotional arousal.

- Personal agency or your capacity to fulfill self-determined choices, can be either positively or negatively influenced by self-efficacy beliefs.

- Attribution theory states that a person's assumed causes for success and failure can influence motivation and achievement.

- Attribution causes are divided into three dimensions: locus of causality, stability, and controllability.

- Expectancy principle emphasizes the relationship between expectations for future success with unstable causes and expectations for future failure with stable causes.
- Mindsets and implicit theories of intelligence reflect whether a person believes his or her ability and intellect is changeable (growth mindset) or set (fixed mindset).

KEY TERMS

- **Attributions** – A person's explanations for success or failure.
- **Attribution Theory** – Theory that states there is a relationship between motivation and three causal dimensions: locus of causality, stability, and controllability.
- **Emotional Arousal** – The impact of physiological feedback on subsequent task persistence, motivation, and self-efficacy beliefs.
- **Fixed Mindset** – A belief that abilities and intelligence cannot be changed.
- **Growth Mindset** – A belief that abilities and intelligence can be developed over time.
- **Mastery Experiences** – The impact of past successes or failures on subsequent task persistence, motivation, and self-efficacy beliefs.
- **Modeling** – The process by which persons serve as an imitative example or to otherwise influence the behaviors of others.
- **Self-Efficacy** – Individual beliefs in the ability or capacity to complete certain tasks or attain specific goals.
- **Sense of Agency** – The subjective awareness that one is initiating, executing, and controlling one's own actions in the world.
- **Social Cognitive Theory** – Psychological theory that explains personality development in terms of thoughts, feelings, actions, and motivations derived from interaction with the social environment.
- **Social Modeling** – The impact of observing others perform tasks, or handle situations, on subsequent task persistence, motivation, or self-efficacy beliefs.
- **Verbal Persuasion** – The impact of either verbal support or discouragement on subsequent task persistence, motivation, and self-efficacy beliefs.

REFERENCES

Bandura, A. (1977). Self-efficacy: Toward a unifying theory of behavioral change. *Psychological Review, 84,* 191–215.

Bandura, A. (1982). Self-efficacy mechanisms in human agency. *American Psychologist, 37,* 122–147.

Bandura, A. (1991). Social cognitive theory of self-regulation. *Organizational Behavior and Human Decision Processes, 50,* 248–287.

Bandura, A. (1992) Exercise of personal agency through the self-efficacy mechanisms. In R. Schwarzer (Ed.), *Self-efficacy: Thought control of action* (pp. 3–38). Washington, DC: Hemisphere.

Bandura, A. (1995). *Self-efficacy in changing societies.* Cambridge University Press.

Bandura, A. (1997). *Self-efficacy: The exercise of control.* New York: W.H. Freeman.

Bandura, A. (2006). Toward a psychology of human agency. *Perspectives on Psychological Science, 1*(2), 164–180.

Bandura, A., Adams, N. E., & Beyer, J. (1977). Cognitive processes mediating behavioral change. *Journal of Personality and Social Psychology, 35*(3), 125–139.

Blackwell, L. S., Trzesniewski, K. H., & Dweck, C. S. (2007). Implicit theories of intelligence predict achievement across an adolescent transition: A longitudinal study and an intervention. *Child Development, 78*(1), 246–263.

Dweck, C. S. (2006). *Mindset. The new psychology of success.* New York: Random House.

Dweck, C. S. (2010). Mind-sets and equitable education. *Principal Leadership, 10*(5), 26–29.

Dweck, C. S., & Leggett, E. L. (1988). A social-cognitive approach to motivation and personality. *Psychological Review, 95*(2), 256–273.

Gecas, V. (2004). Self-agency and the life course. In J. T. Mortimer & M. J. Shanahan (Eds.), *Handbook of the life course* (pp. 369–390). New York: Springer.

Good, C., Aronson, J., & Inzlicht, M. (2003). Improving adolescents' standardized test performance: An intervention to reduce the effects of stereotype threat. *Applied Developmental Psychology, 24,* 645–662.

Hamm, J. M., Perry, R. P., Clifton, R. A., Chipperfield, J. G., & Boese, G. D. (2014). Attributional retraining: A motivation treatment with differential psychosocial and performance benefits for failure prone individuals in competitive achievement settings. *Basic and Applied Social Psychology, 36,* 221–237. doi: 10.1080/01973533.2014.890623

Heider, F. (1958). *The psychology of interpersonal relations.* New York: John Wiley & Sons.

Mueller, C. M., & Dweck, C. S. (1998). Intelligence praise can undermine motivation and performance. *Journal of Personality and Social Psychology, 75,* 33–52.

Pajares, F. (2009). Toward a positive psychology of academic motivation: The role of self-efficacy beliefs. In R. Gilman, E. S. Huebner & M. J. Furlong (Eds.), *Handbook of positive psychology in schools* (pp. 149–160). New York: Taylor & Francis.

Pajares, F., & Schunk, D. (2001). Self-beliefs and school success: Self-efficacy, self-concept, and school achievement. In R. Riding & S. Rayner (Eds.), *Perception* (pp. 239–266). London: Ablex Publishing.

Perry, R. P., Stupnisky, R. H., Daniels, L. M., & Haynes, T. L. (2008). Attributional (explanatory) thinking about failure in new achievement settings. *European Journal of Psychology of Education, 23*(4), 459–475.

Perry, R. P., Stupnisky, R. H., Hall, N. C., Chipperfield, J. G., & Weiner, B. (2010). Bad starts and better finishes: Attributional retraining and initial performance in competitive achievement settings. *Journal of Social and Clinical Psychology, 29*(6), 668–700.

Schunk, D. H. (1991). Self-efficacy and academic motivation. *Educational Psychologist, 26,* 207–231.

Seligman, M. E. P. (1975). *Helplessness: On depression, development, and death.* San Francisco: Freeman.

Swinton, A. D., Kurtz-Costes, B., Rowley, S. J., & Okeke-Adeyanju, N. (2011). A longitudinal examination of African American adolescents' attributions about achievement outcomes. *Child Development, 82*(5), 1486–1500.

Weiner, B. (Ed.). (1974). *Cognitive views of human motivation.* New York: Academic Press.

Weiner, B. (1985). An attributional theory of achievement motivation and emotion. *Psychological Review, 92*(4), 548–573.

Weiner, B. (2010). The development of an attribution-based theory of motivation: A history of ideas. *Educational Psychologist, 45*(1), 28–36.

Weiner, B., Frieze, I. H., Kukla, A., Reed, L., Rest, S., & Rosenbaum, R. M. (1971). *Perceiving the causes of success and failure.* Morristown, NJ: General Learning Press.

Williams, T., & Williams, K. (2010). Self-efficacy and performance in mathematics: Reciprocal determinism in 33 nations. *Journal of Educational Psychology, 102*(2), 453–466.

GAINING AWARENESS AND TAKING CONTROL

CLUSTER 6 OBJECTIVES COVERED IN THIS MODULE

☐ **OBJECTIVE:** Describe the relationship between motivation and other areas (e.g., goals, time management, etc.,) that influence students' educational experiences.

☐ **OBJECTIVE:** Identify strategies to promote and maintain higher levels of motivation.

In the introduction to this cluster, it was suggested that people are not born with some sort of motivation "gene." It may seem like some people are naturally more motivated, but it is likely they have gained an understanding about motivation and its relationship to different facets of their lives. Now that you have an understanding of some key motivational theories and principles, the next step is to gain awareness of how these principles are occurring in your life, and more importantly, how they are affecting your choices and behaviors.

INTRINSIC AND EXTRINSIC MOTIVATION: MASTERY AND PERFORMANCE GOALS

REFLECTION: Do you enjoy all of your academic tasks or are some of them difficult to complete due to lack of interest?

COURSES IN YOUR MAJOR

For intrinsic and extrinsic motivation, it is helpful to gain awareness of where these occur in your academic life. For example, in your courses, do you find that your primary motivation is getting the grade (an extrinsic motivator and performance goal) or are you excited about learning the concepts (an intrinsic motivator and mastery goal)? If the course is primarily content for your major, these questions are significant. Long-term achievement, persistence, and satisfaction will be driven by intrinsic motivators and mastery goals. Alternatively, extrinsic motivators such as grades or career outcomes (such as income) could lead to difficulty in completing academic tasks or more importantly, long-term dissatisfaction with your career choice. As such, it would be helpful to reflect on where each of your major-content courses fall: into the intrinsic motivation/mastery goals or the extrinsic motivation/performance goals category. Depending on your answer, a change may be helpful.

Consider the following example:

As a student, Maria loved the courses in her major. As a result, she read additional books, visited with her professors often and sought out additional ways to develop her skills and knowledge. However, she also recognized that her grades were important to make her competitive for internships and ultimately in seeking a position after graduation.

Now, Maria has graduated and is now working in her chosen profession. She still loves what she does and as a result, seeks out new challenges in her job, continuously looks for ways to develop her skills and quickly volunteers for new tasks. However, Maria is not a volunteer. She still wants the extrinsic rewards of being a professional.

Maria is a good example of how intrinsic and extrinsic motivation can be effectively combined within a major and within a career. The key distinction to recognize is that intrinsic motivation can lead to the possibility of higher performance and subsequent extrinsic rewards. Highly motivated students who seek out challenges, continue to develop new skills, and go beyond what is required, are typically the students who earn higher grades and get hired in their chosen fields.

ACTIVITY 6.3.1 USE THE FOLLOWING TO ANALYZE YOUR MOTIVATION IN YOUR MAJOR-CONTENT COURSES. ON A SCALE FROM 1 (STRONGLY DISAGREE) TO 5 (STRONGLY AGREE), HOW WOULD YOU ANSWER THESE QUESTIONS:	
	Do you have one or more courses in your major where it is difficult to complete the requirements?
	Do you have one or more courses in your major where you are completing the requirements but only doing the bare minimum?
	Do you have one or more courses in your major where you are doing any of the following: procrastinating, skipping classes, cramming for examinations, etc.?
	Do you have one or more courses in your major where you are only concerned about getting the grade?

If you answered with a 4 or 5 on the majority of these questions, you should probably reexamine your interest in your major. Questions to ask yourself:

- Did you select this major for yourself or for someone else?
- Are you focused on the potential future extrinsic rewards (e.g., income, prestige, etc.)?
- Does this major align with your talents and interests?

By ensuring your major taps into your intrinsic motivation, you will likely have less stress, learn more deeply, manage your time better, and achieve more. There are resources (e.g., career services, academic advisers, etc.) on your campus to assist you if a change is necessary.

OTHER COURSES AND ACADEMIC TASKS

What about your other courses that may not include specific major content but are still required? If you enjoy these, most likely you have higher motivation to engage in the coursework and attend class. But, what about those courses you do not enjoy?

- Do you find yourself procrastinating?
- Is it easier to justify missing class?
- Do you do just enough to get by (or maybe your grade has reached a point of real trouble)?
- Do you use learning strategies that are low-level rehearsal strategies?

If the answer is yes to one or more of these questions, there are ways to regain control and help motivate yourself to be more effective in these courses. First, if you have little interest in the content, it can be helpful to try and find connections to areas you do enjoy. Talking with your professor or seeking out other readings around the coursework can help build some interest in the material. If this does not increase interest, reminding yourself of your bigger picture can help. Remember earlier in the cluster, it was suggested that your motivation can shift from extrinsic motivation to more intrinsic forms of motivation (the process of internalization) if you can connect the tasks to your goals and values. For example:

> Deshawn is taking a psychology class as part of his general education requirement. At first, he feels it is not related to his major, electrical engineering. He does not enjoy the class and he recognizes that his motivation continues to diminish. As such, he decides to reflect on how this course and its requirements fit into his big picture and the goals he wants to achieve. First, he has to graduate with his degree to be an engineer and this class is a requirement. When he starts to make poor choices based on his lack of interest, he reminds himself of this important goal. Second, he reflects on the skills the class is trying

to develop. He is learning about people and their behaviors and begins to recognize how some of these concepts will help him work more successfully in engineering teams in the future. As a result, Deshawn's motivation improves.

Deshawn is still extrinsically motivated but it has shifted to an integrated form of extrinsic motivation. In other words, he has built value around this course due to the connections he has made to his goals. The result will most likely be higher motivation, which can then lead to more complex learning strategies, deeper learning, and more effective time management.

This same approach can also work for academic tasks that are dry, time consuming, or even boring. Many times, making the connection to your goals for the particular course can be helpful. For instance:

- I want to earn a 3.0 GPA this semester.
- To make that happen, I need to earn at least a B in my sociology course.
- To earn that B, I need to do each of the readings before lectures.

Ongoing reminders of your goals and how these tasks fit in to achieving them can increase motivation and make it easier to follow through.

GOALS AND TIME MANAGEMENT

In Cluster 2, it was suggested that goals drive motivation and are critical to success in school and beyond. In Cluster 3, there were several suggestions and tips on incorporating goals to help you effectively manage your time. Looking back on the goals you made at the beginning of the semester, are you achieving these goals or at least making satisfactory progress towards these goals? Do you accomplish everything you want each week and maintain a balance between school and leisure? If the answer is no, you may need to make some adjustments. Although many of these suggestions were made previously, this section provides some reminders and connects them directly to motivation theory.

For goals that have stalled consider the following:

	Suggested Task	Likely Result	Example
1. Is the goal missing one of the three characteristic of useful goals: specific and measurable, realistic and challenging and includes a timeframe?	Rewrite your goal to include all three characteristics.	Your motivation will likely increase because you have a specific plan of action and can evaluate progress.	**Original Goal**: I'll finish all of my homework for my courses. **New Goal:** I'll finish all of my homework for my courses at least two days before their due dates.
2. Does this goal feel too big or overwhelming?	Try smaller, short-term enabling goals to help you achieve the bigger goal.	Your *self-efficacy* will increase if you focus on smaller tasks in the immediate short term. These tasks will feel less overwhelming and boost your confidence that you can complete them.	**Original Goal**: I'll earn an A in my biology course. **Enabling Goal:** Every week, I will divide my readings in biology and schedule them over four days. **Enabling Goal:** I will visit the biology tutor at least one day every week.
3. Do you set goals for the week and then do not follow through?	Try incorporating daily and weekly rewards to help you focus on following through.	Rewards can help you tap into *intrinsic* and *extrinsic motivation* and be the force needed to follow through.	**Goal:** Finish all of my weekly requirements/goals by Friday at 5pm. **Reward:** If I finish all of my weekly goals, I will spend Friday night and Saturday with my friends hanging out. If I don't finish, I will continue working until it is done.
4. Are there obstacles getting in the way?	Consider goals that will help you be proactive and move past your obstacles. If needed, seek out resources that can help you such as campus resources (e.g., tutoring), professors, peers, etc.	This will increase motivation by giving you opportunities to take control (helpful *attributions*) and make more progress towards your goal. As you make more progress, your *self-efficacy* will also increase.	**Obstacle**: I get distracted by my dorm mate and the others in my hall and I don't feel like studying. **New Goal:** Each night, I will schedule my study time for the next day and then study in the library and not in the dorm.
5. If you answered no to questions 1–4, have you considered whether this goal should be changed?	Evaluate whether you own this goal and that it aligns with your values.	Attempting goals for others or pursuing goals outside of your values will diminish both your *intrinsic* and *extrinsic* motivation. Many times, this will mean complete termination of efforts.	**Original Goal**: I will get an A in my nursing classes this semester. **Analysis:** My parents want me to be a nurse but I'm not finding it interesting. I don't feel like I own this goal and should probably make a change.

The chart discusses incorporating rewards into your plan. By tapping into your intrinsic and extrinsic motivation, you can take advantage of a very powerful force to manage your own behaviors. What are some potential rewards that you can incorporate? Is it time with friends, going to a movie? Is it spending some time on social media or texting or playing video games? Are there specific treats that you can reward yourself with such as a shopping trip or a visit to your favorite ice cream shop? Not only can you use these for weekly or semester goals, you can incorporate them throughout your day. For example:

> Jose sits down to study one afternoon. He has specific study session goals he wants to accomplish. He needs to read and take notes on 15 pages of his chemistry book, write an introductory paragraph for English, and complete his homework problems for Calculus. He turns off his phone and tablet so that he has no distractions. He decides he will take a 15 minute break after he completes each of these tasks and allow himself some time to text his friends and check his social media. Once the 15 minutes are done, he will turn everything off again and start the next task. When he is completely done, he will go have dinner with his girlfriend.

The additional reward for being intentional with his plan is that Jose can now enjoy his time with his girlfriend without worrying that he should have done more. He has set a plan and accomplished each of his goals so now he can relax and enjoy his evening.

INFORMATION PROCESSING

Cluster 4 described how elaboration strategies allow for deeper processing of information. There is also another advantage to selecting challenging and complex learning tasks and strategies that is related specifically to motivation. Consider how you are supposed to study outside of class one to three hours per every credit hour spent in class. Therefore, for a three-credit class, you should be studying as much as nine hours per week outside of class. Now imagine that you select only rehearsal strategies to complete during those nine hours. This means reading, re-reading, highlighting, flash-cards, reviewing notes, rewriting notes, re-reading, etc. For many students, this could become tedious (i.e., *boring*) and make it difficult to continue. However, by selecting more complex and challenging elaboration strategies, interest and intrinsic motivation can be increased. You are more likely to get deeply involved, and as a result, spend more time on tasks such as creating concept maps or participating in study groups.

Would you rather read your textbook through eight times or create a complex elaborative study guide once?

This then ties into feelings of increased competence (and self-efficacy), which are also linked to higher feelings of intrinsic motivation.

BELIEFS: SELF-EFFICACY, ATTRIBUTIONS AND MINDSETS

REFLECTION: In what areas do you feel you have low self-efficacy? How has this impacted you as a learner?

SELF-EFFICACY

Gaining awareness of your beliefs is also an important facet for promoting and maintaining your motivation. Identifying areas where you have low self-efficacy can help you be proactive and avert some of the more negative consequences. Consider the following:

> During high school, Huan really struggled in her math classes. In fact, she had to repeat one of her semesters to earn her credit. Now, as a second-semester college freshman, she is required to take College Algebra. She recognizes she has low self-efficacy and understands this could affect her motivation, her choice of learning tasks, her persistence, and her time management. However, she is determined to earn her degree and will not let a math class deter her. So she decides she will get a tutor at the beginning of the semester and will go twice every week. During the first week of class, she is going to ask some of her classmates if they would like to meet in a weekly study group. She asks another student if he would like to compare notes after each class. She also goes and visits her professor and asks for suggestions on how to be successful in her course. And lastly, she creates her weekly schedule and sets study times for Algebra six days a week.

Huan has recognized her low self-efficacy in math and has taken immediate specific steps to build her competence and to create a support network. She is not waiting until she experiences difficulties or even failures. As a result, it is likely her self-efficacy will increase over time. At a minimum, she has optimized her opportunities and has provided herself the best chance for success.

The question now is this: In what areas do you have low self-efficacy? What strategies are you using to give yourself the best chance for success?

> Do you think that your abilities and skills are determined by the time you are a teenager in high school? What do failures or successes in high school really mean?

ATTRIBUTIONS AND MINDSETS

Read the following and then select the response that makes the most sense to you:

> Jesse just finished her first mid-term examination in her chemistry class. Although she was very nervous about the examination, she hopes that she did well. However, when she received her results, she failed the examination with a 57%.

Which of the following do you think is the most likely explanation for Jesse's failure?

A. Chemistry is really difficult and Jesse is most likely just not able to pass the examination.

B. Chemistry is really difficult and Jesse most likely did not study enough.

C. If Jesse had studied more she should have been able to pass the examination.

D. Jesse's chemistry professor probably tried to write as difficult an examination as possible because it was the mid-term examination.

If you selected response (A), (B) or (D), you are making external, uncontrollable and stable attributions (i.e., chemistry is really difficult and the chemistry professor). Additionally, in response (A), you are making an internal, uncontrollable and stable attribution (Jesse is most likely just not able to pass). Response (C) focuses on an internal, controllable and unstable attribution (i.e., studied more).

Many times, people will make the same types of attributions for their successes and their failures repeatedly. As with identifying your self-efficacy, it is helpful to become aware of the type of attributions you tend to make. Over time, have you gotten into the habit of explaining your successes and failures with events and circumstances that are not in your control? Does it sometimes feel like you are at the whim of the world with little impact on the outcomes in your life? If the answer is yes, it is likely that your motivation has been minimized. In other words, why try if you cannot change anything?

The key to shifting from these types of attributions is to focus on the areas where you do have control and to recognize that your abilities and intellect can change over time (i.e., a growth mindset). Sometimes people will be in circumstances where they do not have control such as having a poor professor or being in a very difficult class; however, students who succeed in these circumstances ask, "What can I do in spite of these circumstances" or "Where do I have control and how do I maximize my opportunities for success?" Similar to the student described previously with low self-efficacy, students who use proactive strategies and take immediate steps are more likely to face these challenges effectively. Students who make internal, controllable attributions are more likely to:

- Have higher self-efficacy
- Use more complex learning strategies, and
- Overcome difficulties and failures.

Sometimes it may feel better or seem easier to blame a professor, the material or even bad luck; however, you will feel more empowered when you believe that you have the ability to get the results you want. This is highly motivating and can propel you to achieve each of your goals.

1. What is an area where you are experiencing low motivation?

2. What are your behaviors and choices that suggest you have low motivation in this area?

3. What goals have you set for this area? Do they include all three characteristics (i.e., specific and measurable, realistic and challenging, and includes a timeframe)?

4. Using the questions listed in the summary on the next page (e.g., are you linking your tasks with your course goals, are you incorporating rewards, etc.), which of these are potentially contributing to your low motivation?

5. Again, considering these questions, what are specific changes that you can make to positively influence your motivation? Are there new goals that you need to make?

6. Now imagine you have high motivation in this area, what will your life look like and how will it make you feel? How will it contribute to your bigger personal, academic and professional goals?

SUMMARY

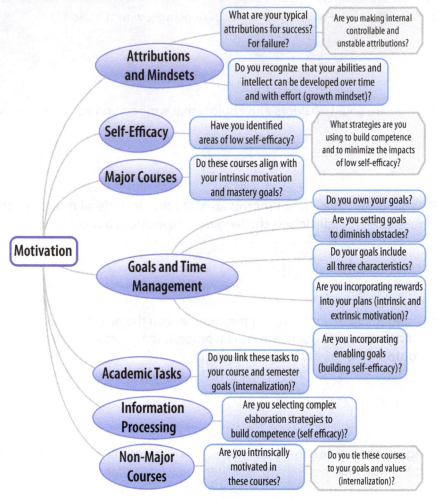

Source: Angela Vaughan and Brett Wilkinson

CASE STUDY

Jessica is a second-semester freshmen. She is majoring in accounting because her mother is an accountant. She never misses classes and turns in all of her work; however, she always waits to the last minute to complete her assignments. Additionally, she only does exactly what is required to get the grade. She does not enjoy her classes, but still manages to go through the motions and get decent grades. When asked about her major, Jessica says: "I guess accounting is alright. I mean, the classes are pretty boring but I still get the work done and my grades are pretty good. And even when I do not understand what the instructors are talking about or why it is important, I still pass the examinations, so that is good too. I don't know. A friend of mine said that I shouldn't worry about remembering this stuff right now anyway because we will review it all in my sophomore classes."

1. What type of motivation do you think is primarily influencing Jessica's behavior?

2. How is this related to her goal orientation?

3. Do you think that her motivation and goal orientation will ultimately affect her persistence and achievement over the long-term? Why or why not?

4. What recommendations would you give Jessica?

POTENTIAL RESPONSES

1. As Jessica is studying accounting because her mother was an accountant it is likely she is extrinsically motivated. This seems to be the case as her behaviors (e.g., waits to the last minute, only does what is required to get the grade) are reflective of someone who is not intrinsically motivated.

2. Additionally, these behaviors are also related to having performance goals. This is exemplified even more by her admitting "even when I do not understand what the instructors are talking about...I still pass the exams." Her focus is not on mastering the content but to get by and make it through this first year.

3. As tasks get more complex and the level of difficulty increases, it will be hard for Jessica to not only maintain decent grades but her lack of interest or enjoyment in the material will most likely make it challenging, or even impossible, to put in the extra effort needed to learn and succeed. She may decide it is not "worth it."

   Furthermore, because she initially is putting in minimal effort and still succeeding, she may decide that new failures in the future are a signal that she is not smart enough for this major and make a change. Her initial attributions in this first semester are most likely that she is smart enough (i.e., internal, stable, and uncontrollable) and the tasks are fairly easy (i.e., external, stable, and uncontrollable). With failure, her attributions could shift to she is not smart enough and the tasks are too difficult for her. Both are uncontrollable and stable and could lead to quitting.

4. Jessica could try to build interest in accounting by talking with her professors and other professionals in the field. Although her mother was an accountant, her experiences may not align with Jessica's interests. This does not mean other pathways within the career would not be interesting to Jessica. Another alternative would be to talk with academic advisors, career services, and other professors about potential career interests. Once she has identified a few possibilities, she could take courses, attend student clubs, and talk with professionals in these areas to see if there is interest. If she makes a change, she should continue to monitor her motivation, achievement orientation, and attributions to see if these align to support long-term intrinsic motivation and achievement.

ADDITIONAL READINGS

Altermatt, E. R. (2019). Academic support from peers as a predictor of academic self-efficacy among college students. *Journal of College Student Retention: Research, Theory & Practice, 21*(1), 21–37. doi: 10.1177/1521025116686588

Bong, M., & Skaalvik, E. M. (2003). Academic self-concept and self-efficacy: How different are they really? *Educational Psychology Review, 15*(1), 1–40.

Midgley, C., Kaplan, A., & Middleton, M. (2001). Performance-approach goals: Good for what, for whom, under what circumstances, and at what cost? *Journal of Educational Psychology, 93*(1), 77–86.

Pintrich, P. R. (2003). A motivational science perspective on the role of student motivation in learning and teaching contexts. *Journal of Educational Psychology, 95*(4), 667–686.

Pintrich, P. R., & Zusho, A. (2007). Student motivation and self-regulated learning in the college classroom. In R. P. Perry & J. C. Smart (Eds.), *The scholarship of teaching and learning in higher education: An evidence-based perspective* (pp. 731–810). New York: Springer.

Reeve, J. (2016). A grand theory of motivation: Why not? *Motivation and Emotion, 40*(1), 31–35.

Rigby, C. S., Deci, E. L., Patrick, B. C., & Ryan, R. M. (1992). Beyond the intrinsic-extrinsic dichotomy: Self-determination in motivation and learning. *Motivation and Emotion, 16*(3), 165–185.

Robbins, S. B., Lauver, K., Le, H., Davis, D., Langley, R., & Carlstrom, A. (2004). Do psychosocial and study skill factors predict college outcomes? A meta-analysis. *Psychological Bulletin, 130*(2), 261–288.

Yeager, D. S., & Dweck, C. S. (2012). Mindsets that promote resilience: When students believe that personal characteristics can be developed. *Educational Psychologist, 47*(4), 302–314.

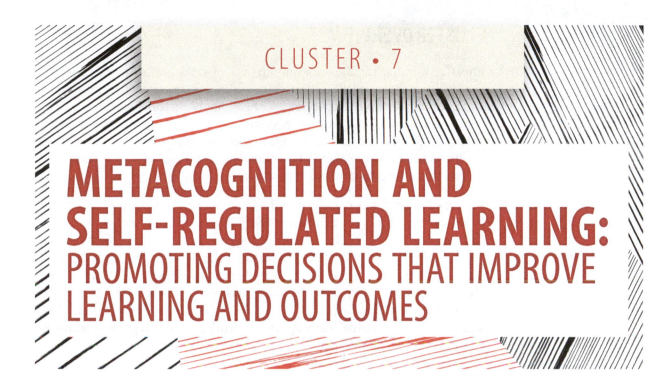

METACOGNITION AND SELF-REGULATED LEARNING:
PROMOTING DECISIONS THAT IMPROVE LEARNING AND OUTCOMES

CASE STUDY

Michael has always been a strong student. He maintained a 4.0 grade point average during high school and arrived at college expecting to do the same. However, his grades have been slipping during his first semester as a freshman. In particular, his grades on both exams and papers in several classes have been consistently lower than he had expected. Michael cannot understand why his academic outcomes are so different from high school. He has not changed anything about his approach to either studying or writing papers, splitting his study time equally among each class, reviewing class notes, highlighting his readings, and using the same memorization techniques that always worked so well before college. Although he decides that simply working harder will probably improve his outcomes, Michael reaches out to his academic advisor for support and direction.

QUESTIONS

1. How might you explain the downturn in Michael's academic outcomes?

2. Going beyond simply "working harder" to improve his academic outcomes, what metacognitive strategies might be helpful for Michael to use?

3. If you were an academic advisor, how might you use the dual processing model of self-regulation and/or the mental contrasting with implementation intentions (MCII) to help Michael address his current problem?

CLUSTER OVERVIEW

Effective learning requires not only the use of skills and strategies but also the ability to thoughtfully assess which skills and strategies are appropriate and useful in different situations. While many basic learning tasks can be completed almost automatically and without much focused thought, more challenging activities tend to engage higher level processing capacities. The ability to refine an approach to task completion involves two important processes: metacognition and self-regulation.

Equipped with a clear understanding of how these two processes influence learning, students can become more intentional in their use of strategies and techniques that can improve academic outcomes. The first module will define metacognition, describe some of the most important features of metacognition, and provide a template for considering ways to implement metacognitive learning strategies in the classroom. The second module will describe self-regulated learning, outline two self-regulated learning models, and provide yet another template for implementing self-regulated learning strategies in the classroom.

CLUSTER OBJECTIVES

- Describe the relationship between cognition, metacognition, and critical thinking as well as their features.
- Describe the characteristics of metacognitive knowledge and metacognitive regulation, including their commonalities.
- Develop an outline for implementing metacognitive strategies on a task.
- Describe characteristics of self-regulated learning.
- Explain the similarities and differences among two major models of self-regulated learning.
- Using the cyclical model of self-regulated learning, develop an outline for approaching a task.

MODULE 7.1

THINKING AND METACOGNITION

CLUSTER 7 OBJECTIVES COVERED IN THIS MODULE

☐ **OBJECTIVE:** Describe the relationship between cognition, metacognition, and critical thinking, as well as their features.

☐ **OBJECTIVE:** Describe the characteristics of metacognitive knowledge and metacognitive regulation, including their commonalities.

☐ **OBJECTIVE:** Develop an outline for implementing metacognitive strategies on a task.

OVERVIEW

REFLECTION: How do you know when a learning strategy is working? Do you recognize when a study approach is effective or when it is not? How do you know?

The Greek term "meta" denotes something that goes beyond, or follows after, something else. In this respect, it is conditional upon something that precedes it or otherwise serves as its basic foundation. Metacognition is therefore a type of cognition because it arises from cognition. Whereas cognition includes reasoning, decision-making, memory processes, attention and the like, metacognition involves thinking about such cognitions, or thinking about thinking. This appears to be a fairly straightforward definition, does it not? Yet, if you stop right now and really try to distinguish between a thought and a thought about a thought, you will likely find yourself somewhat perplexed. Where exactly does one end and the other begin?

This is not a simple distinction. Researchers continue to debate these differences even after 40 years of scholarly inquiry. However, a point of consensus has arisen that will serve as the foundation for this module: cognitions are automatic and unconscious while metacognitions are effortful and conscious (Veenman, Van-Hout-Wolters, & Afflerbach, 2006). For example, consider a

COGNITION:

Mental process of gaining knowledge and understanding by means of thoughts, perceptions, and sensations.

METACOGNITION:

Mental process of gaining knowledge and understanding about cognitions by means of thinking about thinking.

time when you acted without thinking, only to have someone ask "Why did you do that?" Any response to such a question requires effortful introspection, even if you honestly cannot explain your actions. The same principle applies if you were asked to explain how you go about adding two plus two, or how you memorize a brief list of terms. Such automatic cognitions remain unconscious until you deliberately reflect upon your thought process, or consciously engage your metacognitive thinking abilities.

What are some other examples of effortful introspection?

CRITICAL THINKING:
Mental process of purposefully monitoring, analyzing, and reformulating thoughts, beliefs, and judgments.

Under specific circumstances, metacognition also includes the cognitive skill of critical thinking. Metacognitive theorists such as Flavell (1979) and Kuhn (2000) consider critical thinking to be a subtype of metacognition. Critical thinking tends to involve self-reflection by means of questioning your personal beliefs, weighing the evidence for your ideas, or setting aside your preconceptions in order to evaluate new possibilities (Hennessey, 1999). Critical thinking also includes mental habits and attitudes such as curiosity, adaptability, open-mindedness, and fairness (Ennis, 1985; Halpern, 1998). While there are a variety of definitions for critical thinking, most include key terms such as evaluation, analysis, reasoning, and decision-making (Facione, 1990).

Notice that many of these terms are similar to those used earlier to describe cognition. In this respect, critical thinking can be considered a subtype of metacognition which, in turn, is a subtype of cognition. The remainder of this cluster will explore various facets of metacognition as a deliberate and conscious process of thinking. It is proposed that by gaining insight into how metacognition works, students will be in a better position to utilize it as a fundamental and important tool to promote self-regulated learning.

IMPORTANT ASPECTS OF METACOGNITION

The developmental psychologist, John Flavell (1976), is generally considered the pioneer of metacognitive research, having provided the following definition of the term:

> Metacognition refers to one's knowledge concerning one's own cognitive processes and products or anything related to them ... to the active monitoring and consequent regulation and orchestration of these processes in relation to the cognitive objects or data on which they bear, usually in the service of some concrete goal or objective (p. 232).

Notable terms from the above definition include *knowledge* and *regulation*, each of which serves as a core element in metacognitive theory. However, before exploring the importance of these terms in detail, it is important to clarify that Flavell's model of cognitive monitoring was grounded in the work of several notable theorists that came before him. The eminent psychologists Jean Piaget and Lev Vygotsky consistently addressed the value of deliberate, regulated, and goal-directed thinking in child development.

Earlier explorations of information processing and memory (Corsini, 1971; Hart, 1965) also contributed to the metacognitive enterprise, while contemporaneous meta-memory research conducted by Ann Brown (1978) significantly enhanced understanding of student decision-making as well as reading comprehension strategies.

DECLARATIVE AND PROCEDURAL KNOWLEDGE

Flavell (1979) originally designated four classes of metacognitive phenomena, including metacognitive knowledge, metacognitive experiences, goals or tasks, and actions or strategies. However, it was the subsequent work by Kluwe (1982) that emphasized the two general areas of interest in metacognitive research as used today: knowledge and regulation. According to Kluwe (1982), experiences, tasks, and strategies are subdivisions of metacognitive knowledge because each is a type of declarative knowledge.

Declarative knowledge relates to factual understandings and beliefs about how people learn and the variables that impact performance. It consists of both domain knowledge (i.e., stored information about facts and experiences) and cognitive knowledge (i.e., stored assumptions, hypotheses, and beliefs about thinking), each of which are rooted in memory capacities. In other words, declarative knowledge actually uses informational content stored in memory to assess situations and make metacognitive decisions. Therefore, this content directly affects your understanding and beliefs about how cognitive processes work in terms of your metacognitive knowledge of persons, tasks, and strategies.

DECLARATIVE KNOWLEDGE: Fixed information related to facts or verifiable data stored in memory.

Can you think of two basic examples of domain knowledge and cognitive knowledge in your own life experience?

This is contrasted with procedural knowledge, which gives rise to metacognitive regulation. Procedural knowledge, according to Kluwe (1982), includes how people "monitor the selection and application as well as the effects of solution processes and regulate the stream of solution activity" (p. 204). In other words, it involves the executive monitoring of your progress in an activity as well as the executive regulation of your energy and resources in accomplishing tasks. Whereas declarative knowledge is content-based, procedural knowledge is process-based, and thus emphasizes your metacognitive regulation strategies in the areas of planning, monitoring, and evaluating.

PROCEDURAL KNOWLEDGE: Situational information related to performing specific activities.

METACOGNITIVE KNOWLEDGE

Flavell (1979) defined metacognitive knowledge in terms of one's understandings and beliefs about specific cognitive processes. In particular, his model highlights three distinct types: knowledge of person variables, knowledge of task variables, and knowledge of strategy variables. Each follows precisely from its key term, clarifying the distinct ways in which you consider and approach how other people think and behave, what is required to complete a task, and which strategies to leverage in a given situation.

METACOGNITIVE KNOWLEDGE: Personal beliefs and understandings about cognitive processes.

Knowledge of Person

Person variables relate to the understanding of how you yourself *and* how others tend to learn and process information. Such knowledge of person variables influences both your own decision-making (e.g., knowing you study more effectively when listening to music) and how you relate to others (e.g., choosing to wear headphones when studying because music distracts your roommate). It also influences how you approach tasks and implement strategies when collaborating with other people. For example, to effectively work with others in a study group requires that you distinguish between your own learning styles and the learning processes of other group members in order to optimize group outcomes.

Can you pinpoint three different person variables that influence your own learning style?

Knowledge of Task

Task variables relate to knowledge of both what is generally required to complete a task and what challenges the task poses on your own processing capacities. In this respect, it involves not only an understanding of specific features of the task but also how capable you are of accomplishing it. In turn, task knowledge affects your decision-making and motivation because your assessment of how easy or challenging an activity will be often determines your willingness to invest time in that activity. For example, simply thinking about sitting down to complete a difficult reading assignment can serve as a deterrent for a tired student. The assessment of what is required to complete the task (e.g., focused attention) combined with an assessment of how capable you are of meeting that particular requirement (e.g., fatigue) is an example of metacognitive task knowledge in action.

Are there learning situations in which you feel more capable of doing well? What is it about these situations that make you feel confident? How is this related to self-efficacy?

Knowledge of Strategy

Strategy variables relate to knowledge of the strategies that are available for use in certain situations. These include both cognitive strategies and metacognitive strategies. Using cognitive strategies, you can implement specific techniques to accomplish goals, such as memorizing a vocabulary list by reciting the words repeatedly. When using metacognitive strategies, you can decide whether or not a particular cognitive approach is effective and then determine alternative approaches that might be more helpful. This process involves "stepping back" from the situation to evaluate both the task at hand and your own learning processes before choosing to use a different strategy, such as developing a mnemonic to memorize that long list of vocabulary words. Therefore, metacognitive strategies serve as a means of monitoring the use of cognitive strategies.

When reflecting on learning strategies, try to take a third-person point of view, as if you are observing yourself from the outside.

TABLE 7.1.1 METACOGNITIVE KNOWLEDGE

Variable	Definition	Example
Knowledge of person	Knowledge of your own learning processes and how you relate to others	You decide to work in a study group because it is helpful for you to hear a variety of explanations and it is helpful for your peers to be able to explain concepts.
Knowledge of task	Knowledge of how to complete tasks and your own potential obstacles to completing the tasks	You know you need to be able to complete your calculus homework problems to do well on the exam but you tend to struggle getting started. You decide to use a campus tutor to help.
Knowledge of strategy	Knowledge of strategies available to complete tasks as well as monitoring the effectiveness of those strategies	To prepare for your upcoming biology exam, you use flashcards to help memorize the vocabulary; however, after several days, you realize you are still not remembering each term. You decide to try writing out the terms with relevant examples and drawings.

METACOGNITIVE REGULATION

Brown (1987) defined metacognitive regulation in terms of the deliberate, sequential processes used to control and oversee cognitive goals and activities. Fogarty (1994) extended upon this framework by delineating three distinct phases of metacognitive regulation in the learning process: the planning phase, the monitoring phase, and the evaluation phase. Just as with metacognitive knowledge, each key term explains how you regulate your learning outcomes by developing a plan, monitoring your implementation of the plan, and evaluating how effective the plan is in achieving your intended goal. These phases are really the foundation for understanding both metacognition and self-regulation in the learning process. While a similar but far more detailed exploration of these phases is discussed in the self-regulation module, the purpose here is to provide a brief outline of how each stage relates to metacognition. From there, a more nuanced vision of how it all comes together is constructed.

METACOGNITIVE REGULATION: Personal methods by which cognitive processing is directed, controlled, and changed.

Planning Phase

Devising a plan of action before starting a task is an important regulatory learning strategy. The process of planning requires that you assess what precisely needs to be learned, consider various approaches to learning the material, and choose a particular course of action. While it does not take considerable effort to take these steps, many students often overlook the value of preparing for learning tasks by creating a plan. Doing so requires intentionality and thoughtfulness on the part of the learner. Another important aspect of planning is the activation of prior knowledge. Taking time to consider what you already know about a given topic can significantly enhance learning outcomes and make the task of learning new materials easier.

Monitoring Phase

After a plan has been devised and implemented, it is important to monitor how well that plan is working. This is an ongoing process of determining your level of understanding and comprehension of the materials based on the learning approach used. Taking a step back to ask simple questions such as "Am I really understanding the material?" or "Should I continue with this learning approach?" can dramatically improve learning outcomes. Monitoring ensures that you remain both intentional and active in the learning process, making decisions about the strategies you employ and the goals you want to achieve. Perhaps, the most important aspect of monitoring is that it requires you to stop and consider what you have learned so far. Instead of passively reading a chapter only to find out nothing has been retained, the decision to stop and monitor your progress ensures that your time and energy are not wasted.

For example, when monitoring your plan, you might decide to:

- Stop and do a brief "learning check" that tests your comprehension when reading a textbook chapter.
- Stop and assess whether or not your writing approach is relevant and appropriate when working on a paper.

Cluster 5 discusses more specific strategies about monitoring comprehension.

Evaluating Phase

A learning goal has been successfully implemented, monitored, and finished. Now what? It is time to evaluate how well the material was learned and whether or not the plan was really effective. Self-testing can be a simple way to determine understanding and comprehension, such as asking yourself questions about the learning materials or completing review questions at the end of a textbook chapter (see Cluster 5 for more self-testing strategies). However, evaluating the success of the learning strategies used takes a bit more effort. If it appears that the material was not retained or grasped quite as well as expected, the question becomes whether an alternative approach might be more effective. Could something have been done differently? Is there a pattern in what was understood or misunderstood? If so, how might this be addressed in the future? Such questions are an important metacognitive aspect of the learning process.

GOING DEEPER: METATHEORIES OF METACOGNITION

Despite the focus thus far on the differences between metacognitive knowledge and metacognitive regulation, there is also a considerable degree of overlap between them. Schraw (1998) found that numerous research studies reveal a positive correlation between the two, substantiating the claim that knowledge and regulation are mutually interdependent systems (Schraw & Moshman, 1995). In other words, your knowledge of a task informs regulatory planning, monitoring, and evaluation, even as these processes further contribute to your knowledge base. In this back and forth between metacognitive knowledge and regulation, people naturally develop working theories of their own thinking. These are called meta-theories of cognition, and serve to operationalize one's grasp on how individuals learn.

Researchers and theorists have pinpointed three kinds of meta-theories of cognition: tacit theories, informal theories, and formal theories. Tacit theories are developed without any explicit understanding or awareness that a theory has been formed. They operate in the background, influencing your beliefs and decisions at an unconscious level. While tacit theories are a primary mode of operation for young children, older children, and adults tend to rely on them as well. They underlie your preconceptions, biases, implicit attitudes, and automatic judgments. In other words, tacit theories are the driving force behind thoughts, feelings, and behaviors that have not be analyzed or considered in an intentional way.

> What might be a tacit theory you once held about the world but have since thought about and changed?

Informal theories are more explicit than tacit theories, but less explicit than formal theories. They develop from self-musings about your beliefs and assumptions that remain fragmented or incomplete because they have not been systematically explored. This level of metacognitive awareness is a prerequisite for either altering learning styles or establishing learning goals and serves as the baseline for becoming a self-regulated learner (Kuhn, 2000). Formal theories, on the other hand, are complex and explicit and are a thoroughly investigated understanding of your cognitive processes. They provide a strong foundation for cultivating expertise in learning but require a great deal of thoughtfulness and energy to construct (Schraw & Moshman, 1995).

STUDENT SELF-ASSESSMENT

The following is a template for developing metacognitive skills related to a current class assignment. It can be used to systematically guide you toward understanding how to improve the thoughtfulness and intentionality of your academic task approaches.

Activating Prior Knowledge

To assess your prior knowledge about this assignment, answer the following questions:

1. What do you already know about the topics included on this exam?

2. What do you find interesting or useful about better understanding these topics?

3. What previous learnings or experiences have you had related to these topics?

4. What gaps exist in your knowledge of these topics?

5. How might you fill those knowledge gaps? What resources can you access?

Metacognitive Knowledge

To assess how your personal beliefs might directly influence your learning process related to this assignment, answer the following questions:

Person Variables

1. What is your current motivation level for preparing for this exam?

2. What skills do you currently have that can aid you in successfully preparing for this exam?

3. If you imagine preparing for this exam, what barriers come to mind?

Task Variables

1. What is the easiest or least time consuming part of your exam preparation?

2. What is the hardest or most time consuming part of your exam preparation?

3. Based on these responses, how might you choose to approach preparing for this exam in terms of effective time management (see Cluster 4 for some specific suggestions)?

Strategy Variables

1. What are some basic strategies you can use for your exam preparation (see Clusters 4 and 5 for strategy suggestions)?

2. If those strategies are not effective, what alternative strategies might you use?

3. How will you know if a strategy is effective or not?

To determine how your approach to preparing for this exam might be better organized and subsequently enhanced, answer the following questions:

Planning Phase: Describe some efficient steps you can take to complete your exam preparation.

[For example: I will create a test plan that outlines my specific study times and strategies during the two weeks prior to the exam.]

1.

2.

3.

4.

5.

Monitoring Phase: List some ways to monitor your progress on the assignment.

[For example: After each sub-unit, I will answer in writing the unit objectives given by the professor.]

1.

2.

3.

4.

5.

Evaluating Phase: List ways to evaluate how well your planning and monitoring worked.

[For example: Immediately after the exam, I will write down everything I can remember, then identify the sources (e.g., textbook and lecture) of the questions, and then evaluate my performance on each of these sources.]

1.

2.

3.

4.

5.

Although considering some of these tasks and questions may seem peculiar, especially if you have not done this before; using metacognition and being intentional will result in increased efficiency and higher achievement over time. Like most other learning tasks, with practice, thinking about thinking will become a more normal part of your self-regulation process.

MODULE 7.1 SUMMARY

- Cognitions are automatic and unconscious, metacognitions are effortful and conscious, while critical thinking is an objective analysis used to form judgments.
- Declarative knowledge is content-based, while procedural knowledge is process-based.
- Metacognitive knowledge includes three variables: knowledge of person, knowledge of tasks, and knowledge of strategy.
- Metacognitive regulation includes three phases: planning, monitoring, and evaluating.
- There are three types of metacognitive meta-theories: tacit theories, informal theories, and formal theories.

KEY TERMS

- **Cognition** – Mental process of gaining knowledge and understanding by means of thoughts, perceptions, and sensations.
- **Critical Thinking** – Mental process of purposefully monitoring, analyzing, and reformulating thoughts, beliefs, and judgments.
- **Declarative Knowledge** – Fixed information related to facts or verifiable data stored in memory.
- **Metacognition** – Mental process of gaining knowledge and understanding about cognitions by means of thinking about thinking.
- **Metacognitive Knowledge** – Personal beliefs and understandings about cognitive processes.
- **Metacognitive Regulation** – Personal methods by which cognitive processing is directed, controlled, and changed.
- **Procedural Knowledge** – Situational information related to performing specific activities.

REFERENCES

Brown, A. (1978). Knowing when, where and how to remember: A problem of metacognition. In R. Glaser (Ed.), *Advances in instructional psychology* (Vol. 1). Hillsdale, NJ: Lawrence Erlbaum.

Brown, A. (1987). Metacognition, executive control, self-regulation, and other more mysterious mechanisms. In F. E. Weinert & R. H. Kluwe (Eds.), *Metacognition, motivation, and understanding* (pp.65–116). Hillsdale, NJ: Lawrence Erlbaum.

Corsini, D. A. (1971). Memory: Interaction of stimulus and organismic factors. *Human Development, 14*, 227–235.

Ennis, R. H. (1985). A logical basis for measuring critical thinking skills. *Educational Leadership, 43*(2), 44–48.

Facione, P. A. (1990). *Critical thinking: A statement of expert consensus for purposes of educational assessment and instruction.* Millbrae, CA: The California Academic Press.

Flavell, J. H. (1976). Metacognitive aspects of problem solving. In L. B. Resnick (Ed.) *The nature of intelligence* (pp. 231–236). Hillsdale, NJ: Lawrence Erlbaum Associates.

Flavell, J. H. (1979). Metacognition and cognitive monitoring: A new area of cognitive-developmental inquiry. *American Psychologist, 34*, 906–911.

Fogarty, R. (1994). *How to teach for metacognition.* Palatine, IL: Skylight Publishing.

Halpern, D. F. (1998). Teaching critical thinking for transfer across domains: Dispositions, skills, structure training, and metacognitive monitoring. *American Psychologist, 53*(4), 449–455.

Hart, J. T. (1965). Memory and the feeling-of-knowing experience. *Journal of Educational Psychology, 56*, 208–216.

Hennessey, M. G. (1999). *Probing the dimensions of metacognition: Implications for conceptual change teaching-learning.* Paper presented at the annual meeting of the National Association for Research in Science Teaching, Boston, MA.

Kluwe, R. H. (1982). Cognitive knowledge and executive control: Metacognition. In D. R. Griffin (Ed.), *Animal mind, human mind* (pp.201–224). New York, NY: Springer.

Kuhn, D. (2000). Metacognitive development. *Current Directions in Psychological Science, 9*(5), 178–181.

Schraw, G. (1998). Promoting general metacognitive awareness. *Instructional Science, 26*(1–2), 113–125.

Schraw, G., & Moshman, D. (1995). Metacognitive theories. *Educational Psychology Review, 7*(4), 351–371.

Veenman, M. V., Van Hout-Wolters, B. H., & Afflerbach, P. (2006). Metacognition and learning: Conceptual and methodological considerations. *Metacognition and Learning, 1*(1), 3–14.

SELF-REGULATED LEARNING

CLUSTER 7 OBJECTIVES COVERED IN THIS MODULE

☐ **OBJECTIVE:** Describe characteristics of self-regulated learning.

☐ **OBJECTIVE:** Explain the similarities and differences among three major models of self-regulated learning.

☐ **OBJECTIVE:** Using the cyclical model of self-regulated learning, develop an outline for approaching a task.

OVERVIEW

REFLECTION: In what areas of your college studies might you benefit from increased self-control? In what areas might you spend more time monitoring your progress and learning approaches? Are these two areas the same or different? What might this tell you about the value of increasing your self-regulation as a learner?

Self-regulated learning is actually an umbrella term. It refers to the unique way in which cognition, metacognition, critical thinking, and motivation come together to create an optimized learning process. It includes how you control and monitor the aforementioned processes by setting goals, creating detailed plans, developing strategies, and monitoring your progress. Research clearly indicates that highly self-regulated learners in college earn better grades, have higher self-esteem, and are generally more well-adjusted than their peers with lower self-regulatory capacities (Pintrich, 2004; Tangney, Baumeister, & Boone, 2004; Zimmerman & Schunk, 2001). The metacognitive skill of self-monitoring plays a substantial role herein, with research indicating that metacognitive abilities are a strong predictor of overall academic performance (Cassidy, 2011; Dunning, Johnson, Ehrlinger, & Kruger, 2003; Zimmerman & Schunk, 2001).

SELF-REGULATED LEARNING:
Process of assessing, modifying, and evaluating efforts to achieve goals through the use of meta-cognitive skills and self-control strategies.

Schraw, Crippen, and Hartley (2006) define self-regulated learning as "our ability to understand and control our learning environments" (p. 111), while Zimmerman (2002) claims that "self-regulation is not a mental ability or an academic performance skill; rather it is the self-directive process by which learners transform their mental abilities into academic skills" (p. 65).

Both definitions contain important elements for consideration. It is possible to say that self-regulated learners consistently monitor their goals and skills to improve their grasp of academic materials. You might add that self-regulated learners exert control over their attention by using strategies and plans to optimize their academic outcomes. You might also note that self-regulated learners are intentional learners, diligently assessing themselves, their environment, and their learning materials in order to make conscientious choices about their learning process. All of these claims are valid based on the research literature. More importantly, most students will agree that these are valuable academic skills that can significantly enhance the learning experience.

Even though these elements of self-regulated learning make perfect sense on paper, implementing them may seem difficult at first. "If it were easy," you might ask, "then wouldn't all students surely be self-regulated learners?" It is important to keep in mind that these are skills that can become automatic with consistent and repetitive use over time (Pintrich & de Groot, 1990). The greatest challenge—as is the case for so many things—involves taking the first tentative steps. By testing these ideas in your own life experience, you can quickly determine what works and what does not. It is really a matter of effort and thoughtfulness rather than innate ability (Pintrich, 2004). Everyone is capable of becoming a highly effective, self-regulated learner with practice, and due diligence.

TWO MODELS OF ACADEMIC SELF-REGULATION

The following sections will examine two different theoretical models of self-regulated learning. Each has substantial support in the research literature and provides a unique perspective on how students can better understand and bolster their learning outcomes. As noted in the previous module, metacognition and self-regulation are intimately connected. One cannot be adequately understood without the other. All of these theoretical models utilize metacognition as their foundation; yet each incorporates unique elements into its explanation. The first model emphasizes the three phases of metacognitive regulation, and the third concentrates on the role of outcome expectations in goal development (see Cluster 2). Each contributes a unique perspective on how metacognition informs both goal pursuit and self-regulated learning. The following briefly describes each of these models, with more details provided in subsequent sections.

Zimmerman and Moylan (2009) have constructed a model that outlines the phases of self-regulated learning. Based on the groundbreaking work of Brown (1978), the model goes beyond the simple framework of planning, monitoring, and evaluating phases to create a more conceptually detailed approach to self-regulated learning. Their model of a cyclical-phase self-regulatory feedback loop provides a comprehensive understanding of how self-regulated learning occurs and what is required to enact it. Its combination of phases sheds light on how thoughts and feelings contribute to effective self-regulated learning.

Next, Oettingen (1999) developed fantasy realization theory to explain how effective goals can be distinguished from ineffective fantasies by means of mental contrasting, or the ability to consider barriers to success while actively striving for a fantasized goal. The model was combined with the work of Gollwitzer (1999) on implementation intentions, or the use of pre-established plans of action to successfully deal with barriers to goals (Cluster 2 describes the use of implementation intentions and specific plans of action). The result was the model of mental contrasting with implementation intentions (MCII) that has been used around the world to improve academic outcomes for students of all ages.

The model primarily emphasizes how imagination can influence behaviors. The power of free fantasies is that they involve vivid imagery of possible future outcomes. It can be so vivid, in fact, that your brain is tricked into believing the fantasy is a reality! According to fantasy realization theory and the MCII, enacting your goals requires using mental imagery to your advantage by imagining both your fantasy and its barriers in vivid detail. The following sections provide more details about each of these models.

THE CYCLICAL MODEL OF SELF-REGULATED LEARNING

Zimmerman and Moylan (2009) developed a three-phase model of self-regulated learning that is widely viewed as an important contribution to the literature. Each of the three main phases contain two additional sub-phases that are examined below. The purpose of the model is to provide a clear outline of how deep learning occurs so that students and teachers can enhance the learning process and improve learning outcomes.

FORETHOUGHT PHASE

One of the most crucial steps in completing a task occurs before you even begin. Planning and assessing what is required to complete a task requires forethought. Taking the time to formulate goals and strategies, to reflect on past experiences or knowledge about a task, and to consider the level of motivation you bring to a task are important features of self-regulated learning (Zimmerman & Schunk, 2001). Using a systematic learning approach may take more time initially, but the outcomes and results tend to reflect that additional effort (Zimmerman, 1995). During this phase, learners engage in two distinct forms of preparation: task analysis and self-motivation beliefs.

Task analysis involves the development of goals and strategies—often based upon past experiences—that will lead to task completion (Cassidy, 2011). The goals and strategies you choose usually depend on how your performance is going to be assessed (e.g., taking an exam) and the level of performance you want to attain (e.g., satisfied with a B on the exam). Equipped with knowledge of both the method of assessment and the desired level of performance, learners can choose appropriate goals and strategies that fit their needs. For example, studying for a 20-question multiple choice exam and desiring only a passing grade may lead one student to prepare only by scanning the textbook for keywords and definitions on the day before the exam. However, a student preparing for a complex essay exam who wants the highest grade possible will formulate learning goals and study strategies that ensure greater depth of comprehension.

Self-motivation beliefs directly influence the amount of effort and energy you are willing to expend on a task (Zimmerman & Moylan, 2009). There are numerous factors at play in regard to your motivation, all of which stem from your personal beliefs. Students have beliefs about why they are learning the material (goal orientation), the merits and importance of completing the task (personal interest), how capable they are of completing the task (self-efficacy), and finally, what the perceived likelihood is of success (outcome expectation). All of these personal beliefs can change the level of motivation individuals experience as learners. A high level of confidence and interest in a task leads naturally to increased effort (Zimmerman, 1994). Yet when a task is interpreted as irrelevant or not worth the time or simply too difficult, your willingness to expend energy and effort drops off. Furthermore, each of these beliefs can alter what goals and strategies you use in your task analysis.

PERFORMANCE PHASE

Having formulated goals and strategies, the next obvious step in the learning process is to actually perform the task. This performance is guided by decisions made in the forethought phase, such as implementing certain learning goals and strategies (Zimmerman, 2002). However, ensuring that these goals and strategies are effective requires some diligence and intentionality. Therefore, the performance phase is not simply about doing a task. It also involves considering the effectiveness of the goals, strategies, and actions, as well as making changes if necessary (Zimmerman & Schunk, 2001). During this phase, learners engage in two distinct forms of performance review: self-observation and self-control.

Self-observation involves closely considering what is or is not working, or what aspects of your learning approach that are either beneficial or not (Cassidy, 2011). This requires self-monitoring as a metacognitive learning tool. As discussed in the metacognition module, self-monitoring is a process of observing your progress on a task and comparing it to a pre-established standard. Such a standard is typically set in the forethought phase where certain goals and strategies are first considered. It can include monitoring the learning product (e.g., self-testing to determine whether a list of terms have been thoroughly memorized) or the learning process (e.g., assessing whether or not it might be more beneficial to create an acronym or mnemonic device to memorize the list of terms).

Self-control is a matter of concentration and effort, which also ties in closely with motivation. If a lack of motivation is observed in the forethought phase, self-control is probably going to be limited in the performance phase (Zimmerman & Moylan, 2009). However, this can be altered through reminders about the purpose of the task and the goals established (interest incentives), as well as by creating a personal reward system for following through on the task (self-consequences). There are also metacognitive aspects of self-control that revolve around planning and preparation. Using balanced time management strategies, seeking assistance from others when needed, and choosing good environments for studying and learning can improve self-control by eliminating distractions and frustrations. Also, using mental imagery to organize information, describing the necessary steps in the learning process, or simply implementing the basic task strategies formulated in the forethought phase can drastically improve self-control (Zimmerman & Schunk, 2001).

SELF-CONTROL:
Using concentration, effort, and motivation to minimize distractions and frustrations when completing a task.

SELF-REFLECTION PHASE

Once the task has been completed, the post-task analysis begins. While at least some aspects of the forethought and performance phases are typically implemented by students, taking time afterwards to reflect upon the learning process is often ignored. If the task is complete, why be concerned about how it was done? The self-reflection phase is a crucial part of building a strong set of successful learning approaches. When you take the time to consider whether certain goals, strategies, and actions were ultimately effective, your arsenal of learning tools is refined and your ability to attain even better outcomes in the future increases (Zimmerman, 1994). During this phase, learners engage in two distinct forms of outcome review: self-judgment and self-reaction.

How is the cyclical model related to metacognitive regulation?

SELF-JUDGMENT:
Reflective process of self-assessing performance on a task.

Self-judgment is a reflective process of assessing performance on a task. This requires a self-evaluation of how well the task was performed in relation to the method of assessment (e.g., taking an exam) and the performance goals established in the forethought phase (Cassidy, 2011). Even if two students are experiencing the same form of assessment and receive the exact same grade, their self-evaluations can still vary based on how they expected to perform. Causal attributions, or the explanations people create to justify certain outcomes, also play a significant role in self-judgments (Zimmerman & Moylan, 2009). The accuracy (or lack thereof) of causal attributions for performance can change your relationship to the learning process by altering your motivation and heightening your emotions. For example, a student who blames the teacher for a low exam score is less likely to evaluate how their own poor study habits influenced the outcome. At the same time, another student might accurately assess that a bad score resulted from inefficient studying and therefore decide to make a positive and lasting change.

SELF-REACTIONS:
The cognitive, affective, and motivational responses people have to self-judgments.

ADAPTIVE DECISIONS:
Decisions that reflect willingness to try new strategies and set new goals.

DEFENSIVE DECISIONS:
Decisions that reflect an unwillingness to adapt strategies and a preference to avoid tasks.

Self-reactions are the cognitive, affective, and motivational responses you have to self-judgments, or the way you react to and cope with successes and failures (Zimmerman & Moylan, 2009). These influence your future behaviors. People tend to experience self-satisfaction when judging their performance in an affirming manner, which leads to increased motivation and positive affect. Low self-satisfaction has the opposite effect of deterring interest and motivation in the activity. Confronted with feelings of low or high self-satisfaction, the decisions you make can be either adaptive or defensive. Adaptive decisions are related to persistence and flexibility. It is adaptive to reconsider how a learning task was handled in order to try out new strategies and set new goals. Defensive decisions are related to avoidance and rigidity. Instead of seeing the poor learning outcome as an opportunity, it is interpreted as a failure and the task is avoided in the future. When a learner is not satisfied with their performance, the most adaptive decision is to try out new and potentially beneficial approaches to the task.

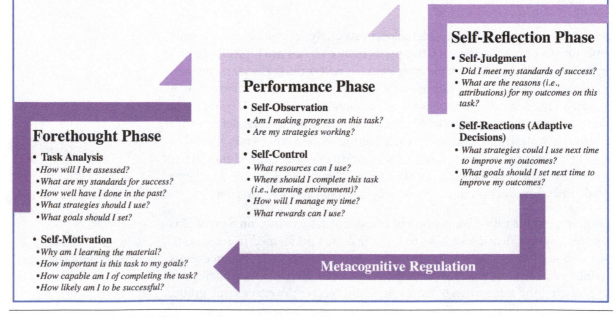

FIGURE 7.2.1: Cyclical Model of Self-Regulation

Source: Angela Vaughan and Brett Wilkinson

FANTASY REALIZATION THEORY

Cluster 2 described in detail how to set useful and effective goals. This module goes further by describing fantasy realization theory and how self-regulation influences goal formation and action (Oettingen, 1999). This theory emphasizes planning, monitoring, and intentionality as basic requirements in the process of reaching goals (Oettingen, Kappes, Guttenberg, & Gollwitzer, 2015). This is called a goal-pursuit approach because it focuses on how wishes or desires determine your motivation to pursue goals. By clearly identifying the way in which certain thought patterns either promote or deter academic goal pursuit, students can determine how their own thought patterns influence their academic outcomes.

According to the theory, thoughts about the future come in the form of either expectations or free fantasies. Expectations are judgments about the likelihood of reaching a future outcome and are based on past experiences. Free fantasies are essentially daydreams about possible future outcomes that are unrelated to actual experiences. Research indicates that the mental imagery of a positive free fantasy mimics actual experiences in the brain, thereby leading to the same feeling of satisfaction that occurs when you really do accomplish a task (Oettingen & Gollwitzer, 2010). Because the human brain does not clearly distinguish between imagined and actual experiences in the world, the emotional content of imagined experiences is unconsciously interpreted as a real event.

EXPECTATIONS:
Judgments about the likelihood of reaching a future outcome based on past experiences.

FREE FANTASIES:
Daydreams about possible outcomes that are unrelated to actual experiences.

Many high level athletes use this to their advantage by employing visualization techniques to improve motivation, focus, and technique. Many writers, artists, and poets use free fantasies to conjure unique and innovative ideas for creative projects. The act of play during childhood is also connected to free fantasies. So it is not as though free fantasies are a bad thing. The problem with free fantasies arises when goal pursuit is delayed or abandoned because individuals experience satisfaction from the fantasy alone. New Year's resolutions are a great example. While many people thoroughly enjoy the fantasy of starting a new exercise regimen or learning to play a musical instrument, the challenges tend to be overlooked in free fantasies.

Can you quickly identify a free fantasy that has not yet become a reality?

Because imagination mimics real experience and a sense of fulfillment arises from merely fantasizing about a goal, the motivation needed to overcome real world obstacles can quickly fade. As a result, such resolutions are often abandoned. It really is much easier to imagine yourself running a competitive marathon or playing the saxophone at a jazz club than it is to train and practice to accomplish such goals. The gap between imagination and reality can seem insurmountable without the proper mental tools for bridging the divide.

The overarching purpose of fantasy realization theory is to explain the difference in how expectations and free fantasies work. Understanding this difference can lead to more intentional decision-making and help people learn more effective ways to pursue goals. Turning fantasies into realities is a matter of diligence, grit, and a willingness to clearly think through the process. Fantasy realization highlights three important styles of thought related to goal-pursuit: indulging, dwelling, and mental contrasting.

INDULGING AND DWELLING

Indulging involves a focus on a positive future fantasy without considering real world barriers to its implementation. It emphasizes fantasies that are not tethered to reality. A basic example of indulging would be fantasizing about becoming a lawyer but never taking the steps to apply to law school. Dwelling, on the other hand, involves focusing on the real world barriers without the motivational impetus of a future-oriented fantasy. It emphasizes reality without the inspirational force of fantasies. An example of dwelling would be thinking only about how much time, money, and effort it would take to become a lawyer while not imagining the experience of defending a client in court. Both styles of thought serve to inhibit efforts to attain goals. It is not helpful to focus only on the fantasy or only on the barriers.

MENTAL CONTRASTING

Mental contrasting includes the very best aspects of both fantasy and realism. It begins with identifying the positive fantasy for a future outcome before identifying the negative barriers that could prevent the outcome. When combined with positive expectations for a successful outcome, mental contrasting is an energizing force that stimulates effort. For example, when the fantasy of successfully graduating or defending a client in court is combined with a realistic assessment of how you can manage your time, finances, and energy to finish a law degree, you are much more likely to complete the law school application.

When combined with negative expectations for a successful outcome, mental contrasting works to preserve your energy (Kuhl, 2000). If you honestly cannot foresee your fantasy becoming a reality, then it may be unreasonable to pursue the goal. If you really want to play professional basketball but genuinely lack the athletic ability to accomplish this goal, then it would be unreasonable to pursue this goal exclusively. Your time and effort would be better spent elsewhere, such as becoming a basketball coach or an athletic trainer, perhaps. Mental contrasting is thus a style of thinking about the future that merges fantasies and realities in a cohesive and meaningful whole.

MENTAL CONTRASTING WITH IMPLEMENTATION INTENTIONS (MCII)

The MCII is a relatively straightforward procedure. It is a goal-pursuit method that merges the tenets of fantasy realization theory (Oettingen et al., 2015) with a self-regulatory implementation model (Adriaanse, Gollwitzer, De Ridder, De Wit, & Kroese, 2011). Equipped with knowledge about the four modes of fantasy realization (i.e., mental contrasting with positive or negative outcome expectations, indulging, and dwelling), learners are encouraged to practice the use of mental contrasting rather than indulging or dwelling. Subsequently, learners should assess the circumstances under which they tend to indulge or dwell rather than using the preferred mental contrasting.

Next, learners are introduced to the idea of implementation intentions as a self-regulatory strategy used to attain goals by means of concrete "if-then" plans (Adriaanse et al., 2011). Research has consistently shown that both persistence and goal attainment increase when "if-then" plans are used to prepare for handling barriers to success (Oettingen & Gollwitzer, 2010). Keep in mind that if-then plans should be reserved for potential barriers rather than routine or unvarying situations. By learning to identify such circumstances, learners have the opportunity to make informed decisions about whether those repetitive barriers need to be more directly addressed as a problem. For instance, an if-then contingency plan for oversleeping is not useful when the oversleeping happens every single morning. It would be more beneficial to set specific and concrete goals that directly address this issue (see Cluster 2 for more discussion about implementation plans and obstacles).

In combination, mental contrasting and implementation intentions are a powerful tool for goal pursuit. Because self-regulation is so closely tied to motivation, it is important to use styles of thought and realistic planning strategies to overcome obstacles while remaining inspired and energized. Therefore, the actual MCII process involves imagining a positive future fantasy, assessing the realistic barriers to achieving that goal, and then developing "if-then" plans for handling those barriers. While this is a straightforward procedure for improving goal attainment, it does require a willingness to observe your own thought patterns and assess how expectations and free fantasies influence your thinking. In this respect, it is a metacognitive skill set that has the potential to enhance self-regulated learning.

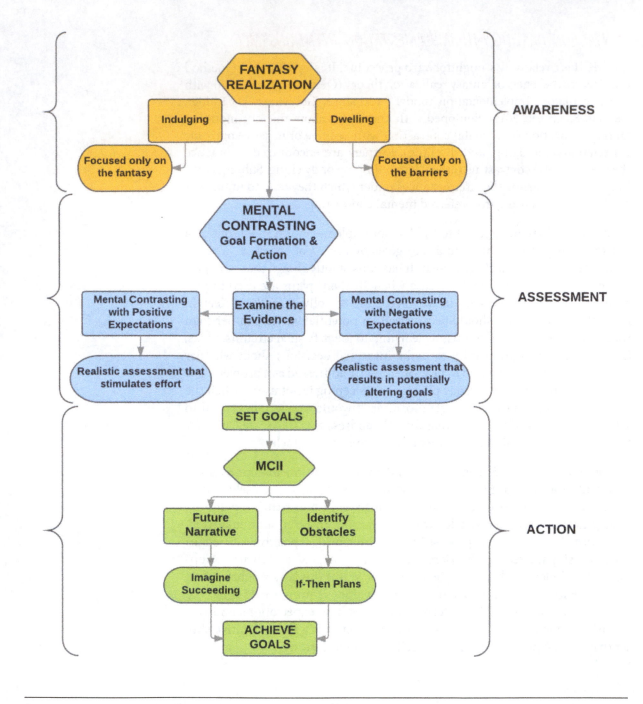

FIGURE 7.2.2: Mental Contrasting with Implementation Intentions

Source: Angela Vaughan and Brett Wilkinson

The following activity is designed to help you understand how past experiences, expectations, and perceived barriers influence your ability to be a self-regulated learner. By working through the template step-by-step, you can gain insight into how your thought patterns largely determine your ability to be self-regulated.

ACTIVITY 7.2.1

A. Choose a goal that you feel confident about accomplishing.

1. What do you value about this goal?

2. What evidence do you have that you can accomplish this goal?

3. Imagine accomplishing this goal. Describe what thoughts and feelings come up for you.

4. Describe how accomplishing this goal can support either a) growth (i.e., seeking ways to enhance mastery), or b) well-being (i.e., seeking ways to avoid threats).

B. Choose a goal that you feel may be too difficult or challenging to accomplish.

1. What concerns you about this goal?

2. What evidence do you have that you might be unable to accomplish this goal?

3. Imagine trying to accomplish this goal and failing. Describe your thoughts and feelings.

4. Now imagine succeeding in accomplishing this goal. Describe your thoughts and feelings.

5. Describe how accomplishing this goal can support either a) growth, or b) well-being.

6. How might accomplishing or avoiding this goal serve a purpose for you?

ACTIVITY 7.2.1 CONT.

C. Think once again about the goal you felt comfortable about accomplishing in (A).

1. Restate your goal.

2. What will be the best result from accomplishing this goal?

3. What is the main obstacle that might keep you from accomplishing this goal?

4. Choose an effective action to overcome this obstacle, using an "If, then" statement.

D. Think once again about the goal you felt may be too difficult to accomplish in (B).

1. Restate your goal.

2. What will be the best result from accomplishing this goal?

3. What is the main obstacle that might keep you from accomplishing this goal?

4. Is there an effective action that might help you overcome this obstacle? If so, address it using an "If, then" statement.

5. With this goal, was it more difficult to identify a realistic "If, then" statement? Why or why not?

6. If you were able to identify a realistic "If, then" statement, do you now feel more confident about pursuing and achieving this goal? Why or why not?

7. If you were not able to identify a realistic "If, then" statement, do you now feel it is time to abandon or change this goal? Why or why not?

By combining metacognitive skills and self-regulation to goal setting, it is more likely that your goals will be realistic (an important characteristic of useful goals) and your implementation plans will be effective.

MODULE 7.2 SUMMARY

- Self-regulated learning is a complex, self-directed goal attainment process that requires the ability to assess, analyze, monitor, evaluate, strategize, maintain self-control, and make decisions in order to improve learning and outcomes.

- The dual-processing model of self-regulated learning describes how environmental factors related to safety and support can influence learning outcomes.

- The cyclical model of self-regulated learning includes the forethought phase, the performance phase, and the self-reflection phase.

- Fantasy realization theory includes five key concepts: evaluations, free fantasies, mental contrasting, indulging, and dwelling.

- The mental contrasting with implementation intentions (MCII) technique combines mental contrasting of free fantasies and realistic barriers with "if-then" contingency plans to improve goal attainment and motivation.

KEY TERMS

- **Adaptive Decisions** – Decisions that reflect willingness to try new strategies and set new goals.

- **Defensive Decisions** – Decisions that reflect an unwillingness to adapt strategies and a preference to avoid tasks.

- **Dwelling** – Focusing only on the barriers to achieving a fantasy.

- **Expectations** – Judgments about the likelihood of reaching a future outcome based on past experiences.

- **Free Fantasies** – Daydreams about possible outcomes that are unrelated to actual experiences.

- **Indulging** – Focusing on a future fantasy without considering real world barriers to its implementation.

- **Mental Contrasting** – Combines a realistic combination of imagining future fantasies and their potential barriers.

- **Self-Control** – Using concentration, effort, and motivation to minimize distractions and frustrations when completing a task.

- **Self-Judgment** – Reflective process of self-assessing performance on a task.

- **Self-Motivation Beliefs** – Beliefs about a task including relevance, value, and ability to finish the task that influence a learner's level of effort to complete the task.
- **Self-Observation** – Closely considering what is working and not working when completing a task.
- **Self-Reactions** – The cognitive, affective, and motivational responses people have to self-judgments.
- **Self-Regulated Learning** – Process of assessing, modifying, and evaluating efforts to achieve goals through the use of metacognitive skills and self-control strategies.
- **Task Analysis** – Development of goals and strategies based on past experiences that will lead to task completion.

REFERENCES

Adriaanse, M. A., Gollwitzer, P. M., De Ridder, D. T., De Wit, J. B. F., & Kroese, F. M. (2011). Breaking habits with implementation intentions: A test of underlying processes. *Personality and Social Psychology Bulletin, 37*, 502–513.

Brown, A. (1978). Knowing when, where and how to remember: A problem of metacognition. In R. Glaser (Ed.), *Advances in instructional psychology* (Vol. 1). Hillsdale, NJ: Lawrence Erlbaum.

Cassidy, S. (2011). Self-regulated learning in higher education: Identifying key component processes. *Studies in Higher Education, 36*(8), 989–1000.

Dunning, D., Johnson, K., Ehrlinger, J., & Kruger, J. (2003). Why people fail to recognize their own incompetence. *Current Directions in Psychological Science, 12*(3), 83–87.

Gollwitzer, P. M. (1999). Implementation intentions: Strong effects of simple plans. *American Psychologist, 54*, 493–503.

Kuhl, J. (2000). A functional-design approach to motivation and self-regulation. In M. Boekaerts, P. R. Pintrich, & M. Zeidner (Eds.), *Handbook of self-regulation* (pp. 111–169). San Diego, CA: Academic Press.

Oettingen, G. (1999). Free fantasies about the future and the emergence of developmental goals. In J. Brandstädter & R. M. Lerner (Eds.), *Action and self-development: Theory and research through the life span* (pp. 315–342). London, England: Sage.

Oettingen, G., & Gollwitzer, P. M. (2010). Strategies of setting and implementing goals. In J. E. Maddux & J. P. Tangney (Eds.), *Social psychological foundations of clinical psychology* (pp. 114–135). New York, NY: Guilford.

Oettingen, G., Kappes, H. B., Guttenberg, K. B., & Gollwitzer, P. M. (2015). Self-regulation of time management: Mental contrasting with implementation intentions. *European Journal of Social Psychology, 45*, 218–229.

Pintrich, P. R. (2004). A conceptual framework for assessing motivation and self-regulated learning in college students. *Educational Psychology Review, 16*(4), 385–407.

Pintrich, P. R., & de Groot, E. V. (1990). Motivational and self-regulated learning components of classroom academic performance. *Journal of Educational Psychology, 82*(1), 33–40.

Schraw, G., Crippen, K. J., & Hartley, K. (2006). Promoting self-regulation in science education: Metacognition as part of a broader perspective on learning. *Research in Science Education, 36*, 111–139.

Tangney, J. P., Baumeister, R. F., & Boone, A. L. (2004). High self-control predicts good adjustment, less pathology, better grades, and interpersonal success. *Journal of Personality, 72*(2), 271–324.

Zimmerman, B. J. (1994). Dimensions of academic self-regulation: A conceptual framework for education. In D. H. Schunk & B. J. Zimmerman (Eds.), *Self-regulation of learning and performance: Issues and educational applications* (pp. 3–21). Hillsdale, NJ: Lawrence Erlbaum Associates.

Zimmerman, B. J. (1995). Self-regulation involves more than metacognition: A social-cognitive perspective. *Educational Psychologist, 30*(4), 217–221.

Zimmerman, B. J. (2002). Becoming a self-regulated learner: An overview. *Theory Into Practice, 41*(2), 64–70.

Zimmerman, B. J., & Moylan, A. R. (2009). Self-regulation: Where metacognition and motivation intersect. In D. J. Hacker, J. Dunlosky, & A. C. Graesser (Eds.), *Handbook of metacognition in education* (pp. 299–315). New York, NY: Routledge.

Zimmerman, B. J., & Schunk, D. H. (2001). *Self-regulated learning and academic achievement: Theoretical perspectives* (2nd ed.). Mahwah, NJ: Erlbaum.

CASE STUDY

Michael has always been a strong student. He maintained a 4.0 grade point average during high school and arrived at college expecting to do the same. However, his grades have been slipping during his first semester as a freshman. In particular, his grades on both exams and papers in several classes have been consistently lower than he had expected. Michael cannot understand why his academic outcomes are so different from high school. He has not changed anything about his approach to studying or writing papers, splitting his study time equally among each class, reviewing class notes, highlighting his readings, and using the same memorization techniques that always worked so well before college. Although he determines that simply working harder will probably improve his outcomes, Michael also decides to reach out to his academic advisor for support.

QUESTIONS

1. How might you explain the downturn in Michael's academic outcomes?

2. Going beyond simply "working harder" to improve his academic outcomes, what metacognitive strategies might be helpful for Michael to use?

3. If you were an academic advisor, how might you use the dual processing model of self-regulation and/or the MCII to help Michael address his current problem?

POTENTIAL RESPONSES

1. It seems that Michael is using learning strategies that are not always effective for college-level work. However, the bigger issue is that Michael is either (a) not aware that more advanced learning strategies can be used to improve his outcomes, or (b) is not monitoring his study process closely enough to determine what is and is not working.

2. Michael can use the cyclical model of self-regulation to help pinpoint which learning strategies are effective and which ones are not. This includes intentional planning with the forethought phase, ongoing monitoring during the performance phase, and then a realistic assessment in the self-reflection phase to determine what specific changes should be made in the future. Does he stop to monitor his progress and check whether or not his strategies are working? By assessing his current study strategies rather than assuming that they should work, Michael will be in a much better position to make intentional and constructive changes in his study habits.

3. As Michael's academic advisor, I would really want to learn more about his academic motivation and how he perceives obstacles to success. First, I would help him assess the obstacles in his way to accomplishing his goals. Using the MCII, we would choose a learning goal, imagine the best outcome of this goal, consider barriers to success, and finally create if-then contingency plans to overcome those barriers.

ADDITIONAL READINGS

Bjork, R. A., Dunlosky, J., & Kornell, N. (2013). Self-regulated learning: Beliefs, techniques, and illusions. *Annual Review of Psychology, 64,* 417–444.

Boekaerts, M. (1999). Self-regulated learning: Where we are today. *International Journal of Educational Research, 31*(6), 445–457.

Cohen, M. (2012). The importance of self-regulation for college student learning. *College Student Journal, 46*(4), 892–902.

Kappes, A., Wendt, M., Reinelt, T., & Oettingen, G. (2013). Mental contrasting changes the meaning of reality. *Journal of Experimental Social Psychology, 49*(5), 797–810.

Mega, C., Ronconi, L., & De Beni, R. (2014). What makes a good student? How emotions, self-regulated learning, and motivation contribute to academic achievement. *Journal of Educational Psychology, 106*(1), 121–131.

Young, A., & Fry, J. (2012). Metacognitive awareness and academic achievement in college students. *Journal of the Scholarship of Teaching and Learning, 8*(2), 1–10.

Zhao, N., Wardeska, J. G., McGuire, S. Y., & Cook, E. (2014). Metacognition: An effective tool to promote success in college science learning. *Journal of College Science Teaching, 43*(4), 48–54.

Zimmerman, B. J. (2013). From cognitive modeling to self-regulation: A social cognitive career path. *Educational Psychologist, 48*(3), 135–147.

UNDERSTANDING AND EXPERIENCING DIVERSITY:
AN INTRODUCTION

CASE STUDY

Sophia is a first-semester freshman who moved across the country to attend college. Leaving her rural mountain community was very difficult for Sophia. After all, in a small town practically everybody knows one another. Over 18 years, Sophia had grown accustomed to being around people who look like her, talk like her, and hold the same beliefs as her. Cultural homogeneity, or sameness, was all she had ever known until arriving at college. Only a month into her college experience, Sophia begins experiencing a great deal of anxiety. She feels as though she is being exposed to ideas and behaviors that she just does not understand. She was raised to be kind and generous but is struggling to feel comfortable around people who seem "abnormal." Sophia feels out of place and is considering going home at the end of the semester.

QUESTIONS

1. What experiences are you currently having that are similar or different from Sophia's first-semester experience?

2. What advice do you have for Sophia to help her understand what she's experiencing?

CLUSTER OVERVIEW

The purpose of this module is to provide an overview of important topics related to diversity while stressing the importance of understanding how personal experiences are socioculturally informed. Module 8.1 explores the meaning of diversity as well as key terms in the diversity literature including culture, ethnicity, race, gender, and spirituality. Module 8.2 examines important concepts that represent barriers to an open and just society including prejudice, discrimination, oppression, and privilege. Finally, the cluster concludes by identifying the benefits of expanding social identity. A case study is provided at the beginning of this module and will be expanded upon in module 8.2 with reflective questions designed to promote a deeper understanding of diversity. This cluster serves as an introduction to these topics to build a foundation of knowledge, which serves to help you think critically and learn more deeply. As a result, this cluster can support higher levels of learning and lead to effective and productive relationships both now in your current educational experiences as well as over the long term in your professional careers.

CLUSTER OBJECTIVES

- Define diversity and describe its implications in terms of diversity and inclusivity.
- Define culture and describe its implications in terms of heritage and identity.
- Identify the difference between race and ethnicity.
- Define gender and describe its implications in terms of gender roles and gender identity.
- Define spirituality and how it differs from religion.
- Define prejudice and discrimination, as well as describe their relationship to stereotyping and in-group socialization.
- Identify the benefits of expanding personal identity and how this can influence your way of thinking about, interacting within, and experiencing the world.
- Describe the personal and social benefits of experiencing diversity.

UNDERSTANDING THE MEANING AND FORMS OF DIVERSITY

CLUSTER 8 OBJECTIVES COVERED IN THIS MODULE

- ☐ **OBJECTIVE:** Define diversity and describe its implications in terms of diversity and inclusivity.
- ☐ **OBJECTIVE:** Define culture and describe its implications in terms of heritage and identity.
- ☐ **OBJECTIVE:** Identify the difference between race and ethnicity.
- ☐ **OBJECTIVE:** Define gender and describe its implications in terms of gender roles and gender identity.
- ☐ **OBJECTIVE:** Define spirituality and how it differs from religion.

WHAT IS DIVERSITY?

REFLECTION: Thinking about your experiences prior to college, how would you have defined diversity? What types of diversity did you experience as part of your daily life and interactions with others? How much of that has changed now that you are at college?

As a noun, diversity means difference or variety. However, diversity also signifies a range of human differences including but not limited to race, ethnicity, gender, gender identity, sexual orientation, age, social class, physical ability or attributes, religious or ethical values system, national origin, and political beliefs. It involves examining individual experiences in the context of an environment comprised of various peoples of different backgrounds (Valadez, 2018). Diversity celebrates the fact that modern society has been made possible by pluralism, meaning the coexistence of different experiences and viewpoints. As a complimentary term, inclusivity signifies the value of going beyond mere coexistence to deliberately welcoming diversity (Banks, 2015). It represents the active embrace of human differences in order to create a social environment that supports and respects the uniqueness of others.

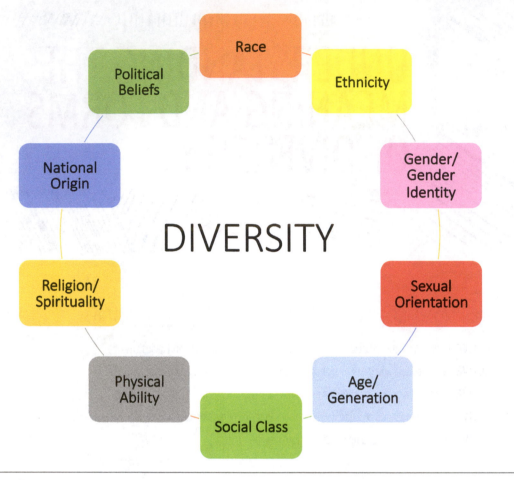

DIVERSITY

FIGURE 8.1.1: Diversity

Source: Angela Vaughan and Brett Wilkinson

DIVERSITY: The range of human differences including but not limited to race, ethnicity, gender, gender identity, sexual orientation, age, social class, physical ability or attributes, religious or ethical values system, national origin, and political beliefs.

INCLUSIVITY: The practice or policy of including people who might otherwise be excluded or marginalized.

From an evolutionary perspective, human beings have an instinctual drive to fear people and situations that appear unfamiliar (Buss, 2015). This fear is clearly observed during infancy in the form of stranger anxiety, as well as during late toddlerhood in the form of separation anxiety. Confronted by a stranger or separated from caregivers, an instinctual fear response kicks in to better ensure physical safety. Such adaptations make sense according to evolutionary psychology because the ancestral environment in which people evolved was extremely dangerous. Fear, distrust, and uncertainty were evolutionarily adaptive responses to a wide variety of potentially harmful situations (Buss, 2015; LeDoux, 2014).

Fearful reactions to loud noises and heights are still reasonable in the modern social environment. Being unresponsive to the honk of an oncoming vehicle when crossing the street is surely problematic, as is being nonchalant when standing atop a two-story house when fixing the roof. Yet, some fears become irrationally overgeneralized (LeDoux, 2014). Although the odds of dying from a snake bite in the United States is incredibly small (about 1 in 50 million, or a nearly no chance) compared to dying in a random car accident (about 1 in 100, or a 1% chance), many people drive vehicles with reckless abandon while developing highly specific snake phobias. A fear of snakes may not make as much sense today as it once did, yet the instinct persists.

The point is that people no longer exist in the ancestral environment and human advancement is as much a consequence of sociohistorical factors as it is a result of evolutionary pressures (Cronk, 2019). The innate tendency to fear strangers is surely a suitable reaction among infants, toddlers, and young children. Yet fear of other people and groups persists among adults in the modern environment as well. While this evolutionary vestige is explainable in theory, it is often quite unreasonable in practice. Additionally, it is not helpful to claim that such fears have been overcome. Instead, educated adults have a responsibility to explore how and why such responses persist in the form of discrimination, marginalization, and oppression. In this respect, diversity calls for a thoughtful examination of how human differences might be appropriately celebrated and embraced. To this end, the following will examine a few of the categories that constitute human differences: culture, ethnicity, race, gender, and spirituality.

> *"Diversity is understood to play a key role in breaking down stereotypes and stigmas, in learning to treat those who are different and those with whom we disagree with respect, and in removing even unconscious prejudice between groups of people with different, typically conflicting, backgrounds and experience. Those who learn with and from each other when they are young, the argument goes, are bound to carry that sense of mutual respect and cooperation with them throughout their lives"* (New & Merry, 2014, p. 206).

WHAT IS CULTURE?

Culture is defined as the shared values, traditions, knowledge, beliefs, language, symbols, behaviors, and forms of artistic expression among groups of people (Cuseo, Fecas, & Thompson, 2010). Human beings are social creatures, and so culture represents the collective social norms and viewpoints held by a community in order to preserve a certain way of life (Cronk, 2019). In other words, cultural communities reflect "the myriad ways of people to preserve society and meet a range of human needs" (Robinson-Wood, 2017, p. 50). Culture can be also viewed as an integral part of personal identity, informing your self-concept and sense of social belonging.

It is important to understand that culture is neither singular nor static (Eller, 2015). Culture is not singular insofar as people tend to participate in many different communities. You are exposed to different cultural expectations whenever you enter new or an unfamiliar environment that has unique customs and traditions. In the case study, Sophia struggles with how to adapt to new cultural experiences after leaving her hometown for college. This is because her heritage is an integral part of her cultural identity. However, culture is also not static and cultural identity can change over time. Adapting to new environments and sharing new experiences with people from different

> What are some of your family's favorite traditions?

backgrounds leads to not only exposure to new ideas, but often to the adoption of new and more complex values, attitudes, and beliefs (Eller, 2015). At the beginning of the next module, you will see how new experiences work to inform Sophia's evolving cultural identity.

WHAT IS THE DIFFERENCE BETWEEN ETHNICITY AND RACE?

ETHNICITY: Identification with the cultural heritage of a group of people who share a common ancestry, language, religion, society, or nation.

ETHNIC IDENTITY DEVELOPMENT: A knowledge of, and sense of belonging to, an ethnic group that develops over time.

SOCIALLY CONSTRUCTED: Ideas that have been invented by, and generally accepted within, a society.

RACE: The idea that the human species consists of distinct groups that can be distinguished according to physical characteristics such as skin color, hair texture, or facial features.

Ethnicity refers to identification with the cultural heritage of a group of people who share a common ancestry, language, religion, society, or nation (Woolfolk, 2011). The phrase ethnic identity development indicates that a knowledge of, and sense of belonging to, an ethnic group is a significant part of personal identity that develops over time (Verkuyten, 2018). Typically, the cultural group you are exposed to during your upbringing comprises your ethnicity. Ethnic identity requires learning the cultural heritage of a group of people and participating in those practices. Since the adoption of an ethnic identity involves learned behaviors, ethnicity is socially constructed rather than biologically or genetically determined (Verkuyten, 2018). Ethnicity, race, and gender are all examples of social constructs, or categories invented within societies to differentiate between groups of people.

Race is rooted in the idea that the human species consists of distinct groups (Smedley, 2018). It is a term used to artificially group people together based on physical traits such as skin color. Yet studies have clearly demonstrated that there is no scientific basis to support the notion that racial categories represent genetically distinct groups (Yudell, Roberts, DeSalle, & Tishkoff, 2016). Studies show that people of the same ethnicity can have more genetic commonalities with people of a different ethnicity than they do with one another (Reich, 2018). In other words, there is far more genetic diversity than homogeneity within socially constructed racial groups. Every human today has the same set of about 25,000 protein-coding genes with minor variations in genetic sequencing, called alleles. For instance, a single gene known as SLC24A5 is responsible for human skin color. Different protein sequences within that one gene account for all unique variations in skin tone (Reich, 2018).

Helpful Video – "The Myth of Race, Debunked in 3 Minutes" at https://www.youtube.com/watch?v=VnfKgffCZ7U

Although race has limited genetic grounding, it does hold significant social and political meaning. The consequence of race as a social construct is observed in both its historical and its modern use to justify oppression and discrimination (Smedley, 2018). Dominant cultural groups have often used race as a means to maintain power through enforced inequality based on the false notion that one major racial group is biogenetically superior to another (Reich, 2018). At the same time, racial identity can serve as a powerful unifying force against discrimination.

For example, the U.S. civil rights movement demonstrated the power and necessity of catalyzing racial identification to enable social justice for African Americans. With all this in mind, scientists have increasingly called for an end to using race as a demographic characteristic due to the lack of genetic homogeneity within broad racial groups (Reich, 2018; Yudell et al., 2016). Ethnicity is considered a suitable replacement because it highlights cultural and ancestral heritage as a self-selected form of identity that bypasses biogenetics.

WHAT IS THE DIFFERENCE BETWEEN SEX AND GENDER?

Gender is another social construct that refers to how the characteristics of masculinity and femininity are ascribed within a culture. Akin to the erroneous belief that human beings can be categorized according to distinct racial groups, the notion that men and women represent a two distinct group is scientifically incorrect (Oakley, 2016). Gender differences actually exist on a continuous spectrum, with individuals falling at a wide variety of places on the masculinity--femininity scale. Whereas sex is assigned at birth based on genitalia and chromosomal makeup; gender indicates the roles that a society expects individuals to perform as a result of their assigned sex. As such, gender is best understood in terms of gender roles and gender identity.

Gender roles are the myriad values, attitudes, and behaviors that are considered socially acceptable for a given sex. Socially sanctioned gender roles tend to be stereotypical, such as expecting women to be homemakers and men to earn a living. Such stereotypes are socially invented rather than innately representative. A curious example of socially constructed gender trends is the association of pink with girls and blue with boys. In the first half of the 20th century in the United States, boys wore pink because it was considered a "more decided and stronger color" compared to the "delicate and dainty" blue assigned to girls (Paoletti, 2012, p. 21)

Gender identity is the way individuals view themselves in regard to socially constructed feminine and masculine characteristics (Oakley, 2016). It represents the identification of one's inner concept of self on the femininity--masculinity spectrum (Helgeson, 2016). As such, self-identified gender can be female, male, some combination of both, or neither. Both gender roles and gender identity are fluid concepts insofar as gender roles vary considerably within and across cultures, while gender identity is self-determined according to the lived experience of the person. *Sexism* tends to be perpetuated by means of sociocultural norms that enforce stereotypical gender roles or prescribe biologically assigned gender identities (Helgeson, 2016).

GENDER ROLES: The values, attitudes, and behaviors considered to be socially acceptable for biologically assigned men and women.

GENDER IDENTITY: The self-selected way in which individuals view themselves in relation to masculine and feminine traits.

SEXISM: Prejudice or discrimination based upon a person's sex or gender.

WHAT IS THE DIFFERENCE BETWEEN RELIGION AND SPIRITUALITY?

Has your religious or spirituality practices changed since starting school? Why or why not?

SPIRITUALITY: Personal engagement in beliefs, traditions, or practices concerned with finding meaning or purpose in life, connecting with the human spirit or soul, and relating to something greater than oneself.

RELIGION: An organized collection of spiritual beliefs, traditions, and doctrines agreed upon by a group of people to explain the cause and purpose of the universe.

Spirituality refers to personal engagement in beliefs, traditions, or practices that tend to be concerned with finding meaning or purpose in life, connecting with notions of the human spirit or soul, or understanding one's relationship to something greater than oneself (Harris, 2014). Spirituality is different from religion, which is an organized collection of spiritual beliefs, traditions, and doctrines agreed upon by a group of people to explain the cause and purpose of the universe. Spirituality is thus a central aspect of religion, but religion or religious practices need not be central to spirituality. Both are related to a process of searching for "a divine being, divine object, Ultimate Reality, or Ultimate Truth as perceived by the individual" (Hill et al., 2000, p. 66). However, a proposed distinction is that spiritual seeking emphasizes that which is sacred and religious seeking emphasizes ways related to the sacred, more broadly (Oman, 2015).

To conclude, the following reflection questions and activity help you to consider these ideas more deeply and how they may align with your own life experience. You will complete part 1 of the activity in this module and then revisit part 2 in Module 8.2.

ACTIVITY 8.1.1

- How does the information presented above resonate with your own life experience?

- What aspects of the socially constructed terms provided do you agree or disagree with?

Activity Instructions (In the next module, you will be asked to return to your responses here):

1. Write your name in the middle circle on the next page.

2. In the surrounding circles, list the groups with which you identify. (Examples: woman, man, African American, age, nursing major, Christian, Democrat, Republican, etc.)

3. Feel free to include additional circles in order to add identities, which feel relevant for you.

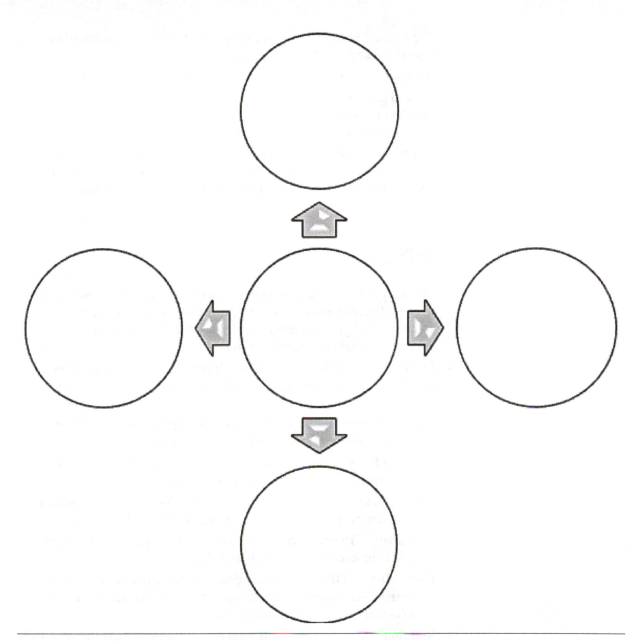

Source: Angela Vaughan & Brett Wilkinson

MODULE 8.1 SUMMARY

- Diversity signifies a range of human differences including but not lim-ited to race, ethnicity, gender, gender identity, sexual orientation, age, social class, physical ability or attributes, religious or ethical values system, national origin, and political beliefs.
- Culture represents the collective social norms and viewpoints held by a community in order to preserve a certain way of life. It is neither singular nor static.

- The cultural group people are exposed to during their upbringing typically comprises their ethnicity.
- Race is a socially constructed idea that has a limited basis on genetics.
- Sex and gender are different concepts where one is assigned at birth based on physical chromosomes and the other is a social construct typically defined within a culture.
- Spirituality is a central aspect of religion, but religion or religious practices need not be central to spirituality. Both are related to a process of searching for a divine being, reality, or truth as perceived by the individual.

KEY TERMS

- **Diversity** – The range of human differences including but not limited to race, ethnicity, gender, gender identity, sexual orientation, age, social class, physical ability or attributes, religious or ethical values system, national origin, and political beliefs.
- **Ethnicity** – Identification with the cultural heritage of a group of people who share a common ancestry, language, religion, society, or nation.
- **Ethnic Identity Development** – A knowledge of, and sense of belonging to, an ethnic group that develops over time.
- **Gender Identity** – The self-selected way in which individuals view themselves in relation to masculine and feminine traits.
- **Gender Roles** – The values, attitudes, and behaviors considered to be socially acceptable for biologically assigned men and women.
- **Inclusivity** – The practice or policy of including people who might otherwise be excluded or marginalized.
- **Race** – The idea that the human species consists of distinct groups that can be distinguished according to physical characteristics such as skin color, hair texture, or facial features.
- **Religion** – An organized collection of spiritual beliefs, traditions, and doctrines agreed upon by a group of people to explain the cause and purpose of the universe.
- **Sexism** – Prejudice or discrimination based upon a person's sex or gender.
- **Socially Constructed** – Ideas that have been invented by, and generally accepted within, a society.
- **Spirituality** – Personal engagement in beliefs, traditions, or practices concerned with finding meaning or purpose in life, connecting with the human spirit or soul, and relating to something greater than oneself.

REFERENCES

Banks, J. A. (2015). *Cultural diversity and education*. New York: Routledge.

Buss, D. (2015). *Evolutionary psychology: The new science of the mind* (5th ed.). New York: Pearson Education.

Cronk, L. (2019). *That complex whole: Culture and the evolution of human behavior*. New York: Routledge.

Cuseo, J. B., Fecas, V. S., & Thompson, A. (2010). *Thriving in college and beyond: Research based strategies for academic success and personal development*. Dubuque, IA: Kendall Hunt.

Eller, J. D. (2015). *Culture and diversity in the United States: So many ways to be American*. New York: Routledge.

Harris, S. (2014). *Waking up: A guide to spirituality without religion*. New York: Simon & Schuster.

Helgeson, V. (2016). *Psychology of gender* (5th ed.). London: Routledge.

LeDoux, J. E. (2014). Coming to terms with fear. *Proceedings of the National Academy of Sciences, 111*(8), 2871–2878.

New, W. S., & Merry, M. S. (2014). Is diversity necessary for educational justice? *Educational Theory, 64*(3), 205–225.

Oakley, A. (2016). *Sex, gender and society*. London: Routledge. (Originally published in 1972)

Oman, D. (2015). Defining religion and spirituality. In R. F. Paloutzian, & C. L. Park (Eds.), *Handbook of the psychology of religion and spirituality* (pp. 23–47). New York: Guilford.

Paoletti, J. B. (2012). *Pink and blue: Telling the boys from the girls in America*. Bloomington, IN: Indiana University Press.

Reich, D. (2018). *Who we are and how we got here: Ancient DNA and the new science of the human past*. Oxford, UK: Oxford University Press.

Robinson-Wood, T. (2017). *The convergences of race, ethnicity, and gender: multiple identities in counseling*. Thousand Oaks, CA: SAGE Publishing.

Valadez, J. (2018). *Deliberative democracy, political legitimacy, and self-determination in multi-cultural societies*. New York: Routledge.

Verkuyten, M. (2018). *The social psychology of ethnic identity*. New York: Routledge.

Woolfolk, A. (2011). *Educational psychology: Active learning edition* (11th ed.). Boston, MA: Pearson Education.

Yudell, M., Roberts, D., DeSalle, R., & Tishkoff, S. (2016). Taking race out of human genetics. *Science, 351*(6273), 564–565.

UNDERSTANDING BARRIERS TO DIVERSITY

CLUSTER 8 OBJECTIVES COVERED IN THIS MODULE

☐ **OBJECTIVE:** Define prejudice and discrimination, as well as describe their relationship to stereotyping and in-group socialization.

☐ **OBJECTIVE:** Identify the benefits of expanding personal identity and how this can influence your way of thinking about, interacting within, and experiencing the world.

☐ **OBJECTIVE:** Describe the personal and social benefits of experiencing diversity.

WHAT IS THE DIFFERENCE BETWEEN PREJUDICE AND DISCRIMINATION?

REFLECTION: Have you ever experienced prejudice or discrimination due to one of your identities? Have you ever felt prejudice or discriminated against someone else?

To be human is to hold beliefs, and to believe is to hold a conviction that certain things are true. Yet the human capacity to believe untrue things is virtually limitless (Kahneman, 2012). This is clearly demonstrated in terms of prejudicial attitudes and discriminatory behaviors. Prejudice is an unjustified negative attitude and stereotyped belief about a social group (Whitley & Kite, 2016). Social identity theory identifies prejudicial attitudes as a consequence of "in-group" socialization, whereby group membership fosters a sense of superiority over other, so called, "out-groups" (Jenkins, 2014). Oversimplified or stereotypical beliefs about out-group members are used to enhance group status as well as the self-image of individuals within the group. In effect, complex human beings perceived as members of an out-group are reduced to stereotypical, and often derogatory, caricatures.

PREJUDICE: An unjustified negative attitude and stereotyped belief about a social group.

STEREOTYPE: An overgeneralization about the appearance, behavior, or other characteristics of all members of a group.

IN-GROUP: An exclusive group of people with a shared sense of identity.

OUT-GROUP: People who do not belong to a specific in-group.

What are common stereotypes that you still see today?

DISCRIMINATION: Actions taken to perpetuate the unequal treatment of a group based on prejudicial attitudes and beliefs.

Prejudices that are continuously affirmed within the psychological safety of in-groups can transform internalized beliefs into externalized behaviors (Jenkins, 2014). In other words, beliefs can lead to actions. Discrimination is any action taken to perpetuate the unequal treatment of a group based on prejudicial attitudes and beliefs (Whitley & Kite, 2016). Discriminatory acts can be levied according to race, ethnicity, sexual orientation, gender roles, gender identity, class, disability, age, marital or employment status, religious or political belief, and other characteristics. As violations of fundamental human rights, discriminatory acts are a form of violence regardless of whether they are expressed in a physical, verbal, emotional, or psychological manner (Whitley & Kite, 2016).

WHAT IS OPPRESSION?

OPPRESSION: A cruel and unjust exercise of power that detracts from physical and psychological well-being.

Prejudice and discrimination are the foundation for cultural, racial, religious, and political oppression. Oppression is a cruel and unjust exercise of power that detracts from physical and psychological well-being. It takes two primary forms: oppression by force and oppression by deprivation. Oppression by force imposes "an object, label, role, experience, or set of living conditions that is unwanted" whereas oppression by deprivation denies access to "an object, role, experience, or set of living conditions that are desirable" (Hanna, Talley, & Guindon, 2000, p. 431). Both are acts of dominance meant to subjugate members of a minority group.

INSTITUTIONALIZED OPPRESSION: The systematic mistreatment of a subjugated or marginalized social group through the use of social institutions controlled by a dominant social group.

SUBJUGATION: The act of bringing a person or group under domination or control.

MARGINALIZATION: The act of treating a person or group as insignificant or peripheral.

Although oppressive acts are generally observed between individuals (e.g., schoolyard bullying, workplace harassment, domestic violence, refusal of services, etc.), it is important to recognize that such individual behaviors are expressions of broader social injustices. History is repleted with examples of how oppression arises from systemic discrimination. From the Spanish Inquisition to slavery in the United States to the rise of Nazi Germany, discriminatory practices have benefited powerful in-groups at the expense of subjugated or marginalized out-groups by means of what is called institutionalized oppression (Young, 2013). The previous historical examples of out-group subjugation, or the act of bringing a person or group under domination, represent institutionalized oppression by force. Oppression by deprivation, on the other hand, is more consistently observed in the form of marginalization, or the act of treating a person of group as insignificant or peripheral.

WHAT IS PRIVILEGE?

PRIVILEGE: When members of a group hold a systemic social right, authority, or advantage that other groups do not hold.

Privilege occurs when a group holds a systemic social right, authority, or advantage that other groups do not hold (Theoharis, 2018). The important term in that definition is "systemic," because holding a position of privilege occurs automatically as a result of in-group socialization. It stems from sociocultural factors that are often beyond the control of individuals. However, this does not mean individuals are not culpable when it comes to recognizing or otherwise benefiting from privileged status (Lawford-Smith, 2016). To the contrary, privilege stemming from being a member of a dominant in-group requires, at minimum, a recognition of its benefits. While there are numerous types of privilege, there are two important forms to distinguish: race-based and class-based privilege.

Race-based privilege includes white privilege, which is a controversial topic because it is widely misunderstood. White privilege means that white people in a predominantly white society can expect to, for example, turn on the television and see white newscasters and actors. It can include expecting to find products or services that are tailored to whites (e.g.; "nude-colored" Band-Aids and baby dolls) whereas non-whites are designated special shopping sections (e.g., ethnic hair products). Such examples might appear trivial to some people, but they reflect a broader cultural sense of what is considered normal, important, or valued in a society. It is about disproportionate representation in mainstream culture, as indicating "the norm, the ordinary, the standard" (Dyer, 2008, p. 11). The privilege in being white is not that it alleviates suffering or magically makes life simple. Rather, it ensures that many systemic barriers are not experienced by whites in the same way as non-whites due to a social system that consistently communicates cultural inclusivity.

Opposition to the idea of white privilege often results from confusing it with class-based, or socioeconomic, privilege. Class privilege means having access to financial resources needed to afford daily living expenses as well as other opportunities that arise from excess resources (Lawford-Smith, 2016), such as vacationing, attending summer camps, or not having to worry about paying rent. It does not necessarily mean being independently wealthy. Rather, class privilege exacts the benefits of security and stability that come from delimited financial stress. However, problems arise when those with class privilege believe that their own successes are solely attributable to personal skill, intelligence, persistence, and the like. By ignoring the role of social class in securing financial and career advantages, it becomes all too easy to attribute states of financial insecurity, including poverty, to personal failures rather than systemic disadvantages.

Read the following scenario and then answer the questions:

A middle-aged, married, Muslim, upper-class, Arabic-speaking, male doctor who lives in Syria successfully migrates to the U.S. seeking asylum.

1. Do you believe this person has privileged identities in Syria? If yes, what are his privileged identities?

2. When he moves to the U.S., would there be any changes to his privilege? Why or why not? What changes do you think may occur?

CASE STUDY—EXPANDED

REFLECTION: How might understanding diversity and oppression benefit you as a college student?

Sophia is approaching midterms and has maintained a high level of academic engagement that provides her with a great deal of self-efficacy as a college student. She does a great job of managing her time and spends every weekday at the library studying when she is not attending classes. However, Sophia has struggled to make friends and establish social supports in part because she believes there is not anyone "like her" on campus. As a result, Sophia has felt increasingly out of place as the semester progresses.

After weeks of invitations, Sophia's roommate finally convinces her to attend a campus organizational event addressing the Deferred Action for Childhood Arrival (DACA) immigration policy. At the event, Sophia listens intently to the testimonials of Hispanic students on campus. She is touched by numerous stories of personal struggles to find social acceptance, of anxiety and uncertainty in daily living, of wanting to meet parental expectations, and of challenges in adapting to the new college culture. Sophia begins to realize that she has more in common with other students than she had ever imagined. After the meeting, Sophia asks her roommate if they can attend another campus event together. She expresses her hope to better understand herself as well as gain new perspectives on how others experience the world.

SUMMARY: THE BENEFITS OF EXPANDING SOCIAL IDENTITY

Social identity theory and identity theory represent two distinct yet over-lapping views in social psychology. Social identity theory posits that group membership is the basis for identity whereas identity theory asserts that social roles are the basis for identity. By merging these two perspectives, Stets and Burke (2000) maintain that "people largely feel good about them-selves when they associate with particular groups, typically feel confident about themselves when enacting particular roles, and generally feel that they are "real" or authentic when their person identities are verified" (p. 234). This statement provides an interesting glimpse into the complex process of personal identity. Being part of an in-group, doing something purposeful within that in-group, and feeling included by group members are all impor-tant contributors to well-being.

As social beings, the value of cultural inclusivity cannot be overstated. Everyone seeks to be a part of something bigger than themselves. It is in everyone's nature. At the same time, as already discussed, in-group member-ship requires out-group counterparts, as well as the potential consequences therein. When a desire for inclusivity and sense of group specialness out-paces mindfulness of common humanity, prejudice and discrimination are often not far behind (Jenkins, 2014). The question everyone must reckon with is whether the wish is to maintain the status quo or to contribute to social justice. To choose the latter requires expanding your social identity. Developing a more inclusive and far-reaching sense of social identity is not a simple task, but the evidence suggests that doing so can enhance life satisfac-tion (Bowman & Denson, 2012).

In the case study, Sophia experienced a great deal of confusion and anxi-ety during her first semester of college. You can observe how Sophia's social identity, rooted in the norms of her hometown, restricted her ability to understand how others operate in the world. However, after hearing the compelling stories of fellow students from a different ethnic background she realized that they had far more in common than she would have ever previ-ously imagined. Embracing diversity is not just a matter of learning about cultural differences. It can lead you to discover commonalities as well. Living in a diverse society provides unique opportunities to learn and grow from other points of view in a manner that cannot be attained in the relative isola-tion of cultural homogeneity (Levin, Sinclair, Sidanius, & Van Laar, 2009).

To benefit from diversity, one must engage in both an internal process of self-reflection as well as an external process of sociocultural participation. College students are presented with a unique opportunity to participate in a diverse community that supports intercultural interactions (Colvin, Volet, & Fozdar, 2014). Engaging in multicultural activities on campus is a great way to over-come prejudicial attitudes and take an active role in promoting the common good for all groups of people (New & Merry, 2014). Meaningful exposure to

What cultural events are hosted on your campus? How can you find this information? What courses are available that would expand these ideas?

diversity forces one to reflect on social identities and to consider alternative ways of seeing the world. By examining personal values and beliefs in the context of diversity, you can expand your self-knowledge and compassion for others in a manner that actively contributes to the common good. Research has also suggested that, "Students who are open to diversity and challenge are more likely to seek out new experiences and to achieve educational success" (Bowman, 2014, p. 288). This includes higher first-term GPAs, retention, and overall engagement. Going further, experiencing diversity enhances learning, grows self-efficacy, strengthens creative thinking, builds leadership skills, and serves as valuable preparation for career success in a pluralistic society (Bowman, 2013; Cuseo, Fecas, & Thompson, 2010).

ACTIVITY 8.2.2

Take a look at your responses in Activity 8.1.1. When thinking about your identities, reflect on the following questions:

1. List the identities you included:

2. Which of your identities do you think of most often? Why?

3. Which of your identities do you think others see most in you? Why?

4. Which of your identities would you like to learn more about?

5. Which of your identities provide you the most privilege? Why?

6. Which of your identities are misunderstood most often? Why do you think that is the case?

7. Are there any identities that subject you to prejudice or discrimination? Why or why not?

8. Change one of your primary identities. How would this change impact your past and/or current experiences? How might it change how you interact with others?

9. Gaining information around diversity, what strategies will you use to expand your self-knowledge?

MODULE 8.2 SUMMARY

- Prejudice is an unjustified negative belief about a social group whereas discrimination is actions taken against a social group based on these beliefs.
- Oppression, an exercise of power, can lead to the domination of persons or groups or to the marginalization of these groups.
- Privilege occurs when a group holds a systemic social right, authority, or advantage that other groups do not hold and can be based on either race or class.
- Developing a more inclusive and far-reaching sense of social identity can enhance life satisfaction as well as academic and professional achievement.

KEY TERMS

- **Discrimination** – Actions taken to perpetuate the unequal treatment of a group based on prejudicial attitudes and beliefs.
- **In-group** – An exclusive group of people with a shared sense of identity.
- **Institutionalized Oppression** – The systematic mistreatment of a subjugated or marginalized social group through the use of social institutions controlled by a dominant social group.
- **Marginalization** – The act of treating a person or group as insignificant or peripheral.

- **Oppression** – A cruel and unjust exercise of power that detracts from physical and psychological well-being.
- **Out-group** – People who do not belong to a specific in-group.
- **Prejudice** – An unjustified negative attitude and stereotyped belief about a social group.
- **Privilege** – When members of a group hold a systemic social right, authority, or advantage that other groups do not hold.
- **Stereotype** – An overgeneralization about the appearance, behavior, or other characteristics of all members of a group.
- **Subjugation** – The act of bringing a person or group under domination or control.

REFERENCES

Andreatta, B. (2011). *Navigating the research university: A guide for first-year students*. Boston, MA: Wadsworth Cengage Learning.

Bowman, N. A. (2013). How much diversity is enough? The curvilinear relationship between college diversity interaction and first-year student outcomes. *Research in Higher Education, 54*, 874–894.

Bowman, N. A. (2014). Conceptualizing openness to diversity and challenge: Its relation to college experiences, achievement, and retention. *Innovative Higher Education, 39*(4), 277–291. doi:10.1007/s10755-014-9281-8

Bowman, N. A., & Denson, N. (2012). What's past is prologue: How pre-college exposure to diversity shapes the impact of college diversity experiences. *Research in Higher Education, 53*, 406–425.

Colvin, C., Volet, S., & Fozdar, F. (2014). Local university students and intercultural interactions: Conceptualizing culture, seeing diversity and experiencing interactions. *Higher Education Research & Development, 33*(3), 440–455.

Cuseo, J. B., Fecas, V. S., & Thompson, A. (2010). *Thriving in college and beyond: Research based strategies for academic success and personal development*. Dubuque, IA: Kendall Hunt.

Dyer, R. (2008). The matter of whiteness. In P. S. Rothenberg (Ed.), *White privilege* (3rd. ed.). New York: Macmillan.

Hanna, F. J., Talley, W. B., & Guindon, M. H. (2000). The power of perception: Toward a model of cultural oppression and liberation. *Journal of Counseling & Development, 78*(4), 430–441.

Kahneman, D. (2011). *Thinking, fast and slow*. New York: Macmillan.

Lawford-Smith, H. (2016). Offsetting class privilege. *Journal of Practical Ethics, 4*(1), 23–51.

Levin, S., Sinclair, S., Sidanius, J., & Van Laar, C. (2009). Ethnic and university identities across the college years: A common in-group identity perspective. *Journal of Social Issues, 65*(2), 287–306.

New, W. S., & Merry, M. S. (2014). Is diversity necessary for educational justice? *Educational Theory, 64*(3), 205–225.

Stets, J. E., & Burke, P. J. (2000). Identity theory and social identity theory. *Social Psychology Quarterly, 63*(3), 224–237.

Theoharis, G. (2018). White privilege and educational leadership. In J. S. Brooks, & G. Theoharis (Eds.), *Whiteucation: Privilege, power, and prejudice in school and society* (pp. 52–61). New York: Routledge.

Whitley Jr, B. E., & Kite, M. E. (2016). *Psychology of prejudice and discrimination.* New York: Routledge.

CASE STUDY

Sophia is a first-semester freshman who moved across the country to attend college. Leaving her rural mountain community was very difficult for Sophia. After all, in a small town practically everybody knows one another. Over 18 years, Sophia had grown accustomed to being around people who look like her, talk like her, and hold the same beliefs as her. Cultural homogeneity, or sameness, was all she had ever known until arriving at college. Only a month into her college experience, Sophia begins experiencing a great deal of anxiety. She feels as though she is being exposed to ideas and behaviors that she just does not understand. She was raised to be kind and generous but is struggling to feel comfortable around people who seem "abnormal." Sophia feels out of place and is considering going home at the end of the semester.

QUESTIONS

1. What experiences are you currently having that are similar or different from Sophia's first-semester experience?
2. What advice do you have for Sophia to help her understand what she's experiencing?

POTENTIAL RESPONSES

1. It is likely that for many of you, being away from home for the first time can result in many of these same feelings. This can be especially strong if you are having to rebuild your support networks. Some students are able to come to college with a large support network of friends and even have home and family close by. The level of anxiety

may be less; however, the greater challenge would be to still seek out opportunities that will expand your self-knowledge and to seek out diversity in terms of other people, cultures and ideas. Essentially, in both cases, you are encouraged to move beyond your "comfort zones" and to gain the benefits of new experiences and ideas.

2. As discussed previously, there are many strategies that Sophia can use. Attending cultural events on campus, seeking out other courses that will expand her knowledge, and engaging with others whenever possible will ease her anxiety while building new support networks. It is also likely that these efforts will lead to more diverse support networks and will provide the greatest opportunities for growth, deep learning, and life satisfaction.

ADDITIONAL READINGS

Collins, P. H. (2002). *Black feminist thought: Knowledge, consciousness, and the politics of empowerment*. New York: Routledge.

David, E. J. R., & Derthick, A. O. (2018). *The psychology of oppression*. New York: Springer.

DiAngelo, R. (2018). *White fragility: Why it's so hard for white people to talk about racism*. Boston, MA: Beacon Press.

Ridarsky, C. L., & Huth, M. M. (2012). *Susan B. Anthony and the struggle for equal rights*. Rochester, NY: University of Rochester Press.

Gallardo, M. E. (Ed.). (2013). *Developing cultural humility: Embracing race, privilege and power*. Thousand Oaks, CA: SAGE.

Hancock, A. M. (2016). *Intersectionality: An intellectual history*. Oxford, UK: Oxford University Press.

Johnson, A. G. (2006). *Privilege, power, and difference*. New York: McGraw-Hill.

King, M. L. (2012). *A gift of love: Sermons from strength to love and other preachings* (7th ed.). Boston, MA: Beacon Press.

McBee, T. P. (2018). *Amateur: A reckoning with gender, identity, and masculinity*. New York: Simon and Schuster.

Mintz, S. B. (2007). *Unruly bodies: Life writing by women with disabilities*. Chapel Hill, NC: University of North Carolina Press.

Patterson, J. (2019). *The bold world: A memoir of family and transformation*. New York: Random House.

Phillips, A. (2007). *Multiculturalism without culture*. Princeton, NJ: Princeton University Press.

Roughgarden, J. (2013). *Evolution's rainbow: Diversity, gender, and sexuality in nature and people*. Los Angeles, CA: Univ of California Press.

Sacks, J. (2007). *The home we build together: Recreating society*. London: Continuum.

Schmidt, L. E. (2012). *Restless souls: The making of American spirituality*. Los Angeles, CA: University of California Press.

Stevenson, B. (2015). *Just mercy: A story of justice and redemption*. New York: Spiegel & Grau.

Winkle-Wagner, R., & Locks, A. M. (2014). *Diversity and inclusion on campus: Supporting racially and ethnically underrepresented students*. New York: Routledge.

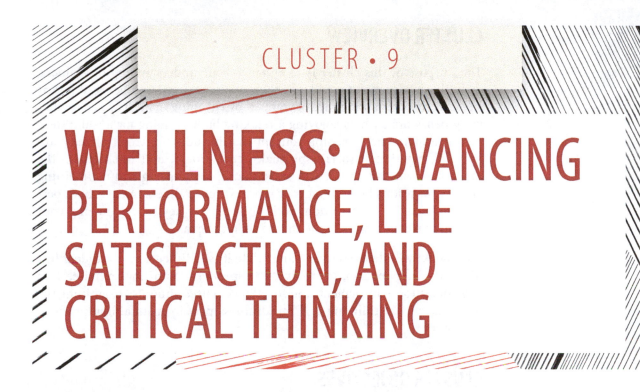

CLUSTER · 9

WELLNESS: ADVANCING PERFORMANCE, LIFE SATISFACTION, AND CRITICAL THINKING

CASE STUDY

Jen is preparing for finals next week in her first semester as a college freshman. Although Jen is excited for winter break, she is also feeling stressed and fatigued. She had set a goal at the beginning of the semester to earn a 3.5 GPA and is determined to attain it. She has pulled two all-nighters this week, drinking far more coffee than usual to stay awake, and eating fast foods multiple times per day. Jen's phone notifies her of a 33% increase in her screen time over the past two weeks. She suddenly realizes that she has been mindlessly scrolling through Instagram again. Jen begins to worry that she won't perform well on her finals next week because she is struggling to maintain her study schedule.

QUESTIONS

1. What areas of wellness are being impacted by Jen's everyday choices?

2. What are two everyday choices Jen can adjust to improve her wellness?

3. What strategies could Jen adjust to increase her wellness?

CLUSTER OVERVIEW

The purpose of this cluster is to enhance your understanding of wellness, including how to monitor and take charge your personal well-being. Whereas self-care involves taking care of yourself by engaging in healthy and revitalizing behaviors such as enjoying a relaxing bath or going for a walk; wellness is a more encompassing concept that includes six broad dimensions: physical, emotional, social, spiritual, occupational, and intellectual. The information in this cluster will assist you in establishing and maintaining all six dimensions by refining your sense of how wellness impacts both performance and life satisfaction, both of which are key to maximizing your educational experiences in the short and long term.

Module 9.1 will define wellness and relate its six dimensions to student life. Module 9.2 applies a holistic wellness perspective to nutrition, exercise, sleep hygiene, stress management, and social media use, while also examining the role that critical thinking and mindfulness play in maintaining personal wellness.

CLUSTER OBJECTIVES

- Identify and define the six dimensions of wellness.
- Describe how the wellness dimensions relate to performance and life satisfaction.
- Define wellness in terms of nutrition, exercise, sleep hygiene, and social media use.
- Describe the relationship between stress management and wellness.
- Describe how critical thinking and mindfulness inform wellness.

THE WELLNESS DIMENSIONS

WHAT IS WELLNESS?

REFLECTION: Have you ever looked at an adult you admire and wonder how they established and then maintain their fulfilling lifestyle?

For much of human history, the term "health" has denoted only a lack of physical illness or disease. However, in 1948 the World Health Organization crafted a multidimensional definition of health as "a state of complete physical, mental, and social well-being, and not merely the absence of disease or infirmity." This definition supports a holistic and preventative view of health as a state of well-being. In turn, wellness has been defined as an active process of gaining awareness and making choices toward a satisfying and fulfilling existence (Hettler, 1984; National Wellness Institute, n.d.). Wellness represents those actions and decisions that lead to a state of health and well-being across physical, emotional, intellectual, social, spiritual, and occupational wellness dimensions.

Studies have also suggested that a person's beliefs and approaches around wellness occur early in life and are formed during the ages of 20 to 24, which for many students include their transition to and performance during college (Idler & Kasl, 1991; Russell-Mayhew, Arthur, & Ewashen, 2007). However, forming habits that lead to short- and long-term healthy existence can be even more difficult during this stressful time of transition (Sallis, Owen, & Fisher, 2008) and increased expectations to perform and achieve success (Beiter et al., 2015; Dyson & Renk, 2006).

Yet, developing awareness and making decisions to support holistic wellness during college has consistently shown improved academic achievement and persistence including higher GPAs (Cereola, Snyder, Cereola, & Horton, 2014; Finkelstein-Fox, Park, & Riley, 2018; Maddi, Harvey, Khoshaba, Fazel, & Resurreccion, 2009). Clearly, understanding, achieving, and maintaining wellness is a worthwhile endeavor with significant benefits for the short and long term.

SIX DIMENSIONS OF WELLNESS

What other dimensions would you include as part of your overall wellness?

The first step is to gain an understanding of the dimensions of wellness as well as to reflect on how these intertwine to promote your holistic wellness. Although there are potentially other dimensions to wellness, the following describes the six primary dimensions designated by the National Wellness Institute (1984).

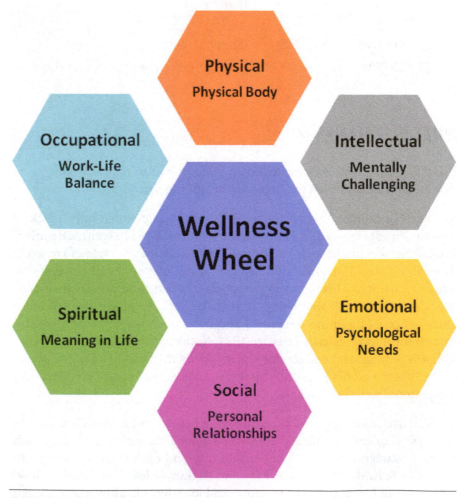

FIGURE 9.1.1: Wellness Wheel   *Source: Angela Vaughan & Brett Wilkinson*

Physical: This aspect of wellness emphasizes taking care of the physical body by means of a healthy diet, regular exercise, sufficient sleep, and good hygiene habits. Physical wellness includes the need for movement as both a means of release and to stay physically fit. It requires self-control related to tobacco, drug use, and excessive alcohol consumption, as well as personal responsibility in terms of regular medical checkups and seeking medical attention when needed.

> What fuels your body? Consider your nutrition choices, daily activities, and hobbies.

Intellectual: This aspect of wellness involves taking part in mentally challenging and creative learning activities that foster curiosity, expand knowledge, demand self-control, and promote open-mindedness. Intellectual wellness signifies the importance of exploring new ideas, discovering new skills, and engaging in unique learning activities that require active problem-solving and critical thinking skills.

Emotional: This aspect of wellness involves being aware of your feelings and psychological needs. Emotional wellness is the foundation upon which self-esteem—the value you place on your own characteristics, abilities, and behaviors (Woolfolk, 2014)—is built. It includes the ability to manage stress, regulate emotional reactions, and cope with life challenges. It requires actively monitoring your expectations and expressing feelings in an appropriate way.

> What are you passionately curious about? How can you dedicate or carve out time to foster the curiosity?

SELF-ESTEEM: The value you place on your own characteristics, abilities and behaviors.

Social: This aspect of wellness emphasizes the value of satisfying personal relationships and the importance of community support in daily life. Social wellness promotes the use of effective communication in an effort to build more intimate relationships and friendships. It also denotes efforts to benefit the community by taking part in activities that support the wellness of others, as well as the natural environments in which you live.

> What strategies do you have to monitor, acknowledge, and let go of your emotions? Think about one new way to regulate your emotions.

Spiritual: This aspect of wellness involves discovering purpose and meaning in life experiences. Spiritual wellness promotes making choices in alignment with values, ethics, and morals drawn upon from religious faiths, spiritual practices, and philosophical ideas. It can involve seeking a balance between inner needs and outer challenges, learning about how your beliefs inform your way of being in the world, discussing different viewpoints with others to promote tolerance and enhance curiosity, and pondering what it means to live in personal harmony.

> Who is your community and how satisfied are you with those connections? What are some strategies to improve these connections?

Occupational: This aspect of wellness recognizes the value of work–life balance as well as the relationship between career satisfaction and personal enrichment. Occupational wellness highlights the benefit of exploring various career options in order to discover a path that aligns with personal values, interests, and beliefs. Factors that influence occupational development may include educational requirements, salary, location, work–life balance, and benefits. Financial wellness is a subcategory of occupational wellness that signifies the necessary balance between work satisfaction and financial security. It is not about accumulating wealth. Rather, it is a state of well-being in which you experience control over current and future finances.

> How does your current educational experiences promote and align with your purpose?

PRIORITIZING WELLNESS IN DAILY LIVING

> Helpful Video – TED: Shawn Achor's "The Happy Secret to Better Work" at https://www.ted.com/talks/shawn_achor_the_happy_secret_to_better_work

The purpose of dedicating a cluster in this textbook to wellness is to highlight the value of building a well-rounded life. Wellness is not simply taking care of yourself. Rather, it represents an intentional and aspirational approach to living. The journey to greater well-being commences anew each day through the choices you make with two vital yet limited resources: time and attention. Seeking wellness entails being thoughtful and selective in determining what you hope to achieve and what kind of person you wish to become.

> If you are depressed, you are living in the past. If you are anxious, you are living in the future. If you are at peace, you are living in the present.
> – Lao Tzu

By dedicating yourself to personal wellness, you are essentially taking the position that your life satisfaction is a worthwhile priority. Attending to wellness is therefore a goal-oriented task. Constructive habits are formed by engaging in healthy, enriching activities on a regularly scheduled basis. Of course, you do not need to tackle everything at once. Even formulating one small goal for each of the six wellness dimensions is a good start. The following assessment and activity will allow you to prioritize specific dimensions according to your personal needs and develop specific plans of action.

ACTIVITY 9.1.1 WELLNESS ASSESSMENT

You can use this self-assessment tool to determine the areas of wellness (physical, intellectual, emotional, social, spiritual, and occupational) where you are thriving, as well as those that may need greater attention. Taking this assessment will also help you to reflect on components of health that you may not have considered before.

Instructions:

1. Answer all the questions for each of the six wellness dimensions.
2. Tally your points for each section and use the guide to interpret the scores.
3. Complete a *Take Action Plan*.

Physical Dimension	Never	Rarely	Sometimes	Usually
1. I engage in physical exercise regularly (e.g., 30 minutes at least 5 × a week or 10,000 steps a day).	1	2	3	4
2. I get 6–8 hours of sleep each night.	1	2	3	4
3. I protect myself and others from getting ill (e.g., wash my hands, cover my cough, etc.).	1	2	3	4
4. I abstain from drinking alcohol; or if I do drink, I aim to keep my BAC < 0.06.	1	2	3	4
5. I avoid using tobacco products or other drugs.	1	2	3	4
6. I eat a balanced diet (fruits, vegetables, low-moderate fat, whole grains).	1	2	3	4
7. I get regular physical exams (i.e., annual, when I have atypical symptoms).	1	2	3	4
Total for the Physical Dimension				

Intellectual Dimension	Never	Rarely	Sometimes	Usually
1. I am curious and interested in the communities, as well as the world, around me.	1	2	3	4
2. I search for learning opportunities and stimulating mental activities.	1	2	3	4
3. I manage my time well, rather than it managing me.	1	2	3	4
4. I enjoy brainstorming and sharing knowledge with others in group projects or tasks.	1	2	3	4
5. I enjoy learning about subjects other than those I am required to study in my field of work.	1	2	3	4
6. I seek opportunities to learn practical skills to help others.	1	2	3	4
7. I can critically consider the opinions and information presented by others and provide constructive feedback.	1	2	3	4
Total for the Intellectual Dimension				

Emotional Dimension	Never	Rarely	Sometimes	Usually
1. I find it easy to express my emotions in positive, constructive ways.	1	2	3	4
2. I recognize when I am stressed and take steps to manage my stress (e.g., exercise, quiet time, meditation).	1	2	3	4
3. I am resilient and can bounce back after a disappointment or problem.	1	2	3	4
4. I am able to maintain a balance of work, family, friends, and other obligations.	1	2	3	4
5. I am flexible and adapt or adjust to change in a positive way.	1	2	3	4
6. I am able to make decisions with minimal stress or worry.	1	2	3	4
7. When I am angry, I try to let others know in non-confrontational or non-hurtful ways.	1	2	3	4
Total for the Emotional Dimension				

Social Dimension	Never	Rarely	Sometimes	Usually
1. I consciously and continually try to work on behaviors or attitudes that have caused problems in my interactions with others.	1	2	3	4
2. In my romantic or sexual relationships, I choose partner(s) who respect my wants, needs, and choices.	1	2	3	4
3. I feel supported and respected in my close relationships.	1	2	3	4
4. I communicate effectively with others, share my views, and listen to those of others.	1	2	3	4
5. I consider the feelings of others and do not act in hurtful/selfish ways.	1	2	3	4
6. I try to see good in my friends and do whatever I can to support them.	1	2	3	4
7. I participate in a wide variety of social activities and find opportunities to form new relationships.	1	2	3	4
Total for the Social Dimension				

Spiritual Dimension	Never	Rarely	Sometimes	Usually
1. I take time to think about what's important in life—who I am, what I value, where I fit in, and where I am going.	1	2	3	4
2. I have found a balance between meeting my needs and those of others.	1	2	3	4
3. I engage in acts of caring and goodwill without expecting something in return.	1	2	3	4
4. I sympathize/empathize with those who are suffering and try to help them through difficult times.	1	2	3	4
5. My values are true priorities in my life and are reflected in my actions.	1	2	3	4
6. I feel connected to something larger than myself (e.g., supreme being, nature, connectedness of all living things, humanity, and community).	1	2	3	4
7. I feel like my life has purpose and meaning.	1	2	3	4
Total for the Spiritual Dimension				

Note: As many of you are in school to pursue a career (and not yet working in your career), you can consider the academic work you are completing now for your chosen degree as you respond to these items.

Occupational Dimension	Never	Rarely	Sometimes	Usually
1. I get personal satisfaction and enrichment from work.	1	2	3	4
2. I believe that I am able to contribute my knowledge, skills, and talents at work.	1	2	3	4
3. I seek out opportunities to improve my knowledge or skills.	1	2	3	4
4. I balance my social life and job responsibilities well.	1	2	3	4
5. I effectively handle my level of stress related to work responsibilities.	1	2	3	4
6. My work load is manageable.	1	2	3	4
7. I explore paid and/or volunteer opportunities that interest me.	1	2	3	4
Total for the Occupational Dimension				

Calculate your Scores

Wellness Dimension	Ideal Score	Your Score
Physical	28	
Intellectual	28	
Emotional	28	
Social	28	
Spiritual	28	
Occupational	28	

Scores of 20–28: *Outstanding! Your answers demonstrate that you're already taking positive steps in this dimension of wellness. You're improving your own well-being and also setting a good example for those around you. Although you achieved a high overall score in this domain, you may want to check for low scores on individual items to see if there are specific areas you might want to address. You might also choose to focus on another area where your scores weren't so high.*

Scores of 15–19: *Your behaviors in this area are good, but there is room for improvement. Take a look at the items on which you scored lower. What changes might you make it improve your score? Even a small change in behavior can help you achieve better health and well-being.*

Scores of 14 and below: *Your answers indicate some potential health and well-being risks. Review those areas where you scored lower and review resources provided in today's Wellness Resources handout to help you develop and set achievable goals.*

ACTIVITY 9.1.2 TAKE ACTION PLAN

Review your scores, both overall for each dimension of wellness and for individual statements. For those areas where you scored lower, consider what might have a significant impact on your daily life (e.g., interferes with your performance, causes distress, etc.) and focus on those behaviors. Then ask yourself what you feel capable of changing.

1. Which aspects of which dimensions are you ready and willing to work on?

2. Select <u>one</u> of the behaviors you listed above and take action by setting a *USEFUL* goal:

> • Specific – develop the details of your goal (what, where, when, why).
> • Measurable – define a quantity (frequency, amount, etc.) that you can measure.
> • Challenging – will this goal require higher levels of effort that will help develop new skills and competence?
> • Time-bounded – by what deadline or time frame do you wish to accomplish this goal?

Useful Goal:

3. What are/would be the benefits of working on this behavior? (e.g., better time management skills, improve quality of relationships)

4. What could get in the way of achieving your goal? (e.g., struggling to find time, difficulty feeling motivated)

5. How can you reward yourself for achieving your desired goal? (e.g., host a get-together, treat yourself to a new outfit)

6. What can help you achieve your goal? (e.g., support of family or friends, seeing results)

7. On what date will you start? (e.g., next Monday, at the end of the school year)

MODULE 9.1 SUMMARY

- Wellness can be understood in terms of six primary dimensions: physical, intellectual, emotional, social, spiritual, and occupational.
- Everyday choices and personal priorities impact overall wellness.

KEY TERMS

- **Self-Esteem** – The value you place on your own characteristics, abilities, and behaviors.
- **Wellness** – A continual active process of gaining awareness and making choices toward a satisfying and fulfilling existence.

REFERENCES

Beiter, R., Nash, R., McCrady, M., Rhoades, D., Linscomb, M., Clarahan, M., & Sammut, S. (2015). The prevalence and correlates of depression, anxiety, and stress in a sample of college students. *Journal of Affective Disorders, 173,* 90–96. doi:10.1016/j.jad.2014.10.054

Cereola, S. J., Snyder, C. S., Cereola, R. J., & Horton, B. W. (2014). Holistic wellness and its impact on first-semester grades. *Journal of the First-Year Experience & Students in Transition, 26*(2), 89–106.

Dyson, R., & Renk, K. (2006). Freshmen adaptation to university life: Depressive symptoms, stress, and coping. *Journal of Clinical Psychology, 62,* 1231–1244. doi:10.1002/jclp.20295

Finkelstein-Fox, L., Park, C. L., & Riley, K. E. (2018). Mindfulness and emotion regulation: Promoting well-being during the transition to college. *Anxiety, Stress, & Coping, 31*(6), 639–653. doi:10.1080/10615806.2018.1518635

Hettler, B. (1984). Wellness: Encouraging a lifetime pursuit of excellence. *Health Values, 8,* 13–17.

Idler, E. L., & Kasl, S. V. (1991). Health perceptions and survival: Do global evaluations of health status really predict mortality? *Journal of Gerontology: Social Sciences, 46*(2), 55–65.

Maddi, S. R., Harvey, R. H., Khoshaba, D. M., Fazel, M., & Resurreccion, N. (2009). Hardiness training facilitates performance in college. *The Journal of Positive Psychology, 4*(6), 566–577. doi:10.1080/17439760903157133

National Wellness Institute. (n.d.). *The six dimensions of wellness.* Retrieved from https://www.nationalwellness.org/page/Six_Dimensions

Russell-Mayhew, S., Arthur, N., & Ewashen, C. (2007). Targeting students, teachers and parents in a wellness-based prevention program in schools. *Eating Disorders, 15*(2), 159–181.

Sallis, J. F., Owen, N., & Fisher, E. B. (2008). Ecological models of health behavior. In K. Glanz, B. K. Rimer, & K. Viswanath (Eds.), *Health behavior and health education: Theory, research, and practice* (4th ed., pp. 465–486). San Francisco, CA: Jossey-Bass.

Woolfolk, A. (2014). *Educational psychology: Modular active learning edition* (13th ed.). Boston: Pearson.

TAKING CHARGE OF PERSONAL WELLNESS

CLUSTER 9 OBJECTIVES COVERED IN THIS MODULE

☐ **OBJECTIVE:** Define wellness in terms of nutrition, exercise, sleep, and social media use.

☐ **OBJECTIVE:** Describe the relationship between stress management and wellness.

☐ **OBJECTIVE:** Describe how critical thinking and mindfulness inform wellness.

WELLNESS IN PRACTICE

REFLECTION: Think back to a goal you set at the beginning of the semester. How is it going? What are the road blocks? Are you still motivated to complete the goal? If not, what has changed?

The broader purpose of this textbook is to provide students with knowledge, strategies, and skills that enhance learning in the college environment and beyond. In order to accomplish both personal and professional goals, students must learn how to monitor behaviors to determine what works and what does not, as well as learn how to form effective habits that lead to better outcomes. In this manner, wellness is actually a central underlying premise of every module in this textbook. Creating intentional goals, improving metacognition and critical thinking skills, increasing motivation, and learning time management set you up for long-term career success.

A balanced approach to maintaining personal wellness is thus a prerequisite for optimal learning outcomes. Understanding how daily functioning is impacted by particular lifestyle choices can help students grasp the relationship between learning and daily decision making. For example, Cluster 4 describes how information processing models are concerned with storing, encoding, and retrieving information from memory. However, effective memory retrieval strategies are contingent upon daily wellness choices related to nutrition, exercise, sleep hygiene, and stress management because learning is an integrative neurobiological process (see Figure 9.2.1). If students wish to succeed in learning how to learn, they must learn how to take care of their physical and mental health needs as well.

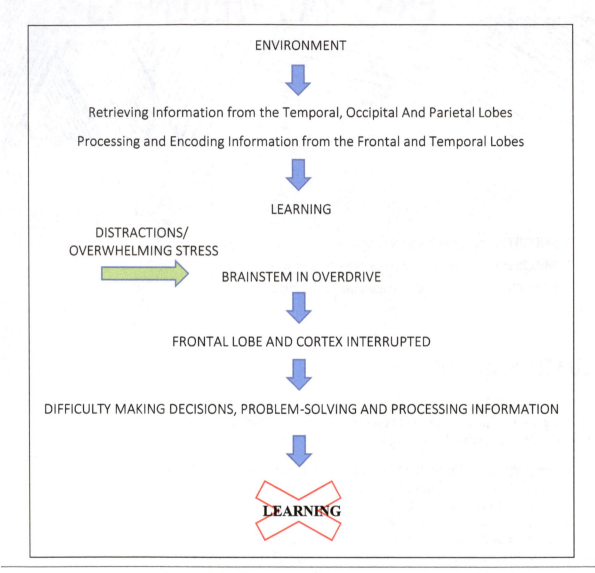

FIGURE 9.2.1: Information Processing: A Neuroscience Perspective (Stiles & Jernigan, 2010)

WELLNESS ROUTINES: SLEEP, NUTRITION, AND PHYSICAL ACTIVITY

REFLECTION: Have you ever "woken up on the wrong side of the bed" leaving you to go about your day groggy, grouchy and unfocused?

In terms of physical well-being, college students tend to grasp the importance of getting restful sleep, eating nutritional meals, and exercising regularly to enhance daily functioning. Yet there is often a large gap between knowing that something is healthy for you and acting upon that knowledge. In terms of nutrition, poor eating habits established in college are linked to dire health consequences across the lifespan (Plotnikoff et al., 2015). Physical activity declines precipitously between high school and college, with only 40% of college students exercising regularly (Kim & Cardinal, 2019).

The U.S. Center for Disease Control and Prevention has declared insufficient sleep a public health epidemic, with research indicating that 50% of college students report daytime sleepiness and 70% report insufficient sleep (Hershner & Chervin, 2014). Short-term sleep deprivation impacts the cortex's overall functioning and the temporal lobe's ability to consolidate and encode into long-term memory. All of this leading to an increased struggle for students to focus, thus affecting the student's ability to learn and retain new information.

The importance of establishing wellness routines that take sleep hygiene (see Table 9.2.1), nutritional intake, and physical activity into consideration cannot be overstated. In addition to sleep as described above, deficits in any of these areas can significantly detract from mood stability, memory consolidation, and attentional capacity, making it more difficult to process information, retain memories, make decisions, and solve problems. Furthermore, poor wellness habits tend to increase the risk of anxiety, burnout, depression, and illness (Plotnikoff et al., 2015). As such, it is clear that physical needs impact every dimension of wellness, including the regulation of emotional responses to stress and anxiety, the management of intellectual endeavors in terms of focused problem solving and curiosity, and the enhancement of social wellness in terms of patience and attentiveness in relationships. In turn, occupational and spiritual wellness tend to suffer when one lacks the energy needed to engage in meaningful personal or work-related tasks.

TABLE 9.2.1 SLEEP HYGIENE—COMMON RECOMMENDATIONS
(CENTER FOR CLINICAL INTERVENTIONS, N.D.; CUSEO, FECAS, & THOMPSON, 2010)

Do:	Don't:
Establish a daily routine: • Go to bed at the same time • Wake up around the same time • Have a bedtime routine (e.g., reading, warm bath, etc.) • Keep your daily routine the same even when tired or if you didn't get enough sleep	Stay in bed awake. It is better to go find something to do, boring is better, and then return to bed when you are sleepy.
Make sure the room is comfortable with a cooler temperature and blankets to keep warm. If noise and light are a problem, use earplugs and an eye mask.	Drink caffeine or alcohol or exercise before bedtime for approximately 4 to 6 hours.
Use your bed for only sleep or sex.	Read, watch TV, pay bills, or other activities in bed.
Get regular exercise, earlier is better.	Take afternoon naps, or limit them to 20 minutes only.

Improving wellness across the domains of sleeping, eating, and exercising demands a self-regulated learning process of setting goals, applying strategies, monitoring changes, and evaluating outcomes. Students can use self-monitoring strategies such as journaling, smartphone applications, and physiological monitoring devices (e.g., fitbit, watches, etc.) to gain insight into how current habits impact their well-being, as well as how new routines might lead to improvement in overall functioning (see Cluster 2 for additional ideas on using technology to increase accountability). By means of evaluating and prioritizing such habits, students can drastically improve their sense of wellness.

Figure 9.2.2 and Textbox:

REFLECTION: Have you ever wondered why being "hungry" can be such an intense experience?

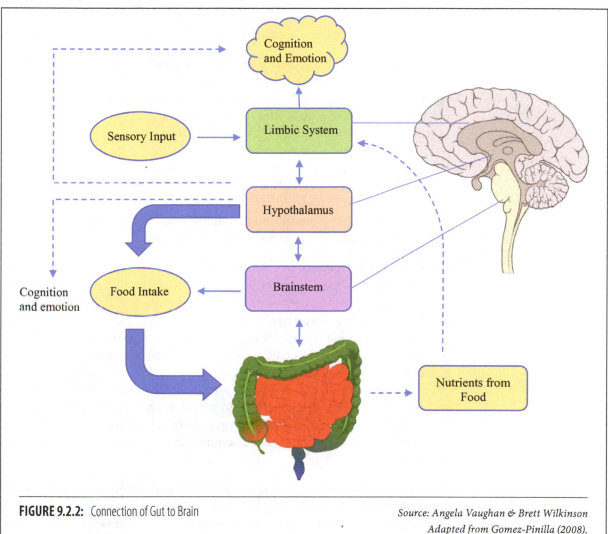

FIGURE 9.2.2: Connection of Gut to Brain

Source: Angela Vaughan & Brett Wilkinson
Adapted from Gomez-Pinilla (2008).

The experience of being hungry can overtake cognitive functioning, reducing the ability to monitor and regulate emotions, work effectively and focus. The vagal nerve is directly connected to the brain centers maintaining energy homeostasis and cognitive functioning. Vagal nerve stimulation (VNS) impacts digestion initiating the messages to activate digestive enzymes and food absorption (Gómez-Pinilla, 2008). The sensory process of preparing a meal is where this process begins entering through the visual and olfactory centers of the brain (Occipital and Parietal lobes). Mood can be impacted when this process starts as the vagal nerve begins to dump enzymes and to prepare the digestive track for food ingestion creating stomach aches and rumbling. Once food has been ingested and hormones, such as insulin, are released into circulation centers of the brain, synaptic activity increases aiding in memory and learning. Food is a direct link to learning and retaining information.

How was food viewed in your home growing up? How could your view of food be impacting your wellness? What does mindful eating mean to you?

Helpful Video – TED: Kelly McGonigal's "How to Make Stress your Friend" at https://www.ted.com/talks/kelly_mcgonigal_how_to_make_stress_your_friend

Stress reactions tend to occur when the perceived demands of a situation exceed personal resources (Lazarus, 2006). The experience of stress corresponds with the release of the hormone cortisol, which exerts an influence on three key areas of executive functioning: working memory, inhibition, and cognitive flexibility (Shields, Sazma, & Yonelinas, 2016). Although individual responses to stress vary widely, research has shown that emotional regulation, memory retention, planning, and impulse control tend to be impaired by chronically stressful conditions. In relative moderation, however, stress can actually improve performance (Kohn, Hermans, & Fernandez, 2017; see Cluster 5). Duration, intensity, and source of stressors are important to consider when reflecting on your own response to stress.

Considering the ubiquity of stress in daily life, stress management strategies are a crucial component of wellness. Anxiety and stress management skills related to test taking can be found in Module 5.2. Time management practices (i.e., ideal schedules, master calendars, etc.) outlined in Module 3.2 represent another way to manage stress by creating consistency and predictability amidst busy schedules. Routines related to sleeping, eating, and exercise also serve to manage stress. In all of these cases, the importance of establishing organized routines is met in equal measure by the need for self-awareness. Personal wellness thus involves using mindfulness strategies to manage stress. Mindfulness is the practice of self-awareness that requires noticing one's thoughts, emotions, actions, and experiences in the present moment.

MINDFULNESS: The practice of self-awareness through noticing one's thoughts, emotions, actions, and experiences in the present moment.

Reflect for a moment on your morning routine. Are you consistent? To be mindful, begin by considering the order of your routine and how long it takes to complete. This is a method of mindful self-observance, so it should be done without judgment. Repeat this process with your bedtime routine. Is it effective? The predictability of a bedtime routine prepares the body for sleep in the same way a morning routine prepares us for the day. Planned routines are critical to feeling in control of your time, which tends to reduce stress. You may notice that this practice of mindful reflection is akin to the visualization exercises presented in Module 4.1 that enhance memory retention. Visual imagery is also a powerful tool for emotional regulation and stress management. When done mindfully, active visualization practices can help increase wellness by, for example, imagining you are someplace calm, or even imagining placing stress "in a box". Try one of the visualizations in Activity 9.2.1.

Beach Visualization

Imagine you are lying on a beach, your back is laying on the cool sand as the sun hits your front. Your toes are touching the water and just like your breath, the ocean ebbs and flows. With each breath in, the water moves up your body a little more, with each breath out you begin to float away. First your toes . . . [inhale, exhale] . . . moving up to your knees [inhale, exhale]. With each exhale, allow your body to feel light and relaxed as you float away in the ocean. Moving up your legs to your hips and stomach . . . [inhale, exhale] to your chest, shoulders, and finally your head. As you float in the sea, scan your body noticing any tension or clinching. Enjoy the peaceful ebb and flow of your breath. Now with each inhale and exhale imagine the ocean is gently placing you back on the beach. First your head and shoulders . . . [inhale, exhale] . . . moving to your arms, chest, and stomach . . . [inhale, exhale] . . . to your hips, knees, and finally down to your toes. You are back on the beach, enjoying the cool sand on your back and the sun on your face. Slowly blink your eyes open, moving slowly and returning to a seated position.

Container Visualization

Imagine a container. This container will be strong enough to hold all this distressing stuff—the memories, images, thoughts, physical sensations, sounds, smells, emotions. Now describe this container. What would this container have to be like in order to securely hold your distress? (e.g., a safe, office drawer, shipping container, crate, etc.) Can you describe it to me? What is it? What color is it? How big is it? What does it look like? What is it made of? What makes it safe and secure?

Now imagine taking the distressing images and putting them inside or sending them to the container, then shutting the door. Take the distressing thoughts . . . . . . (including any of the sounds, physical sensations, smells, and emotions with these thoughts) and place them in the container.

Anything else that needs to go in there? Now shut the door securely. How do you make the door more secure? OK, can you do that now? Is it secure now? Is there anything else you need to do to make it more secure? How does this feel now? Shall you leave this container in the room here, or is there a different secure place where you can leave this container? During the week (or until next time), if anything disturbing comes up, just imagine sending it there and putting it all in this container.

Progressive muscle relaxation is a stress management strategy designed to calm your mind and body by tensing and relaxing muscle groups in a systematic way. As a mindfulness exercise, it can be helpful to visualize the tension flowing away from each muscle group when it is relaxed. Follow the instructions in Activity 9.2.2.

ACTIVITY 9.2.2 MUSCLE RELAXATION

To start, sit up straight in a seat and place your feet flat on the floor. Take a deep yet gentle breath in through your nose, hold it for three seconds, and then exhale gently through your mouth. Feel your body relax. Notice the rising and falling of your rib cage with each breath. As you move through the relaxation exercise from the top of your body down, remember to breath.

Raise your eyebrows and hold for five seconds, then release. Feel the tension move away from your forehead. Pause for ten seconds. Smile widely and hold for five seconds, then release. Feel the tension move away from your cheeks and mouth as you pause for five seconds. Squint your eyelids tightly and hold for five seconds, then release. Feel the tension move away from your eyes as you pause for ten seconds. Gently tilt your head up to look at the celling, then release. Feel the tension move away from your neck as you pause for ten seconds. Repeat this process of tensing a muscle group for five seconds and then relaxing for ten seconds with each of the following muscle groups, in order: shoulders, upper back, chest, upper arms, hands, stomach, lower back, thighs, and feet.

Finally, creating and establishing boundaries related to time, mental space, and substance use is an important aspect of stress reduction. A house has physical walls, windows, doors, and locks that serve as protective boundaries against the weather, intruders, and the like. Similarly, people establish physical boundaries to ensure safety and stability. However, attending to emotional, occupational, and social boundaries is of equal importance. Take a moment to reflect on personal boundaries you have established. How do they relate to your values, ideals, and goals? Are you consistent in maintaining your personal boundaries? Might you benefit from mindfully reflecting on how clear boundaries across all six of the wellness dimensions can enhance your life?

WELLNESS ROUTINES: CRITICAL THINKING

According to Elder (2007), "Critical thinking is self-guided, self-disciplined thinking which attempts to reason at the highest quality in a fair-minded way. People who think critically consistently attempt to live rationally, reasonably, and empathically." Becoming an effective learner clearly requires critical thinking skills, as demonstrated throughout this book. Building personal wellness also requires critical thought. The process of critical thinking can be applied to personal wellness in much the same way as it is applied to academic pursuits since the same basic steps are taken to monitor, analyze, and reformulate plans. However, building a greater sense of wellness across the six dimensions also requires applying mindful self-awareness to personal thoughts, feelings, values, perceptions, and beliefs. Below are suggested critical thinking steps drawn from previous clusters that can be used to formulate and then assess a wellness plan or approach toward areas of concern. These descriptions are then followed by an example for practice.

CRITICAL THINKING: Mental process of purposefully monitoring, analyzing, and reformulating thoughts, beliefs, and judgments (Cluster 7).

- **Metacognitive Knowledge** (Knowledge of Self, Task, and Strategy, Module 7.1): Students are asked to increase their awareness surrounding situational information, personal beliefs, and understanding of boundaries before creating a plan for change.

- **Establish a Goal** (Goal Setting, Cluster 2): Students are asked to create a plan to tackle the problem and establish concrete, challenging, though attainable, goals for change.

- **Gather Resources** (Goal Setting, Cluster 2): Establishing enabling goals as well as proactive and reactive steps, students are asked to plan for roadblocks such as low motivation and lacks in accountability, among other obstacles.

- **Monitor the Plan** (Metacognitive Regulation, Cluster 7): Students are challenged to honestly assess how well their plan is working by monitoring each area of wellness and how it is being impacted by their established plan.

- **Analyze the Outcome** (Metacognitive Regulation, Cluster 7): Students are asked to check-in with each area of wellness utilizing resources such as the wellness assessment provided in Module 9.1 to assess progress. Was the plan effective and were outcomes achieved?

- **Reformulate Plan and Repeat the Process**: The final step of critically thinking about your wellness is to make adjustments and changes to your first plan. Making adjustments to your plans and goals is an important process for maintaining a balanced well-being. Students are asked to recognize the active and ongoing process of critically thinking through personalized processes.

TABLE 9.2.2 CRITICAL THINKING AND SOCIAL MEDIA WELLNESS

Critical Thinking Steps	Definition	Example – First Case Study
Metacognitive knowledge	Personal beliefs and understandings about cognitive processes	Jen believes she has been spending too much time on her phone and is thinking about creating some boundaries around her phone screen time.
Establish a goal	Establish a concrete, challenging, attainable goal for change	Jen's goal is to ignore social media until her final exams are completed. As such, she removes all social media apps from her phone and will reload them once she has finished her final exams.
Gather resources	Plan for roadblocks and barriers by filling in gaps of metacognitive knowledge	Jen is worried she will download social media again onto her phone, so she told her friend Sarah to check-in on her at least once a week through final exams. She decides to reward herself each day of successful studying by spending dinner time with her best friend.
Monitor the plan	Honestly check-in about effectiveness of plan and strategies	Jen has been off social media for two weeks, Sarah has been checking in with Jen and she is so proud of herself. However, Jen hasn't been getting more sleep, instead is watching more TV since she doesn't have social media to mindlessly scroll through.
Analyze the outcome	Evaluate your level of satisfaction with the outcome	The outcome surrounding sleep is not what Jen was hoping for but she has made progress with her goals of staying off social media until finals.
Reformulate and try again!	Make changes and adjustments based on your evaluation	Jen has established a concrete goal of going to bed by 11 pm on weeknights, so she can get 8–9 hours of sleep per night during the week. Jen added this time to her iCal app.

WELLNESS ROUTINES: SOCIAL MEDIA

Although social media is not typically listed as a wellness dimension, it can be argued it contributes, or detracts from the social dimension as well as impacting many of the other areas. In fact, social media culture can exert an overall powerful effect on student wellness. There is certainly evidence to suggest that social media use benefits students by facilitating social connectedness. However, recent studies also indicate an increase among young adults in what has been termed problematic social media use, or PSMU. PSMU is a maladaptive pattern that denotes excessive concern with, and use of, social media to the exclusion of other activities (Andreassen, 2015). Research indicates that upward of 44% of young adults self-report PSMU (Shensa et al. 2017), which has ALSO been linked to an increased risk of anxiety and depression (Shensa, Sidani, Dew, Escobar-Viera, & Primack, 2018).

As with so many activities, the use of social media is not problematic in itself. Rather, social media use appears to become a problem among young adults when it actively interferes with relationships, community involvement, and academic or career achievement (Shensa et al., 2017). In terms of academic achievement, both multitasking and the use of social media for non-academic purposes while studying has a detrimental impact on college student performance, including grade point average (Lau, 2017). In terms of wellness broadly speaking, excessive social media use is associated with reduced physical activity (Barkley & Lepp, 2017), poor sleep habits (Levenson, Shensa, Sidani, Colditz, & Primack, 2016), and lower self-reported scores of life satisfaction (Andreassen, 2015).

As such, critically thinking about how you use social media is an important consideration when it comes to personal wellness (see Table 9.2.2 for an example). Applying the various mindfulness and critical thinking skills previously discussed in this module may prove a beneficial way to determine how your own relationship with social media platforms influences your wellness. Do you find that time spent on social media enhances your intellectual and emotional well-being? Or, do you find yourself in constant comparison to others or seeking information that already confirms your beliefs, values, and prejudices?

Are you using social media to facilitate social engagement opportunities in offline settings? Or, is this the sole means for engaging with others? How might social media use inform and promote your physical, occupational, and spiritual wellness? Each of these questions requires ongoing critical thinking and thoughtful reflection to help maintain holistic wellness and ultimately increase performance and life satisfaction.

> What boundaries do you want to have around your social media use to protect your mental health? How do you plan to implement?

The following is a template for developing critical thinking skills related to wellness. As adapted from Cluster 7, it can be used to systematically guide you toward understanding how critical thinking and mindfulness impacts your well-being. Module 9.1 asked you to start formulating a plan around an area of wellness. It may be helpful to choose the same wellness area and reflect more deeply using these questions.

ACTIVATE PRIOR KNOWLEDGE

To assess your prior knowledge and awareness of this area of wellness, answer the following questions:

1. What are of wellness, will you reflect on?

2. What are you unsatisfied with in this area of wellness?

3. What previous things have you tried that did and did not work?

4. What gaps exist in your knowledge of this area of wellness?

5. How might you seek to fill those gaps? What resources can you access?

METACOGNITIVE KNOWLEDGE

To assess how your personal beliefs might directly influence your ability to maintain balanced wellness in this area, answer the following questions:

Knowledge of Person Variables

1. What is your current motivation level for making change in this area of wellness?

2. What skills do you currently have that can aid you in successfully making this change?

3. If you imagine this area of wellness, what are the perceived barriers to change?

Knowledge of Task Variables

1. What is the easiest or least time consuming part of maintaining this area of wellness?

2. What is the hardest or most time-consuming part of maintaining this area of wellness?

3. Based on those two answers, how might you choose to approach planning for change in this area of wellness?

Knowledge of Strategy Variables

1. What strategies do you use to maintain satisfaction in the identified area above?

2. What strategies have you tried that make maintaining this area more difficult?

3. Based on the above answers what strategies can be adapted to promote this area of wellness?

4. How will you know if a strategy is effective or not?

MODULE 9.2 SUMMARY

- Information processing is contingent upon daily wellness choices related to nutrition, exercise, sleep hygiene, and stress management.
- Poor wellness habits tend to increase the risk of anxiety, burnout, depression, and illness.
- Wellness is a self-regulated learning process of setting goals, applying strategies, monitoring changes, and evaluating outcomes.
- Mindfulness is the practice of self-awareness that requires noticing one's thoughts, emotions, actions, and experiences in the present moment.
- Progressive muscle relaxation is a stress management strategy designed to calm your mind and body.
- The process of critical thinking can be applied to personal wellness using the basic steps of monitoring, analyzing, and reformulating plans.
- Critically thinking about how you use social media is an important consideration when it comes to personal wellness.

KEY TERMS

- **Critical Thinking** – Mental process of purposefully monitoring, analyzing, and reformulating thoughts, beliefs, and judgments.
- **Mindfulness** – The practice of self-awareness through noticing one's thoughts, emotions, actions, and experiences in the present moment.

REFERENCES

Andreassen, C. S. (2015). Online social network site addiction: A comprehensive review. *Current Addiction Reports, 2*(2), 175–184.

Barkley, J. E., & Lepp, A. (2016). Mobile phone use among college students is a sedentary leisure behavior which may interfere with exercise. *Computers in Human Behavior, 56,* 29–33.

Center for Clinical Interventions. (n.d.). Sleep hygiene. Retrieved from www.cci.health.wa.gov.au

Cuseo, J. B., Fecas, V. S., & Thompson, A. (2010). *Thriving in college and beyond: Research-based strategies for academic success and development.* Dubuque, IA: Kendall Hunt.

Elder, L. (2007). Defining critical thinking. Retrieved from https://www.criticalthinking.org/pages/defining-critical-thinking/766

Gómez-Pinilla, F. (2008). Brain foods: The effects of nutrients on brain function. *Nature Reviews Neuroscience, 9*(7), 568–578.

Hershner, S. D., & Chervin, R. D. (2014). Causes and consequences of sleepiness among college students. *Nature and Science of Sleep, 6,* 73–84.

Kim, M. S., & Cardinal, B. J. (2019). Differences in university student motivation between a required and an elective physical activity education policy. *Journal of American College Health, 67*(3), 207–214.

Kohn, N., Hermans, E. J., & Fernández, G. (2017). Cognitive benefit and cost of acute stress is differentially modulated by individual brain state. *Social Cognitive and Affective Neuroscience, 12*(7), 1179–1187.

Lau, W. W. (2017). Effects of social media usage and social media multitasking on the academic performance of university students. *Computers in Human Behavior, 68,* 286–291.

Levenson, J. C., Shensa, A., Sidani, J. E., Colditz, J. B., & Primack, B. A. (2016). The association between social media use and sleep disturbance among young adults. *Preventive Medicine, 85,* 36–41.

Plotnikoff, R. C., Costigan, S. A., Williams, R. L., Hutchesson, M. J., Kennedy, S. G., Robards, S. L., & Germov, J. (2015). Effectiveness of interventions targeting physical activity, nutrition and healthy weight for university and college students: a systematic review and meta-analysis. *International Journal of Behavioral Nutrition and Physical Activity, 12*(1), 45–58.

Shensa, A., Escobar-Viera, C. G., Sidani, J. E., Bowman, N. D., Marshal, M. P., & Primack, B. A. (2017). Problematic social media use and depressive symptoms among US young adults: A nationally-representative study. *Social Science & Medicine, 182,* 150–157.

Shensa, A., Sidani, J. E., Dew, M. A., Escobar-Viera, C. G., & Primack, B. A. (2018). Social media use and depression and anxiety symptoms: A cluster analysis. *American Journal of Health Behavior, 42*(2), 116–128.

Shields, G. S., Sazma, M. A., & Yonelinas, A. P. (2016). The effects of acute stress on core executive functions: A meta-analysis and comparison with cortisol. *Neuroscience and Biobehavioral Reviews, 68,* 651–668.

Stiles, J., & Jernigan, T. L. (2010). The basics of brain development. *Neuropsychology Review, 20*(4), 327–348.

CASE STUDY

Jen is preparing for finals next week in her first semester as a college freshman. Although Jen is excited for winter break, she is also feeling stressed and fatigued. She had set a goal at the beginning of the semester to earn a 3.5 GPA and is determined to attain it. She has pulled two all-nighters this week, drinking far more coffee than usual to stay awake and eating fast foods multiple times per day. Jen's phone notifies her of a 33% increase in her screen time over the past two weeks. She suddenly realizes that she has been mindlessly scrolling through Instagram again. Jen begins to worry that she won't perform well on her finals next week because she is struggling to maintain her study schedule.

QUESTIONS

1. What areas of wellness are being impacted by Jen's everyday choices?
2. What are two everyday choices Jen can adjust to improve her wellness?
3. What additional strategies could Jen adjust to increase her wellness?

1. Several dimensions of wellness are being impacted including physical and emotional wellness. It is also likely that Jen's intellectual wellness is suffering as her cognitive and information processing abilities are diminished due to higher levels of stress, too much caffeine, poor nutrition, and lack of sleep. This will most likely affect her performance on her final exams.

2. Jen could prioritize healthier eating choices to help sustain her as well as committing to a sleep schedule that will support her efforts. If both of these areas are improved, it is more likely she will be more efficient and her study sessions will be more effective.

3. Jen could use technology as a means to help her with her time management, removing distractions from her technological space through deleting social media apps, and prioritizing sleep by establishing a strong sleep routine. Additionally, she could include her bedtime on her iCal app, tell a friend or roommate about her plans for change, and maybe invite someone to join in on her goals with her. She could also include some physical exercise breaks in her study sessions such as short walks to help her become reenergized and refocused.

ADDITIONAL READINGS

Glowacki, E. M., Kirtz, S., Hughes Wagner, J., Cance, J. D., Barrera, D., & Bernhardt, J. M. (2018). HealthyhornsTXT: A text-messaging program to promote college student health and wellness. *Health Promotion Practice, 19*(6), 844–855.

Higgins, W. J., Lauzon, L. L., & Bratseth, A. Y. (2009). University student's wellness: What difference can a course make? *College Student Journal, 43*(3), 766–777.

Jennings, M. L., & Slavin, S. J. (2015). Resident wellness matters: Optimizing resident education and wellness through the learning environment. *Academic Medicine, 90*(1), 1246–1250.

Karaman, M. A., Lerma, E., Vela, J. C., & Watson, J. C. (2019). Predictors of academic stress among college students. *Journal of College Counseling, 22*(1), 41–55.

Lee, Y. L. (2018). Nurturing critical thinking for implementation beyond the classroom: Implications from social psychological theories of behavior change. *Thinking Skills and Creativity, 27,* 139–147.

Lentz, T. A., & Brown, C. (2018). Mindfulness and health behaviors in college students: The moderating role of sleep. *Journal of American College Health,* 1–10.

Martin, G. L. (2015). "Tightly wound rubber bands": Exploring the college experiences of low-income, first-generation white students. *Journal of Student Affairs Research and Practice, 52*(3), 275–286.

Montalto, C. P., Phillips, E. L., McDaniel, A., & Baker, A. R. (2019). College student finance wellness: Student loans and beyond. *Journal of Family and Economic Issues, 40,* 3–21.

INDEX

adequate sleep, 114

assignments, start and finish of, 117–118

case study, 121–122

meals, avoid skipping, 114

overview, 113–114

personal belongings and work area, management of, 116

physical health with exercise, 114

procrastination, avoid, 114

schedule smaller work blocks, 115–116

studying for examination, 117

test plan, 117

Transferrable learning skills, 8

Triggers, recognizing of
external triggers, 190–191
internal triggers, 188–189

Trivium, 9

True/false items exams, 198

Unit objectives, self-testing strategy, 178

Useful goals, 42–47

case study, 309

definition, 311–312

dimensions of, 312–313

emotional, 313, 316

financial, 313

intellectual, 313, 315

occupational, 313, 317

overview, 310

personal. *See* Personal wellness

physical, 313, 315

prioritizing, in daily living, 314

social, 313, 316

spiritual, 313, 317

wheel, 312

Working memory, 128–129

Writing to learn strategy, 134

CPSIA information can be obtained
at www.ICGtesting.com
Printed in the USA
LVHW021602140720
660692LV00001B/1